ALL
THESE VOWS

Kol Nidre

Other Jewish Lights Books by Rabbi Lawrence A. Hoffman

My People's Prayer Book: Traditional Prayers,
Modern Commentaries, Vols. 1–10

My People's Passover Haggadah: Traditional Texts,
Modern Commentaries, Vols. 1 & 2
(coedited with David Arnow, PhD)

The Art of Public Prayer: Not for Clergy Only, 2nd Ed.
(A book from SkyLight Paths, Jewish Lights' sister imprint)

Rethinking Synagogues: A New Vocabulary for Congregational Life

Israel—A Spiritual Travel Guide:
A Companion for the Modern Jewish Pilgrim

The Way Into Jewish Prayer

What You Will See Inside a Synagogue
(coauthored with Dr. Ron Wolfson)

Also in the Prayers of Awe Series

Who by Fire, Who by Water—Un'taneh Tokef

PRAYERS OF AWE

ALL THESE VOWS

Kol Nidre

Edited by
Rabbi Lawrence A. Hoffman, PhD

JEWISH LIGHTS Publishing

All These Vows—Kol Nidre

© 2011 by Lawrence A. Hoffman

For information regarding permission to reprint material from this book, please mail or fax your request in writing to Jewish Lights Publishing, Permission Department, at the address / fax number listed below, or e-mail your request to permissions@jewishlights.com.

Library of Congress Cataloging-in-Publication Data
All these vows : Kol Nidre / edited by Lawrence A. Hoffman.
p. cm. — (Prayers of awe ; v. 2)
Includes bibliographical references.
ISBN978-1-58023-430-6 (hardcover)
ISBN978-1-68162-975-9 (pbk.)
1. Kol nidrei 2. Yom Kippur—Liturgy. 3. Judaism—Liturgy. 4. Vows (Jewish law)
I. Hoffman, Lawrence A., 1942–
BM670.K6A77 2011
296.4'532—dc23
2011025799

Front Cover: Jeff Miller
Cover Mechanical Design: Grace Cavalier

Published by Jewish Lights Publishing

www.jewishlights.com

Contents

Acknowledgments

Acknowledgments begin with the many High Holy Day worshipers for whom *Kol Nidre* has proved important. To these worshipers in general, I add the many colleagues, artists, composers, poets, philosophers, theologians, and critics who added more technical voices to the conversation. Many of them are included here. To them—to all the contributors whose commentaries found their way into this volume—I am grateful.

Whenever I finish editing a volume, I am struck by how much I owe to all the others included in it, but that is especially the case here. Midway through the volume, I had to undergo eye surgery; as a result, I misplaced files, misdirected emails, and delayed the book enormously. I was overwhelmed by the patience and understanding that I received from everyone. I cannot adequately express how grateful I am for the support accorded me during those long hard months.

The support came also from my extraordinary publisher, Stuart M. Matlins, founder of Jewish Lights, and from Emily Wichland, vice president of Editorial and Production at Jewish Lights. My profound thanks go to them both. Stuart continues to demonstrate his extraordinary commitment to Jewish literacy, spirituality, and renewal. In fact, it was Stuart who first approached me with the idea for the Prayers of Awe series, as suggested to him by Dan Adler in response to a High Holy Day program developed by Rob Eshman, editor in chief of the *Jewish Journal of Greater Los Angeles*, and David Suissa. Their program sprang from an idea first conceived by Rabbi Elazar Muskin of Young Israel of Century City. Emily continues to amaze me in all she does: her abundant wisdom, skill, patience, and perseverance are precisely what an author most desires. For her copyediting and proofreading, my thanks go again to Debra Corman. I happily include as well all the others at Jewish Lights, especially Tim

Holtz, director of Production, who designed the cover for this book and typeset the English text.

Authors rely on other authors who have come before, and from time to time, particular books stand out as guides without which one's own work would not have been possible. In this case, I relied to an extraordinary degree on the work of Moshe Benovitz, whose *Kol Nidre: Studies in the Development of Rabbinic Votive Institutions*, Brown Judaism Studies, 315 (Scholars Press, 1998) informed every aspect of how I understand the halakhic implications of the various vows and oaths included in *Kol Nidre*. I record my debt to him in my own essay on the subject, but wish here, as well, to acknowledge his extraordinary accomplishment. The overall history of *Kol Nidre* is widely known by now, but credit goes to Stuart Weinberg Gershon for supplying it early on in a readily readable format that is widely cited by others here as well (*Kol Nidre: Its Origin, Development and Significance* [Lanham, MD: Jason Aronson, 1994]). My thanks go also to Marc Saperstein, who made many valuable suggestions that have been incorporated into this book; and to Eliezer Diamond, Alyssa Gray, Charles Middleburgh, and Dvora Weisberg with whom I consulted regarding the translation.

PART I
Kol Nidre and History

Morality, Meaning, and the Ritual Search for the Sacred

Rabbi Lawrence A. Hoffman, PhD

It is hard for us to appreciate how seriously people took oaths in the days when they thought the universe was a moral, not a scientific, thing. We assume a universe run by mathematical principles with which there is no bargaining: $E = MC^2$, for example, is simply "true," whether we like it that way or not. Periodic hurricanes devastate the Caribbean because it lies in the path of tropical storms, not because the Haitians who live there deserve punishment. Bad things sometimes happen to good people because that is just the way the world is. The laws of nature are not whimsical. No guru, shaman, sage, or sorcerer can compel the universe to be other than what it is.

Rabbi Lawrence A. Hoffman, PhD, has served for more than three decades as professor of liturgy at Hebrew Union College–Jewish Institute of Religion in New York. He is a world-renowned liturgist and holder of the Stephen and Barbara Friedman Chair in Liturgy, Worship and Ritual. He has written and edited many books, including *My People's Prayer Book: Traditional Prayers, Modern Commentaries,* winner of the National Jewish Book Award; *Who by Fire, Who by Water—Un'taneh Tokef,* the first volume in the Prayers of Awe series; and he is coeditor of *My People's Passover Haggadah: Traditional Texts, Modern Commentaries,* a finalist for the National Jewish Book Award. He is a developer of Synagogue 3000, a transdenominational project designed to envision and implement the ideal synagogue of the spirit for the twenty-first century.

Understanding all of this, we try whenever possible to enlist science in our own defense. We wear seat belts, wash our hands, wear sunscreen, and eliminate transfats from our diet. All species scramble to be on the cutting edge of evolutionary success. We have added scientific knowledge to our defensive weaponry.

Our ancestors made do with a smaller arsenal. It was not simply that they didn't know as much as we do. They were ignorant of what would even count as proper knowing, in that they thought the world responded to moral rather than mathematical necessity. They lived in fear of forces beyond themselves who might punish moral failure by redirecting nature to cause them harm.

They were not unscientific, in the sense of not understanding cause and effect. They just had the list of causes wrong. No less than we, they employed what knowledge they had to ward off disaster. But for them, that knowledge included sacrifice and, later, prayer, that they judged sufficient to change the natural course of things. They also fasted to atone for sin, not as a matter of moral improvement or spiritual discipline (these are modern rationales) but as self-affliction, a prophylactic against punishment from on high. And they avoided vows that might activate supernatural punishment if they were not kept.

We still pray, fast, atone, and avoid making wholesale vows that we may not keep. But we harmonize these practices with our scientific understanding of the universe. Depending on our view of God, we call these practices commandments, virtues, traditions, or moral training for the soul. Beliefs entrenched from childhood do die hard, however, so even we, sometimes, suffer a sense of divine foreboding, which we link to inadvertent breaches of character, like making promises that we cannot or do not fulfill. Our world is not rife with superstition, but it is not utterly without it either.

Kol Nidre, however, arose in the premodern world where superstition was still rampant. As such, it came under attack by nineteenth-century critics who had assimilated a scientific temperament and who "knew better."

It is not the only prayer or practice to attract critique. There are lots of medieval customs that we too are just as happy to do without. How many people even know that prior to the twelfth century, Jews customarily examined the bedsheets after a couple's wedding night and, upon finding blood there, said a blessing (*birkat b'tulin*) thanking God for bridal virginity. We didn't have to wait for modernity to deplore that—Maimonides did it for us, declaring the ritual "exceptionally ugly" and saying, "No one of good sense would be found anywhere near such a custom." Similarly, the *Alenu* (a Rosh Hashanah prayer composed in late antiquity and used since the fourteenth or fifteenth century to close every service) once included a phrase categorizing other faiths as "praying to emptiness and vanity and to a god who cannot save them." However much the line originally denoted pagan polytheism, Jews in medieval Europe were convinced it meant Christians. So again, we got rid of it, this time, perhaps, because we were afraid of retaliation by the church; today, however, reprisal is not an issue, yet except for some ultra-Orthodox prayer books, our liturgy still omits the line simply because this is not something we wish to say. So too, most Jews today do not wave chickens over their heads as Rosh Hashanah scapegoats. The religious landscape is cluttered with ritual detritus that we have abandoned along the path from medieval superstition to modern religious consciousness.

In cases of moral revulsion (the virginity blessing, the *Alenu* line), most of us would agree that we are better off without yesterday's liturgical debris. When we talk nostalgically of the good old days, the only thing we can be sure of is that they were old, not that they were good. The romantic urge to retrieve the past should be tempered—it is a romance after all, and not all love affairs are healthy.

But some of them are. Rational ritual housecleaning can go too far. Classical Reform Judaism in North America once looked askance at praying in Hebrew, for example. It abandoned the traditional prayer garb of *tallit* and *yarmulke* because newly acculturated Jews were trying to make it in the West and didn't want to look too "oriental." Whatever the wisdom of that rationale back then, Reform Jews today have recovered ritual garb as *meaningful*.

"Meaningful," not "moral"—these are two separate criteria for ritual entanglement. Morality is outer-directed; it measures a ritual's impact on others. It makes a claim upon us, sometimes against our will. Meaning, by contrast, measures our internal ritual temperature—whether a ritual leaves us hot or cold, as it were. It may be a matter of taste; there are people who like oatmeal or olives and people who do not. Tastes change.

Sometimes, however, "meaning" comes closer to "moral," in that it places internal demands upon us—as when the tradition is very old, commanded by halakhah (Jewish law), practiced worldwide, and so on. The concern here is not exactly ethical, but it is more than taste. Meaning may thus make demands upon us—not moral demands, but demands nevertheless. Still, meaning, more than morality, is reversible. For classical Reform Jews, wearing a *yarmulke* was once meaningless: they neither liked it (taste) nor felt impelled to continue it (obligation). Many of their descendants feel differently (on both grounds).

Ritual decisions are easier to make when something is morally offensive and without meaning. But what if the two conflict? What do we do when we have moral problems with a tradition that, on other grounds, we like a great deal? Or when our moral reservations conflict with obligation—the responsibility to obey halakhah, retain tradition, or honor the customs of generations past? Here is where the conflict emerges. On the one hand, we would love to do without it; on the other hand, we dearly love it or feel obliged to have it.

Kol Nidre is as good an example of this conflict as one can find. The negative pole is our moral disgust with the very idea that we can blithely cast aside promises as empty. Do any of us really believe that responsibility for promises we have made in the past can be canceled at will? Or that promises we may make in the future can come with a footnote indicating that we proactively took steps to dismiss them in advance? Other issues emerge too, halakhic ones (as we shall see). But halakhah has had several centuries to appropriate *Kol Nidre* as valid, so it is usually its moral consequences that make us pause today.

The positive pole of the conflict comprises several components. Loyalty to halakhah is one. Fealty to the past is another: how many generations have been coming faithfully to this Yom Kippur service above all others! It even bears *Kol Nidre*'s name: "the *Kol Nidre* service," as we call it. And then there is the music, especially the haunting melody introduced into the Ashkenazi repertoire by the sixteenth century, if not earlier (see Mark Kligman, pp. 67–70); but also, by now, melodies in some Sephardi communities that have joined the Ashkenazim in valuing *Kol Nidre* as a haunting symbol of new year piety. *Kol Nidre* is at one and the same time both less and more than a prayer: "less than" a prayer in that it is actually a legal formula with none of the formal characteristics that designate prayers as a distinctive outcry of the human spirit; but "more than" a prayer in that it is an entire ritual in and of itself. Indeed, in most congregations, it is such a high point of the evening that everything else following can seem like background liturgical muzak for the *Kol Nidre* melody, which echoes in our souls long after it is sung.

The conflict is not new, however. It has been going on for a long time now!

Kol Nidre: Anatomy of a Conflict

The history of *Kol Nidre* is generously referred to throughout this book and can be easily summarized here.

Its origins are tied conceptually to oaths (*sh'vu'ot*; singular: *sh'vu'ah*) and vows (*n'darim*; singular: *neder*), two broad categories of sacred affirmations that go back to the Bible. As we shall see, *Kol Nidre* refers to both, as well as to subcategories of them, like *esarei* and *charamei*, technical terms that are best left untranslated, because there is no commonly accepted English equivalents. Since the language of the prayer is Aramaic, the categories of oaths and vows appear in the Aramaic rather than the Hebrew plural (*nidrei*, for example, not *n'darim*). *Kol nidre* is Aramaic for *kol han'darim*, "all the vows." (Throughout this book, we will adhere to the conventional spelling, *nidre*; when transcribing the Aramaic within the prayer itself, however, we will obey the technical rules that render the spelling *nidrei*.)

Kol Nidre annuls these varieties of sacred affirmations, either *misrepresentations of fact* (I swore that I knew nothing about a shady business deal, when in fact I did) or *affirmations of behavior*—promises of what I would or would not do, made to myself, to God, or to other people. Some versions stipulate promises made in the past (from last Yom Kippur to this one); others denote the future (from this Yom Kippur to the next one). We have already looked briefly at the moral problem of annulment. There is, in addition, a set of halakhic problems, which vexed the Rabbis more than the moral ones did, not because they cared so little for morality, but because, as legalists, their language of discourse was Jewish law and because Jewish law (like other legal codes) was itself a reflection of moral considerations.

The practice of *Kol Nidre* arose in response to the seriousness with which Rabbinic law treats oaths and vows—two different things, legally. *Vows* (*nidrei*) were originally the means of donating possessions to God, that is, in practice, to the Temple, God's representative institution on earth. *Oaths* (*sh'vu'ot*) could be of any sort (e.g., "I swear, by God, that I was home yesterday"; "... that I'll never talk to you again"; "... that I'll work till the day I die"). Oaths were more serious than vows in that they invoked the name of God—at least implicitly, because even if the actual name was not mentioned, it was assumed that the oath included it by intent. Oaths had grave consequences, not unlike an oath made in court today, but even worse, because breach of the latter is punishable by human law, while falsity to the former calls down the much more powerful authority of the divine. But people do, in fact, abuse God's name regularly, so the Rabbis sought legal means to avoid divine recrimination.

Some vows were written off as unintended—exigencies of the marketplace, for example, where two sides negotiate a bargain by swearing they will not sell the item for a dollar less (or buy it for a dollar more) even though neither one of them means it; or vows of exaggeration, where you swear by all that's holy that the fish you almost caught was really, really, big! A further regulation, however, permitted a Rabbinic sage to annul a person's vows, in a process called *hatarat n'darim*, literally, "annulment of vows" (for details, see Eliezer Diamond, pp. 73–79). Rabbinic opinion differed on the relationship between these two stipulations. Was the rabbi who oversaw *hatarat n'darim* just a lawyer to whom one went to find out if a given vow fell into the categories of promise that could be annulled? Or was he more like a shaman, gifted with the power to annul other vows as well under certain circumstances? In either case, a wholesale annulment of all oaths as a matter of public ritual is recognized by neither the Bible nor the Talmud.

Yet that is what *Kol Nidre* is. How and where did it arise?

Kol Nidre is connected to the ancient belief in the power of magical adjuration—the act of making a spirit or demon swear that it will harm someone. The Babylonians of late antiquity and the early Middle Ages used magic bowls that were believed to undo the oath that the demons had been forced to make, thereby undoing also the damage they promised to cause. If I believe my enemy has enlisted demons by making them swear they will harm me, I take a bowl and write on it a formula that remits the demon's vow; I then smash the bowl and bury it in my home. Freed from its promise to hurt me, the demon will leave me alone. The formulas on these bowls are remarkably similar to what we find in *Kol Nidre*. The most convenient conclusion is that *Kol Nidre* emerged among the folk as a popular adaptation of the magic bowls, which would explain why the custom is unknown to the Talmud, why it does not obey Talmudic law, and why (as we shall see) post-Talmudic authorities who first heard of it opposed it as foolish and tried to get rid of it.

It may be, however, that *Kol Nidre* emerged independently, with or without the same magical outlook as that represented by the bowls. Any Jewish use of the bowls may have derived from *Kol Nidre*, not the other way around: that is, Jews already had a formula that released themselves from oaths they had taken; they then adopted the magic-bowl practice of their culture and applied the same formulas to release evil spirits from promises enforced upon them. Scholars are divided on the subject of which was the cause and which was the effect.[1] Either way, the bowls on one hand and the prayer on the other are more different from each other than they are similar (see Dalia Marx, pp. 26–30).

The key to knowing which came first may lie in knowing where *Kol Nidre* arose. The bowls are from Babylonia, whereas *Kol Nidre* is Palestinian, as we can see from a close look at the post-Talmudic authorities mentioned earlier.

The authorities in question are called *geonim*. The geonic era probably began with the coming of Islam (early seventh century CE) but reached its golden era only after 747, when a new dynasty moved the caliphate from Damascus to Baghdad, where the Talmudic academies had the good fortune to be located. The rabbis of these academies benefited from the steady flow of money and power to the dynastic capital and began claiming the same authority over world Jewry that the caliph claimed over worldwide Islam. The gaonate was, therefore, like a chief rabbinate, located in what is now Iraq, but claiming authority over Jews everywhere. Its holders were *geonim* (singular: *gaon*, a biblical term originally, which eventually came to mean something like "Your Honor"). It was the *geonim* who successfully championed the Babylonian Talmud at the expense of its rival, the Palestinian Talmud, and who introduced responsa, still the primary way of applying halakhah to the changing times. One such responsum, by Rav Amram bar Sheshna Gaon, is our first comprehensive prayer book, composed around the year 860. In it, Amram refers to his predecessor, Natronai Gaon, who had already heard of *Kol Nidre* from his own distant predecessor, Yehudai (middle of the eighth century). None of the *geonim* liked the custom, since it ran counter to the carefully controlled practice of *hatarat n'darim*, which canceled certain vows only, under certain circumstances only, and purely at the discretion of a legally constituted halakhic court.

All three *geonim* agree that within the official circles over which they preside, *Kol Nidre* is unknown; they even call it a "foolish custom" that is to be avoided. They say, however, that it is the practice of "other lands," thus solving our problem of the country of *Kol Nidre*'s origin. It cannot be Babylonia. From other sources, primarily, a legal responsum from the rabbis of Eretz Yisrael, we can see that the practice was Palestinian.

In the early period of the gaonate (from Yehudai to Amram, mid-eighth to ninth centuries CE), Babylonian practice had yet to emerge as dominant among Jews worldwide. Palestinian rabbis still maintained the priority of their own Talmud and of customs based upon it, going back, as they saw it, farther than the relative upstarts in Babylonia. Even if *Kol Nidre* had not run counter to Rabbinic law, these *geonim* would likely have opposed it, as they did every other liturgical custom that marked Palestinian, but not Babylonian, practice. But as it happens, it did run counter to that law, so they had good halakhic reason to object to it. The version we now use is in Babylonian Aramaic, but the one cited by Rav Amram is in Hebrew, and there is reason to believe that at some point, alternative Aramaic and Hebrew versions circulated simultaneously.

In any event, these early geonic demands to eradicate *Kol Nidre* fell on deaf ears. Other opinions followed, as Rav Amram's successors took their own aim at the "foolish" innovation, some accepting it with stipulations, and some recording their own preferred version of it.

By the thirteenth century, *Kol Nidre* had gained enough momentum to be taken for granted as a Yom Kippur staple. The MaHaRaM (an acronym for *M*oreinu [our teacher] *H*arav *R*abbi *M*eir [of Rothenberg]) supplied it with its introductory liturgical context by composing the lines that set it in a cosmic courtroom: sinners and innocent pleading alike before the "*yeshivah* on high and the *yeshivah* below." Our familiar Ashkenazi melody may not have come about until as late as the sixteenth century (see Mark Kligman, pp. 67–70), but it was being chanted in some manner as early as eleventh-century Ashkenaz. By then, it was apparently here to stay. As we saw, the original prayer addressed vows made in the past. The shift to specify vows of the future came about in the thirteenth century, as yet another means to harmonize the conflict between Jewish law, on one hand, and a popular custom that had gone mainstream, on the other.

By the nineteenth century, *Kol Nidre* came under attack again, this time by Enlightenment-trained rabbis in Central Europe who led the religious fight for Jewish civil rights and who knew enough about history to know they had ample precedent in denouncing a prayer that was not Talmudic to begin with and that the *geonim* themselves had opposed. Parallel reform did not occur in Sephardi lands, most of which were in the Mediterranean and well protected from the influences of modernity. The possibility of achieving full civil rights for Jews did not arise there; nor was there a university-trained Jewish middle class that objected to premodern liturgical customs.

But even in synagogues where these modern Ashkenazi rabbis ruled with great authority, *Kol Nidre* proved hard to exclude. People loved the melody. In addition, they had the Ashkenazi cantorate to contend with. In Ashkenazi countries, cantorial solos had become central to the service. To some extent, cantors commanded salaries based in part on their performance at the High Holy Days, in which *Kol Nidre* played a central role. When, therefore, rabbis suggested eliminating *Kol Nidre*, they were opposed by the congregation as a whole and by the cantor in particular, who sometimes simply refused to go along. That is not to say *Kol Nidre* went unchallenged. Rabbis persisted, and a number of options developed: everything from performing the piece on a musical instrument (without the offending words) to substituting a psalm (or similar passage) sung to the *Kol Nidre* melody (for details, see Annette M. Boeckler, pp. 39–66).

In the latter half of the twentieth century, new liturgies came into being throughout the Jewish world. Their editors too had to decide what to do with *Kol Nidre*, and their decisions are examined in part 4. For traditional prayer books, *Kol Nidre* was a given. Not so the liturgies of progressive Jewish movements, which had done without it for decades. Only rarely did the editors of these volumes worry about the halakhic implications of each and every word in the prayer; they did not, by and large, consider themselves bound by the laws of vows and oaths to which the prayer referred. But historically speaking, each and every word mattered, and before looking further at *Kol Nidre* today, we should consider why each word is there. The halakhic meaning of *Kol Nidre* is the subject of part 2, but we should at least summarize the matter here.

Kol Nidre: The Anatomy of Sacred Promises

The more interest we have in something, the more we study it, and the more we study it, the more we organize it. The respect that biblical and Rabbinic society paid to oaths and vows is therefore evident in the complexity with which they dissected the subject. *Kol Nidre* reflects centuries of detailed legal wrangling. Its several terms listed in succession are a taxonomic shorthand for an entire catalogue of verbal promises that the prayer was meant to nullify.

I say "prayer," for, by now, it is that; but as we have seen, *Kol Nidre* is, in form, a legal statement—that is one reason it appears in Aramaic, the language of Jewish legal documents generally (marriage documents [*k'tubot*], for example). By the geonic era, people hadn't spoken Hebrew for centuries; it was considered sacred, the language of revelation and of prayer. The lingua franca was Arabic, the language of the empire that encompassed both major Jewish communities of the time: the Land of Israel and Babylonia. Before that, it had been Latin, Greek, and Aramaic. But both Talmuds were in Aramaic, which remained the internal language of Jewish law, as it does to this day. *Kol Nidre*, then, is an Aramaic legal formula that covers all its bases by listing the various biblical and Rabbinic terms likely to be used for making vows or oaths of any sort. Each term has its own history.

Yehudai Gaon (eighth century) tells us that the laws of vows had long ceased to be a serious part of the curriculum in the academies. If his remark reflects the situation in Eretz Yisrael as well, it is likely that only the very learned in either Jewish center fully understood the complexities of the laws on vows. From its very inception, therefore, the consequences of *Kol Nidre* were never understood very well even by the rabbis (whoever they were) who drew it up, never mind the average people who recited it. They probably comprehended *Kol Nidre* about as well as most people today understand the niceties of boilerplate legal documents downloaded off the Internet. The litany of terms was just a formulaic attempt to include all possible legal eventualities.

Nonetheless, each term does mean something, and it is quite fascinating to see what that meaning is. If *Kol Nidre* is about the power of words, nothing better illustrates its truth than its own obsession with the words it chooses. Words constitute worlds, social facts that do not exist until words are invented to describe them. Vows are such social institutions; they exist only because we say they do. We, today, have our own rather meager catalogue: marriage vows differ from oaths we take in court, and swearing on oath in court is not the same as a profanity sworn in anger. The world of our ancestors was much richer in defining the various ways that words entail commitment. Our knowledge on that score has been greatly enriched by Moshe Benovitz, whose detailed study provided the basis for the discussion that follows.[2]

Most of the terms go back to the Bible, but the Bible was written over a long period of time, and the meaning of the various oaths and vows changed with time and circumstances. The earliest usage comes from those parts of the Bible that can be dated prior to the seventh century BCE; they are called pre-Deuteronomic, because they came before Deuteronomy. Deuteronomy is usually associated with a legal reform initiated by King

Josiah in 621 BCE, and it has its own approach to things. Last, we have exilic and post-exilic writings associated with the priests who established the theocracy of the early Second Temple period, following the return from exile in 538 BCE. Terms are used differently in these various eras.

The Rabbis codified the Bible and added their own post-biblical understanding of what the Bible had to say. We customarily divide this post-biblical period into two: the Mishnaic era (culminating in the Mishnah, our first great compendium of Jewish law, in about 200 CE); and the period that gave us the Talmud (sometimes called Gemara) about three to four hundred years later. There were actually two Talmuds, a Palestinian Talmud (the Yerushalmi) promulgated about 400 CE, and the Babylonian Talmud (the Babli), which is usually dated somewhere between 550 and 650 CE. The final understanding of *Kol Nidre*'s legal niceties comes from the two Talmuds, particularly the Babylonian Talmud, which became dominant after the Babylonian *geonim* managed to make it so.

The two most basic biblical terms are *sh'vu'ah* ("oath") and *neder* ("vow").

The more serious of the two is the *sh'vu'ah*, an oath taken in the name of God and punishable, should the oath not be fulfilled, for taking God's name in vain. The Ten Commandments (Exodus 20:7) guarantee that "Adonai will not hold guiltless the one who swears falsely by his name." A *sh'vu'ah* may refer to the past or present, an oath that such and such is (or was) the case, in which case it is *assertory*—it *asserts* something that already is either true or false. An obvious case would be an *assertory* testimony attempting to clear yourself of a criminal charge. But it may refer to the future, in which case it is *promissory*, because it promises that you will or will not do something.

You might simply swear and be ready to pay the penalty for falsely doing so. Alternatively, however, you might go so far as to have recourse to an *executor* oath. Here, you would say to a king or other powerful person (or even to God), "As you live, I swear such and such." Should the oath prove false, the named person (or God) is given the authority to execute the punishment. By the Rabbinic era, we find *surety* oaths also, cases where I say to you, "As you live, swear such and such to me." You might respond, "As I live, I swear it," thereby guaranteeing expressly that your life is being put up as surety for the validity of the oath. Surety oaths are Rabbinic, however, not biblical; the Rabbis borrowed the custom from Roman culture, where it was common. You need not put up your actual life as surety; it might be just your property, but it could also be another human being, a loved one over whom you have control ("By the life of my son," you might say, for example), although, for obvious reasons, the latter was frowned upon.

Sh'vu'ot ("oaths") were avoided in general, because they required taking God's name in vain and had, therefore, such terrifying consequences: should the oath be broken but the sanction not put into effect, God would rain down punishment. We saw above that God's name did not have to be explicitly mentioned. It was enough for the Rabbis that a person said, "*Sh'vu'ah* that …" ("This is an oath that …"). In such cases, the name of God was considered implicit, so that the curse entailed by the oath came provisionally into effect. Fearing such consequences, the Rabbis avoided oaths altogether, and in their place, they construed a clever use of the *neder*.

What then is a *neder*? In the Bible, a *neder* is the act of dedicating something (or someone) to God. In effect, this amounts only to donating it to the Temple, after which the donor may not use it anymore. It becomes sacred, the property of God, and may be used only by the priests, who are likewise sacred (by dint of birth and inheritance), not by the original owner, who is not. The use of sacred property in a non-sacred state is a kind of theft known as *m'ilah*. Such a *neder* is called a *dedicatory* vow.

The Rabbis, however, extended the concept to include a *prohibitive* vow, a *neder* that prohibits the use of something to someone. Conceptually, the prohibitive vow is an easy next step, because if something belongs to the Temple, it is, in effect, prohibited for normal use. In Rabbinic times, then, a person did not actually have to give it to the Temple, which, in any case, was impossible after the Temple was destroyed in 70 CE. One could simply vow not to use something, *as if* it were given to the Temple, as if (that is) it were a *korban* ("a sacrifice").

But the matter is slightly more complicated. I might normally make such a vow by saying something like, "This wine of mine from which you benefit is like a sacrifice [*k'korban*]." This looks like a dedicatory vow donating the wine to God (were the Temple still standing). But as the careful wording indicates, it is only so dedicated when and if you benefit from it, not before. Until such time, I still own it and may use it for myself or for others—just not for you. The practical effect of such a *neder* is that even though I may keep on using it, you may not, because if you do, it becomes the equivalent of Temple property at that moment, and you are guilty of *m'ilah*. As a matter of personal piety, I might equally prohibit my own use of something in this roundabout way. By saying, "This wine of mine [or of someone else's] is *k'korban* when I use it," I vow (in effect) not to use it, but unless and until I use it, it remains available to serve to you or to others. I alone have sworn off it, without, however, having to swear an actual oath. The *prohibitive vow* (the *neder*) takes the place of a *prohibitive oath* (a *sh'vu'ah*) that would have accomplished the same thing but at the cost of invoking God's name and risking a possible curse if I later break my word and use it. I have simply erected a legal fiction that if and when I do use it, at that moment it becomes "like" the Temple's, in which case I would be guilty of misusing Temple property (*m'ilah*).

This prohibitive *neder* is sufficiently extendable to take the place of any *sh'vu'ah* imaginable. Suppose I have a business partner who has cheated me; I want to break off the relationship and never do business with her again. Rather than a *sh'vu'ah*, I can simply say, "All the world is like a *korban* to me if I use it and if I ever do business with her again." The double conditional ("if I use it" and "if I ever do business with her again") effectively accomplishes my goal, since I can hardly live without getting some benefit from the world.

We saw above that a *sh'vu'ah* can be *assertory* (testifying to a condition of fact, past or present) or *promissory* (testifying to a planned course of behavior for the future). As it occurs in the primary biblical instance (Numbers 30), the *issar* is similar to the promissory *sh'vu'ah*—indeed, it is shorthand for a larger term, *sh'vu'at issar*, meaning "an *issar* oath." The Hebrew root for *issar* has the connotation of "being bound," and a person can be bound either to act or not to act in some manner or other. The *issar*, therefore, can be positive ("I bind myself to come on time") or negative ("I bind myself not to come at all").

By the Mishnaic period, however, some Rabbis could not believe that *sh'vu'ah* and *sh'vu'at issar* were identical. Believing that each and every word of Torah has its own meaning, so that nothing can be redundant, they sought specific meaning for the *sh'vu'at issar* and found it. A *sh'vu'at issar*, they argued, is a subcategory of an ordinary *sh'vu'ah*, namely, a prohibition that one takes upon oneself, but without the use of any specific formulaic language. As such, it did not take God's name in vain, so was a relatively mild promise without real sanctions. It was eventually limited to a relatively specific case of taking on the obligation to fast under certain circumstances. In Eretz Yisrael, it took on yet another meaning—a generalized term to imply a vow.

The *issar*, therefore, was a relatively unimportant term, just a synonym of a *sh'vu'ah* in the Bible and, among the Rabbis, either a promise to fast or a synonym for a prohibitive vow (a *neder*).

Cherem, however, was a different matter. Nowadays, we think of *cherem* as the noun for "excommunication": we speak, that is, of placing heretics (for example) "in *cherem*," by which we mean that they are to be treated as completely outside the fold; no one may have anything to do with them. That use, however, is relatively late, occurring only in late strata of the Talmud and beyond. In the Bible, *cherem* does not yet have that connotation. Rather, it is a dedicatory vow like a *neder*, but promulgated by entire communities, not individuals. A community would dedicate its joint property to God under two circumstances: first, the spoils of war—entire cities, for example, and even the populations within them. The act of military devastation was thereby likened to a sacrifice in which the damage wrought by the warring Israelite army was considered the equivalent of an offering to God. A second use of *cherem* related to a campaign against idolatry, in which case the idolatrous objects, cultic accoutrements, and so on would be destroyed outright. The two uses are obviously related, since the war against the Canaanite nations was conceptualized as a war against idolaters. Unlike a *neder*, however, which also would have dedicated the captured items to God, the *cherem* consigned everything (with minor exceptions) to destruction by fire, like a real sacrifice offered up upon an altar.

By the late biblical period, in the post-exilic writings of the priests, *cherem* is no longer associated with either of these uses, neither with warfare, that is, nor with idolatry. Indeed, it is no longer a communal matter at all. Instead, it has been commuted into a particularly stringent type of personal dedicatory *neder*. If I vow something to God by a *cherem*, even the priests may not use it because it has to be destroyed by fire or, if a live animal or human being, killed. The item vowed could indeed be a human being, as long as the person named gave permission to be included in the *cherem*. It was used, for instance, by conspirators in the Second Temple period as a conditional vow to kill anyone in the group who became a turncoat.

The *cherem* of excommunication is an altogether different thing, derived, in fact, from an altogether different verb that sounds the same and that means "cut off." The *cherem* of warfare and idolatry has ceased, as has the *cherem* that demands burning or killing. What we have left is *cherem* as excommunication—not *cherem* as a vow at all, but *cherem* as cutting someone off from the body politic.

We are left with a variety of terms that are similar in that they are substitute words for the various terms we have already looked at. In general, *Kol Nidre* calls them *kinuyei*, the Aramaic form of the parallel Hebrew noun *kinuyim*, meaning "epithets" or "names" given to something or other. *Konamei* (singular: *konam*) and *konasei* (singular: *konas*) are two particular *kinuyim* that *Kol Nidre* mentions—it calls the latter *kinusei*—but there were many others, which the use of the generic *kinuyei* is supposed to cover. In general, people hesitated to use the various terms for oaths and vows, the same way people today avoid expressly mentioning the name of God, or even the way people pronounce certain swear words to avoid saying the actual word by substituting something that sounds like it: "darn" instead of "damn," for example. In its anxiety to cover all conceivable cases of vows and oaths we might make, *Kol Nidre* stipulates the most common euphemisms to which we might have recourse (*konamei* and *konasei*) and then subsumes everything else that we might come up with as simply one of the *kinuyei*.

In general, the specific *kinuyei* mentioned in the Mishnah follow prescribed linguistic patterns. Two euphemisms cited for *sh'vu'ah*, for example, are *sh'vutah* and *sh'vukah*. In both cases, the substitute term is grammatically shaped to sound like the original, except that one of the three Hebrew root consonants has been changed (the final *ayin* of *sh'vu'ah* has become a *tav* or a *kuf*). In addition, however, the substitute is not utter nonsense; it has something to do with the original *sh'vu'ah*. *Sh'vutah* (from the Hebrew root that gives us *Shabbat*) means "to cease" and is, therefore, related to an oath that prohibits something to the person making the declaration. *Sh'vukah* comes from the Aramaic root meaning "to abandon," a similar play on meaning, since someone under oath must abandon using whatever the oath prohibits.

The most common case mentioned, however, is *konam* (plural: *konamei*), intended as a substitute for *korban*, in the *neder* introduced by the statement that an object that we forbid to ourselves be considered "as if it is *korban* ['sacrifice']." *Konas* (plural: *konasei*) is used similarly. In both cases, the substitute word is shaped to sound like *korban*—thereby following the pattern of *sh'vutah* and *sh'vukah* relative to *sh'vu'ah*. But unlike these latter terms, neither *konam* nor *konas* comes from Hebrew or Aramaic. It turns out, however, that they come from the Greek *koinon*, meaning "something given to charity," a perfect parallel to a *neder* in which something is "as if a *korban*" (given to the Temple). *Koinon* (the masculine) appears also as *koinos* (feminine). *Koinon* and *koinos* have become *konam* (it is not the only case where an "n" sound becomes an "m") and *konas*.

Kol Nidre is therefore a perfectly normal legal document like anything a lawyer might draw up today to protect a client from damages. She would make a list of every possible eventuality—the usual formulas of vows and oaths to which the client might be liable, as well as whatever euphemisms there are—and then, for good measure, stipulate that the list is not exhaustive but includes any other words (*kinuyei*) that the client might have recourse to for whatever reason. For good measure, we get not only the nouns—*nidrei*, for example—but the verbs too—*dindarna*, from *n.d.r*, meaning "to make the *neder*." If the formula is not particularly poetic or moving, well, what legal contract is?

It may be that originally, people would say *Kol Nidre* in front of a sage or *bet din* (an actual court—Jewish law empowers several judges to act together as a court). This would be a midway stage between the original practice of *hatarat n'darim*—an individual consulting with a sage about certain oaths or vows that might be voided—and *Kol Nidre* as we have it—a prayer said in community as a blanket pardon for vows. The interim stage still featured individuals and a tribunal, but the specified oaths have become formulary.

If that is the case, it may be that the individual making the statement said the first part—in effect, "May all vows and oaths ... that I have vowed be null and void," and the tribunal answered with the second half, "All vows and oaths ... are null and void." When the formula became a prayer with no tribunal present, the two parts were combined in a ritualized performance by the prayer leader, who eventually chanted or sang it as a whole.

The occasion for *Kol Nidre* is itself interesting: the twilight hour that is more than "everyday" in its feeling tone, but is still not Yom Kippur yet. How did it get there? Why then, that is, instead of after nightfall, when Yom Kippur has actually begun?

The Palestinian *Kol Nidre* that the *geonim* had heard about was being recited on Rosh Hashanah or Yom Kippur. But even in Palestine, there were rabbinic objectors. An anonymous Palestinian responsum takes issue with the practice, not because oaths and vows may not be annulled, but because the annulment, halachically speaking, cannot occur on holidays. Babylonians too forbade annulment of any sort on Shabbat and holidays. So when *Kol Nidre* became a staple even in Babylonia, it had to be moved. Scheduling it just before Yom Kippur solved the problem. The holiday had not yet officially begun; during the twilight hour just before, annulment could still take place and, simultaneously, set the right tone for the Day of Atonement.

Kol Nidre: The Anxious Search for the Sacred

The amazing thing about *Kol Nidre* is that we insist on saying it. It is not just that we disagree with it on moral grounds. There are ways to get around that: to explain, for instance, that only vows with God are meant, or to invoke one of the many spiritual rationales that are offered by this book's contributors. The question is why we care enough even to offer those rationales—why, that is, we go on saying *Kol Nidre* when most of us do not even believe in the sacred power of the oaths and vows that are mentioned and when we never have recourse to them anyway. Why does *Kol Nidre* retain its hold on us? Why is it as sacrosanct an entity as anything else in all of Jewish liturgy?

The various essays that form the second half of the book consider this very question. Is it the music? Surely. Is it also the high drama of the occasion—Torah scrolls dressed in white and held aloft while *Kol Nidre* is chanted? Yes, no doubt it is that as well. But it is surely more. To some extent, it is the nature of Yom Kippur itself. Like no other holiday, Yom Kippur puts us in touch with the sacred; and like no other prayer, *Kol Nidre* puts us in touch with Yom Kippur. Desperately searching for the sacred, we attend *Kol Nidre* even though we neither understand it nor believe in it.

By "sacred," I mean the opposite of "secular." Ever since the middle of the nineteenth century, we have been on a road toward greater secularity. That is not necessarily a bad thing, if by "secular" we mean the discovery that the world is devoid of magical forces and that everything runs by an immutable set of scientific laws. Life has become incomparably better than it was when we thought the universe operated by moral rather than mathematical calculus.

But we have paid a price. Without inviolably sacred days on our calendar, holidays move to long weekends when we may conveniently contemplate sales rather than eternity. If places are not sacred, we can visit them on our own terms—no need to dress up, act differently, or open ourselves to the possibility of mystery. If we ourselves are not made in the image of God, because there is no God in whose image to be made or because we have decided to reduce God to whatever image we think we are easily capable of generating, then what is the point of the whole human enterprise? Not that there has to be a point. But we would like there to be one. That is why we have eulogies: to hear how those we love transcended pettiness. We will eventually get a eulogy of our own. What do we hope people will say about us?

The conversation about secularity has a long history. Its founding prophets of the heady nineteenth century, the era when all seemed possible and we didn't yet know what a world war was, predicted a demystified world where progress would be quite enough to satisfy our sacred yearning. Progress we have had. For most of us, however, it is not enough. So people seek the transcendent wherever they can find it.

The problem is that secularization really has thrown us back on our own devices. It is not that the sacred doesn't exist—it does. But like so much else, it is not so much discovered as it is created. In point of fact, the sacred has always been something we manufacture to some degree: great cathedrals, Bach's B Minor Mass, the music for *Kol Nidre*—we make these up. But we used to pretend that we didn't, and we cannot do that anymore. Secularization is the process of yanking at the curtain and finding out who the Wizard of Oz really is. The curtain is gone, and we are the wizard.

That's called disenchantment, and an increasing number of people wish they still had a wizard to do the magic tricks. Some of them become terrorists who wage holy war against science, the secular, and everything modern. Others are the peaceful variety who go about their business but want more than business to go about, and spend an inordinate amount of time explaining why the curtain never really came down after all: Darwin was wrong; materialism is evil; the Bible had it right. Their loyal opposition all too easily become reductionists who confuse the wizard with the sacred and pronounce both of them missing. But secularity is no enemy of all that's holy. Disenchantment need not entail demoralization. A universe that operates by natural law can still have mystery. The purpose of life, our vision of an ultimate, the insistence that we matter, and the search for meaning are as real as ever. The wizard is gone, but the yellow brick road is still well populated. Get rid of the recidivists who utterly reject modernity; dispense also with the reductionists who utterly reject the sacred. Join the masses on the yellow brick road, striving for meaning without wizardry.

Yes, the old order of supernatural wonder has had its day, but listening in on the conversations, it is hard to tell just who is secular and who is not. Take Charles Taylor, Jane Bennett, and George Levine, three prominent philosophers on the subject. Taylor contends that "the theory of evolution has, in fact, given us further, deeper cause to wonder at the universe."[3] Bennett and Levine write whole books on "the enchantment of modern life" and "the re-enchantment of the world."[4] Are these thoughtful men and women religious or secular? The very dichotomy of secular versus religious has to be abandoned.

Overwhelmingly, we pilgrims on the yellow brick road have converged onto a path toward meaning, a search that has become a veritable cottage industry by now. The *New York Times Book Review* of January 23, 2011, for example, features two lead articles on "What It All Means."[5] Other philosophical titles in the last several years include "The Meaning of Life," "On the Meaning of Life," and "What's It All About."[6] Is "meaning" all that different from "sacred"? What about "mystery" and "transcendent," two other terms that come up from time to time? Whatever word we use, we are all on the road together wanting desperately to know that we can be modern, secular, scientific, and savvy without giving up on the sense that life still matters.

More than any other occasion in the entire Jewish calendar, Yom Kippur eve has been our Jewish time that matters. Out of nowhere, crowds materialize and actually sit in silence. The synagogue is quiet too. Energy runs high; memories go deep. As if nothing has changed since the beginning of time, we get ready for *Kol Nidre*. For a very short while, it is as if nothing has eroded our certainties, because nothing has changed in a thousand years or more.

People make the mistake of thinking that belief precedes prayer, as if they cannot pray because they cannot believe. The reverse is more likely the case. Prayer compels belief, not the other way around. The communal worship of Yom Kippur establishes realities of which daily life is only dimly capable of grasping. For a very brief moment, we are in touch with the sacred, with our finitude, with those we love, with the broader human universe that calls us to our better selves, and with the God we are not even sure we believe in.

◦◦◦

The Heavenly Assembly

Dr. Marc Zvi Brettler

Although its haunting melody and years of association make *Kol Nidre* very meaningful, it is a very odd prayer. About half of it is composed of Aramaic synonyms for "vows" and "annulling." It concludes with a medley of biblical verses. Yet strangest of all is its beginning, invoking "the authority of the heavenly court [or: assembly]," the *yeshivah shel ma'alah*. What is this *yeshivah*? What a remarkable contrast the opening of the Yom Kippur liturgy is to its clear and appropriate conclusion, in which we affirm our monotheism by reciting the *Sh'ma*, declaring God our ultimate ruler and announcing, "Adonai is the (only) God"!

The concept of this *yeshivah* goes back to the divine councils of the ancient Near East. Mesopotamians, living in what is now Iraq, believed in councils as gathering places for the fifty great gods or, at times, just seven gods who met in a type of executive session. The most senior deity, Anu, the sky-god, would preside. Closer to Israel, in Ugarit (a city in ancient Syria), the council convened atop a mountain and was led by El (related

---

Dr. Marc Zvi Brettler is the Dora Golding Professor of Biblical Studies at Brandeis University and has published and lectured widely on metaphor and the Bible, the nature of biblical historical texts, and gender issues and the Bible. He contributed to all volumes of the *My People's Prayer Book: Traditional Prayers, Modern Commentaries* series, winner of the National Jewish Book Award, and to *My People's Passover Haggadah: Traditional Texts, Modern Commentaries* and *Who by Fire, Who by Water—Un'taneh Tokef* (all Jewish Lights). He is coeditor of *The Jewish Study Bible*, which won the National Jewish Book Award; and author of *How to Read the Jewish Bible*, among other books and articles. He has also been interviewed on National Public Radio's *Fresh Air* by Terry Gross.

22

to the Hebrew word for "god," *el*; plural: *elim*, and a variant *elohim*). In some cases, the chief deity was the Canaanite deity, Ba'al, well-known from biblical texts as well. These councils or assemblies decided issues concerning kingship, who among the deities would have children, and other important matters.

This council is referred to often in the Hebrew Bible as the "hosts" (*tz'va'ot*) whom Adonai controls, as in the frequent expression *Adonai tz'va'ot*, "the Lord [or: Adonai] of hosts." Sometimes, following ancient Near Eastern precedents, where the senior god headed the council comprising his children, the other members of the council are called "sons of God" (e.g., Psalm 29:1, when they are told to praise Adonai). Like Adonai, who was typically viewed anthropomorphically in the Bible, these "children" too were human-like; indeed, Genesis 6:2 states that "the divine beings [literally 'sons of God,' *b'nei ha'elohim*] saw how beautiful the daughters of men were and took wives from among those who pleased them." As a group, these heavenly beings were called by various names: *sod k'doshim*, "the council of the holy ones" (Psalm 89:8); *k'hal k'doshim*, "the assembly of the holy ones" (Psalm 89:6); and *b'nei elyon*, "the divine assembly" or "the assembly of El" (Psalm 82:1).

Psalm 82 (especially verses 6–7) suggests that these beings were once immortal but are now mortal: "I had taken you for divine beings, sons of the Most High, all of you; but you shall die as men do, fall like any prince." Their mortality, along with the fact that they need approval from Adonai before acting, fundamentally differentiates them from Adonai. As Psalm 82 reflects, the Bible sometimes depicts a multiplicity of deities with Adonai as the supreme, incomparable deity who has full power over the others. Eventually, perhaps, as radical monotheism took hold, these other godlike beings were understood as semidivine. In this sense, even these sections of the Bible should be considered monotheistic.

Several biblical texts depict this council in action. 1 Kings 22:19 portrays "Adonai seated upon his throne, with all the host of heaven standing in attendance to the right and to the left of Him," and God asking advice of the council. In Isaiah 6:8, the prophet stands amidst this council, as God asks for a volunteer: "Whom shall I send? Who will go for us?" The most detailed description of the council is in the first two chapters of Job, where "one day the divine beings presented themselves before Adonai, and the Adversary came along with them" (1:6). The Hebrew for "the Adversary" is *hasatan*. In Hebrew, personal names (like

Moses, Deborah, Satan) cannot take a definite article (the prefix *ha*), so it is clear that *satan* here is not this individual's name, but a common noun depicting his role as bad guy or troublemaker within the council on high. Indeed, until late in the Second Temple period, most members of the council are unnamed and often undifferentiated. This adversary, the *satan*, has enough power to control nations, to alter the weather, and to bring on cataclysmic plagues, but only with Adonai's permission. He is also sly and clever enough to convince God to afflict the guiltless Job. In post-biblical literature (Rabbinic and other) and in one late biblical text (1 Chronicles 21:1, most likely from the fourth century BCE), he is explicitly called Satan (without the definite article *ha*), though he is not there red and horned. That popular image comes about only later by way of Christian art during the Middle Ages.

The idea of a heavenly council is further developed in late Second Temple and Rabbinic literature by various delineations of its angelic members. In the Bible, the only named angels (Hebrew: *malachim*, literally, "[divine] messengers") are Michael and Gabriel, and they are found only in Daniel, one of the latest biblical books (second century BCE); many more angels are named later, some with specific roles. Angels play a significant role in some of the Dead Sea Scrolls, and many angels are named in the late Second Temple extra-biblical book of 1 Enoch, which, for example, names seven angels who taught people knowledge (chapter 8) and lists six archangels: Suruel (or Uriel), Raphael, Raguel, Michael, Sarakael, and Gabriel (chapter 20). Similarly the Talmud knows many angels—Raphael, for example, the angel of healing, and Uriel, the angel of light. Under the influence of Maimonides (1135–1204) and other rationalist Jewish philosophers, the role of angels and the divine council was diminished in many Jewish circles. Yet it lives on in the opening of *Kol Nidre*.

As I think of the words *yeshivah shel ma'alah*, two Rabbinic midrashim come to mind. One is based on Daniel 7:9, where "Thrones were set in place, and the Ancient of Days [a name of Adonai] took his seat." Sensitive to the plural "thrones"—for Adonai certainly needs only one throne—the Babylonian Talmud (Sanhedrin 38b) suggests, "One throne is for Justice, and the other is for Mercy." Another midrash (see *Sefer Ha'aggadah* 513:77)—based on the words of Job 25:2 (which appear in the *Kaddish*), "He imposes peace in his heights" (*oseh shalom bimromav*)—states, "Michael is the prince of snow, and Gabriel the prince of fire. Yet Michael does not quench Gabriel, nor does Gabriel incinerate Michael. Even when half of an angel is fire and the other half is snow, the Holy One, blessed be He, makes peace between the two parts."

There is much that I find comforting about the divine council that introduces the *Kol Nidre* prayer. It is easier for me to believe in a God who (as in Job) is misled by bad advisors than to believe in an entirely good, omniscient, and omnipotent deity who works altogether independently. I want to invoke the council with the hope that one of its members, named "Mercy," will be active on my behalf. And finally, I hope that my calls for repentance will not be received by one of the lower members of the highly hierarchical council, but by Adonai directly. A deity who is great enough to make fire and snow coexist is great enough to remember that I am human, and great enough to forgive.

What's in a Bowl?

BABYLONIAN MAGIC SPELLS AND THE ORIGIN OF KOL NIDRE

Rabbi Dalia Marx, PhD

The Jews of late antiquity had a rich and nuanced practice of magic. We might depict them as rational and logical, but any perusal of the Babylonian Talmud will show a preoccupation with *mazikin* ("harmful beings") and other supernatural powers. Indeed, Jews no less than their non-Jewish neighbors believed in the existence of these types of forces in the world around them, some of them beneficial but others harmful. The positive and sometimes even the malignant forces might be harnessed to a person's advantage. But a person needed protection from them as well, toward which end people depended on professionals to create spells against illnesses, enemies, and the realm of the sinister in general.

Rabbi Dalia Marx, PhD, is a professor of liturgy and midrash at the Jerusalem campus of Hebrew Union College–Jewish Institute of Religion and teaches in various academic institutions in Israel, the United States, and Europe. Marx earned her doctorate at the Hebrew University in Jerusalem and her rabbinic ordination at HUC–JIR in Jerusalem and Cincinnati. She is involved in various research groups and is active in promoting progressive Judaism in Israel. Marx contributed to *Who by Fire, Who by Water— Un'taneh Tokef* (Jewish Lights). She writes for academic journals and the Israeli press, and is engaged in creating new liturgies and midrashim.

Spells such as these have been unearthed in various locations in Mesopotamia, especially in the Babylonian city of Nippur (today's Iraq). They were written in 300–700 CE on clay bowls, buried in and around domestic environments, sometimes in graveyards. The incantations are composed of recurring phrases, words, verses, and various types and styles of formulae, to call upon different names of God and angels, who were believed to have positive powers (though occasionally also malignant ones), and to protect against the demonic as well. The bowls were usually buried upside down under the floor in and around the house, to prevent the powers that they held from escaping as they worked their magic promoting prosperity, health, and protection, especially for the young. They represent the vivid popular culture that is only partially reflected in the contemporary Rabbinic sources.

Scholars have shown interesting similarities between some texts of these magic bowls and *Kol Nidre*, both in vocabulary and style. For example:

> Overturned are all the vows [*kol nidre*] and curses and spells and sorceries and curses and sorcerers and evil knocks that may lodge in this man.[1]

The pronounced parallel to *Kol Nidre* ("All vows, obligations, oaths," etc.) and the shared vocabulary in general are remarkable because *Kol Nidre* is known to us only from much later sources, from the geonic literature of the ninth century. Not all the words typical of *Kol Nidre* are found in the bowls, but we do have interesting similarities that go beyond just the actual words *kol nidre*. In some bowls, we see long chains of annulment and banning phrases, just as in *Kol Nidre*: for example, "Bound, seized, attached, pressed down, trashed, exorcised are all [the evil powers]."[2] Both the bowls and the prayer use certain key Aramaic nouns and verbs, such as "vow," "swear," "bound," and "annulled," and both utilize a common style and syntax. We cannot help but conclude that formulae quite similar to our liturgy were in Jewish use centuries before the appearance of *Kol Nidre* in the liturgy, even if they were composed and used in a completely different context.

The linguistic and stylistic resemblances between the magical bowl formulae and the prayer are striking enough for many scholars to conclude that *Kol Nidre* originated in the world of magic. No wonder geonic authorities were not overjoyed finding *Kol Nidre* appearing in the various liturgies that came their way. But despite the parallels in formulaic style, prayer is not magic, and we should pay equal attention to the way the two differ. Scholars have been less careful to explore the differences in psychological and cultural function served by the magic bowls on one hand and the liturgical prayer on the other.

Some differences between *Kol Nidre* and magic bowls are clear:

1. *Kol Nidre* is used in a legal-liturgical context. The bowls were used for magic.
2. *Kol Nidre* is an oral ritual. The bowls relied on a written text. True, the installation of bowls in the home may have had an oral component of which we are ignorant, but the formula inscribed upon them functioned thereafter as a written charm acting in its own right.
3. Although *Kol Nidre* might not have begun as a communal practice, our sole knowledge of it is as a public synagogue ritual. The bowls were entirely personal and private, a function of each individual home.
4. *Kol Nidre* corresponds to a specific calendrical moment (Yom Kippur). The bowls were utilized at any time, presumably as needed.
5. Although normally sung by a cantor, *Kol Nidre* may be led by any adult Jew. The bowls were produced by experts of magical ritual.
6. Despite their common language ("all vows"), *Kol Nidre* is general, annulling all the vows and oaths that the people present in the synagogue take. The magic bowls were specific, each one designed to protect a particular client (or clients) from demons and from bad wishes of other human beings and powers—it was meant to annul any vows that could harm the client made primarily by foe but presumably also by friend or even the client him- or herself. *Kol Nidre*, that is, annuls the vows and oaths of each individual Jew present in the synagogue, while the magic bowls compelled external powers.
7. *Kol Nidre* makes no sense unless the participant understands its content or at least its aspects and implications. It requires intentionality (*kavvanah*) and earnestness, if not in the strict halakhic sense, then in the manner that it is perceived. A client who ordered a magic bowl did not have to understand it at all; on the contrary, the efficacy of the incantation may have been enhanced by its cryptic and secret nature.

To sum up, *Kol Nidre* has both personal and communal aspects, in that it negates individual oaths but only from its communal ritual setting. It corresponds to annual calendrical time and relies on no special technical knowledge. The magic bowls were dependent on individual whim; they were made by experts for private and domestic use in order to fulfill personal needs.

Even if *Kol Nidre* is a direct descendant of magic practices in Babylonia of late antiquity, we can detect a crucial developmental difference between the two. The magic bowls operated in a world full of harmful external powers, in which case all one could do is to protect oneself, one's family, and one's property; *Kol Nidre* does not deal with fear of demonic powers, invoked by other people's vows, but, rather, with the fear of unfulfilled oaths and vows made by each worshiper. It revolves about the human being who says it, not a world of demons from whom the person saying the prayer must fear retaliation.

If the differences between the two practices are so great, however, what is the use of comparing the two? What can be learned from their relationship and possible common origin?

First, it is important to acknowledge the stylistic and linguistic similarities between the two. The magic bowls reveal much older linguistic forms and an older practice as well, perhaps, than what we see in *Kol Nidre*. It is, at the very least, fascinating to watch a domestic magical practice become a communal liturgical ceremony. Second, however, is the realization that the two practices together attest to the enormous gravity people ascribed to vows and the consequences of making them—so much so that a formal means to deal with them was instituted in both private and public domains. Taking vows was considered a serious act with cosmic ramifications, binding on both human and supernatural beings, who share a common world of cause and effect.

Most importantly, the two practices exhibit profound features of human nature, especially when confronting the unknown. Both reveal elemental concerns rooted in human vulnerability, the sense of ultimate helplessness in a world that is beyond our control or comprehension. Both reflect anxieties in a reality that is beyond the human ken, and a craving for control in a world that is all too often out of control. Like prayer, both *Kol Nidre* and the magic bowls are ways of using speech formulaically to achieve certain ends. But neither one is actually a prayer. Both appeal to law more than to God, in that the bowls access the arcane laws that govern hidden forces of nature, while *Kol Nidre* has its place in the legal context of Rabbinic Judaism. The bowls obey magical laws that banish evil forces from one's immediate universe; *Kol Nidre* prescribes a legal means to prevent one's own ill doing through vows made in error or in haste.

Did the people who ordered a bowl from a professional actually stop worrying about the dangers that made them order them once the bowl was placed in its proper place under the doorpost of the house? I dare say that the anxiety did not completely evaporate. Do Jews who, even today, depart crowded synagogues after hearing *Kol Nidre* leave behind their regrets, guilt, and shame over wrong decisions, unkept promises, and unfulfilled expectations? Probably not entirely—fears and anxieties have a persistent nature. These two practices are designed to ease distress and attain peace of mind: the bowls, because of danger directed by others at the person deploying the incantations; *Kol Nidre*, because of danger caused ultimately by the worshipers themselves. Both acknowledge the insecurities of life and the haunting realization that we can never gain full control over our lives.

And to be honest, do any of the modern precautions we take to overcome our fears and anxieties have a total effect? Do any of the "self-help" books, shows, and specialists, diets, psychological therapies, physical exercises, Eastern and Western practices, not to mention the excessive medications and drugs many of us consume, remove distress and fears? I bet that in most cases the answer would have to be negative here too.

One can finish "unfinished business" only to some extent. Our existential fears remain with us, and we can only pray that we may confine them and gain some control over them. Yom Hakippurim is the day our tradition designates for *cheshbon nefesh*, "soul-searching," but every time we stand in prayer, not only on the High Holy Days, we have an opportunity for reflection and modest empowerment. Yom Hakippurim and *Kol Nidre* provide us with a language and tools to help us cope with our finite and fragile nature. This is a redemptive language, and it grants us *nechamah purta*, "minor consolation," and a chance for growth.

∽∾

I thank Dr. Dan Levene and Professor David Levine for their help and valuable suggestions.

Sermons and History

THE "MARRANO" CONNECTION TO KOL NIDRE

Rabbi Marc Saperstein, PhD

It is not uncommon, even today, to hear that *Kol Nidre* refers back to the period of the Spanish Inquisition, when Jews who had been forcefully converted to Christianity felt it necessary to seek divine pardon for the vows that they had made to live as Christians. Where did this view come from? And is there any truth to it?

One way of tracing the diffusion of any idea within the Jewish community is to look at sermons delivered on occasions of large synagogue attendance. The evening of Yom Kippur is an obvious example. For the first four decades of the twentieth century, however, *Kol Nidre* was rarely addressed from the pulpit, especially within American Reform Jewish synagogues. This pattern of neglect seems to have changed in the early 1940s, when *Kol Nidre* was being heard for the first time by many Reform Jews. It had virtually disappeared from American Reform liturgy, on account of its content: a bald statement that Jews may successfully nullify their vows and promises in advance! A large hostile literature had attacked

---

Rabbi Marc Saperstein, PhD, is principal of Leo Baeck College in London. Previously he taught and headed Jewish studies programs for twenty-nine years at Harvard University, Washington University in St. Louis, and George Washington University in Washington, D.C., and was vice president of the American Academy for Jewish Research. He contributed to *Who by Fire, Who by Water—Un'taneh Tokef* (Jewish Lights).

Jews for this apparent unreliability in their commitments. Already in Germany, reformers attempted to eliminate the *Kol Nidre* text, and American Reform rabbis followed suit. It was not until the *New Revised Union Prayer Book II* of 1945 that the words *Kol Nidre* even appear in the evening liturgy for Yom Kippur.[1]

Until that time, *Kol Nidre* was replaced by other material considered more suitable for this most holy day of the Jewish year.[2] If *Kol Nidre* was mentioned at all, it would be in a passing and somewhat disdainful reference, as in a 1928 sermon by Joseph Stolz of Chicago, who describes Psalm 130 as "set at the head of this night's solemn service in place of the antiquated *Kol Nidre*."[3]

In 1940, however, sermons drawing on the *Kol Nidre* liturgy became considerably more prevalent, many of them asserting a historical link between *Kol Nidre* and the Spanish conversos, then generally known by the older term "Marranos." In 1940, Sidney S. Tedesche of Brooklyn's venerable Union Temple introduces the Marrano hypothesis in passing: "The meaning of *Kol Nidre* was that all vows which a loyal Jew might be forced to make against his faith imposed by harsh inquisitor or assassin were to be forgiven." He then transitions quickly to a more general point about the hypocrisy of the gentile world:

> A nation can violate treaties, override boundaries, rain death and destruction from the skies, rob and slay and kill, deceive, betray and act in general as though there is no such thing as a moral law, yet they proclaim in utter cynicism that the only unforgivable crime is to be a Jew.

The allusion to Nazi Germany would have been unmistakable at a time when Yom Kippur observances in England were being curtailed because of the German bombing of London and other cities.[4]

More detail about the Marrano connection was given on the same 1940 Yom Kippur evening by the distinguished New York rabbi Louis I. Newman, a published historian with strong Zionist sympathies. He begins with substantial background information to the effect that *Kol Nidre* was introduced into the liturgy by the common people despite the opposition of the rabbis. But he continues to emphasize a different point—not that *Kol Nidre* was a misplaced piece of popular superstition, but that it is "associated with Jewish heroism and Jewish martyrdom." With utter cer-

tainty, he proclaims, "We know that the *Kol Nidre* prayer is closely identified with the history of ... the Spanish Marranos," actually *instituted* for
the benefit of the Iberian crypto-Jews. At the same time, he concedes that
Cecil Roth, perhaps the leading contemporary authority on the Marranos
and the Spanish Inquisition, had dismissed this entire theory as "fanci-
ful."[5] Like Tedesche, Newman is more concerned about the resonance
with contemporary Jewish suffering: the plight of Jewish refugees, especially those deported to the "Lublin Reservation" in Nazi-occupied eastern
Poland.[6] He concludes, "Out of horrors such as these, *Kol Nidre* was born
in days gone by." The association of *Kol Nidre* with historical Jewish suffering, replete with poignant resonance, is central to the sermon.[7]

By the early 1950s, the chanting of *Kol Nidre* had been officially
reintroduced into the High Holy Day volume of the *Newly Revised Union
Prayer Book* (1945). The text was missing, but the traditional words were
sung to the familiar melody, following a rabbi's prayer in English having
nothing to do with the original *Kol Nidre* content. With *Kol Nidre* back,
rabbis were free to turn to the association with the Marranos, which, by
then, seems to have become widely accepted. Norbert L. Rosenthal,
preaching in 1951 in Tulsa, Oklahoma, on the topic "*Kol Nidre*: The
Song of the Heart," asserts that the simple and unvarnished legal terminology with no beauty of diction or elevation of content once "served to
liberate from a nightmare of fear and self-reproach the *Anusim*, the
'forced ones,' who had chosen conversion in preference to the alternatives
of exile or execution."[8]

Two years later, on Yom Kippur 1953, Louis I. Newman gave
another sermon on *Kol Nidre*, in which he abandoned his 1940 historical
reservations about the theory's veracity. With newfound certainty, he
describes the process by which *Kol Nidre* must have come into being:

> Out of pity, the Jewish people evolved a formulation of
> absolution for the Marranos—the formula known as "*Kol
> Nidre*." In order that no Crypto-Jew need be recognized,
> the men of the Congregation covered their heads with the
> *Tallit* or Prayer-Shawl from the beginning to the end of the
> Service. Thus a compassionate and clement community
> made it possible for those whose conscience prompted
> them to join their brother-Jews at divine worship, to
> answer the summons of tradition and of their better self."[9]

The following year, Max Nussbaum, himself a refugee from Nazi Germany, entitled his Yom Kippur eve sermon "Hail the Marrano." Recapitulating the historical background material, he raises the familiar problem of the *Kol Nidre*'s power and appeal despite the dry legal terminology of its words. Recognizing, however, that scholarship had demonstrated the impossibility of *Kol Nidre* being composed as late as the "Marranos," he reconstructs the historical account somewhat:

> It is only recently that historical studies have begun to shed light on the whole mystery of all three: the melody, the text, and the prologue. We know today that the *Kol Nidre* is indeed a unique memorial to important historical events. It has its origin in Spain—not in the Spain of the Middle Ages, but in the one of the 7th century....
>
> Because of its peculiar origin, *Kol Nidre* thus assumed special significance, centuries later, during the Spanish Inquisition. The Marranos used to assemble during Yom Kippur in some concealed place in order to renounce their vows and ask forgiveness and absolution for their "sins" as did their forefathers centuries before.[10]

Despite the fact that *Kol Nidre* is documented in medieval Ashkenaz much more than in Spain, the association of Iberian crypto-Jews with a prayer that annuls vows or with the proclamation that it is permissible to pray with sinners (*avaryanim*) has at least a superficial plausibility. But the link of Marranos with the *Kol Nidre* melody is totally far-fetched. As Newman himself had noted in his 1940 sermon, the consensus of musicologists is that it originated in Germany. Yet for Nussbaum, even the melody is connected to the plight of Spanish Jews in the Inquisition:

> It is the outcry of a people, crushed and broken, haunted and hunted. More specifically, the song of the forced convert, the lamentation of the martyr, who poured all the sentiments of his heart into music. And yet I believe it is also a *monument* to the loyalty of the Marrano. Mingled with the notes in minor are those in major key—thus expressing his joyous exultation when he could rejoin his brothers and embrace the Torah. The *Kol Nidre* is both a chant of grief and a song of triumph....

The whole life pattern of generations of Marranos—a pattern simultaneously horrible and heroic—was compressed in the *Kol Nidre,* the words and the melody, replete with both serenity and hope. Thus *Kol Nidre,* the first movement in the Yom Kippur symphony of devotion, becomes a religious salutation to the Marrano."[11]

All this is based upon the vague reference to recent "historical studies" that result in what "we know today" about the origin and subsequent role of *Kol Nidre.*

That not only Reform rabbis emphasized the Marrano connection can be seen in two Orthodox rabbinical sermons from the same period. The first, by Rabbi Leo Jung of New York, was delivered in 1952:

> Intrigued by the contrast between the beautiful music and the cold paragraph which was set to it, a scholar of the last century offered this explanation. For hundreds of years, Jews in the Iberian peninsula lived in the shadow of the Inquisition with its ruthless cruelty. Its officers enforced baptism on them and punished the slightest deviation from Christian custom or practice with unimaginable torture. Some of our brethren accepted a specious conformity and vowed abrogation of Jewish loyalty in order to save their own lives.... [By means of *Kol Nidre*], they begged forgiveness for the vows made under frightful duress when they escaped from the cage that was Spain into freedom. They declared all such extorted promises false and pleaded to be re-accepted into the House of Israel.[12]

The historical accuracy revealed here is not at the highest level. Iberian *Jews* lived under the shadow of the Inquisition not for centuries but for fewer than thirteen years, from its establishment in January 1480 until the Expulsion; officers of the Inquisition did not enforce baptism, but rather enforced faithful observance of Christianity by those who had been baptized; torture was used not to punish deviations from Christian practice but for refusal to confess such deviations. It is the association with Jewish suffering rather than the details that is paramount.

Three years later, Leon Stitskin, another Orthodox rabbi, made the same historical connection at the beginning of his Yom Kippur evening sermon:

We have ushered in the most solemn day of the year with the prayer of *Kol Nidre*. It is related to the wretched life of the Marranos—the Spanish Jews of the 15th century, forced to embrace a strange faith, but in secret, holding steadfastly to their own traditions and loyalties. On *Kol Nidre* night, the Marranos assembled in cellars and attics and pronounced this vow, asking G-d to nullify the oaths to renounce Judaism made to the inquisitors. This hymn brings to mind a picture of a people huddled in hidden places, bearing with endurance untold persecution and barbaric atrocities. It is a picture of Israel in deep pain, agony and anguish. Alas, the threat of human suffering runs through the entire course of Jewish history unrelentingly and undiminishingly.[13]

Note also that while Jung spoke of former New Christians who had left the Iberian Peninsula to re-affiliate with Jewish life, Stitskin, like Nussbaum before him, speaks of Marranos gathering in some concealed place while still in Spain for *Kol Nidre*. Neither scenario is especially plausible, nor can it be documented by historical evidence.

Why did the Marrano connection with *Kol Nidre* become so appealing to preachers in the middle of the past century? Perhaps most obvious is the context of Nazi persecution. The sermons from the early 1940s and 1950s depict the Marrano as the very model of a Jewish martyr, willing to die (if necessary) out of loyalty to Judaism—a potentially inspiring association for Jews gathered in the hush of Yom Kippur eve.

A second relevant phenomenon of the time is assimilation. Nussbaum makes this explicit in the continuation of his sermon "Hail to the Marrano." When he excoriates Jews who spend Friday evening at baseball games rather than in synagogue, he characterizes his generation as gradually becoming "Marranos in reverse: Jews from without and Gentiles from within."[14] Nineteen years later, Eugene Borowitz would publish *The Masks Jews Wear*, expanding this formulation: "We are Marranos in reverse, for we have repressed our inner identity."[15]

Finally, these rabbis were able to draw on a growing body of historical literature becoming available at the time. The theory that *Kol Nidre* emerged in seventh-century Visigothic Spain with the first mass forced conversion had been proposed by the German rabbi and scholar Joseph S.

Bloch in 1917; it became more widely known a decade later (1927), when Bloch referred to it in a book published in English.[16] Critics pointed out that the Visigothic connection was supported by no evidence and was unknown to ninth-century Babylonian Rabbinic authorities (the *geonim*) in their discussion of the text.[17] The later Marrano connection with *Kol Nidre* had been proposed by Leon Mandelstamm, for example, in 1860.[18] But that too had been challenged as having no supporting evidence.

In addition to the *Jewish Encyclopedia*, the most likely source of information about the "Marranos" would have been the highly influential British historian Cecil Roth, whom, as we saw, Rabbi Newman actually cited in his sermon. Roth's 1931 article "The Religion of the Marranos" (incorporated into his 1932 book *A History of the Marranos*, reprinted in 1941) began by dismissing the "popular fantasy" of a complete "subterranean Judaism" as "far removed from the truth," and his discussion of crypto-Jewish observance of the Day of Atonement makes no mention of *Kol Nidre*.[19] Nevertheless, his book contains a chapter entitled "Saints, Heroes and Martyrs," and in his foreword to the 1958 third edition of his book, Roth wrote that "years have diminished, though it is to be hoped not entirely obliterated, the author's high romanticism of a quarter-century ago." That was an image with obvious appeal to Jewish preachers.[20]

This idealized portrait was strongly challenged in 1958, when Ellis Rivkin—who would teach Jewish history to two generations of rabbinical students at Hebrew Union College, Cincinnati—published a seminal article entitled "The Utilization of Non-Jewish Sources for the Reconstruction of Jewish History."[21] Rivkin presented an alternative picture of the Iberian converso and the Inquisition: not all Jews who accepted baptism in the wake of the 1391 riots were compelled to do so, and many who converted in subsequent years did so voluntarily; by the 1470s and 1480s, three to four generations later, most of the "New Christian" conversos were quite content to be accepted into Christian society and retained Jewish folkways more out of family tradition than out of a secret Jewish loyalty; accusations documented in Inquisitional records had to be read skeptically; some of those who were burned at the stake died proclaiming their faithfulness to Christianity, insisting that the accusations of Judaizing were slanders.

This alternative presentation of converso religious identity put a damper on the enthusiasm for including Marranos in Yom Kippur sermons, as it became more problematic for preachers to present them as models of inspiring heroism and a way to salvage the legalistic content of the *Kol Nidre* text.

But old mythic images die hard. The idealized notion of a prevalent secret Judaism, reinvigorated by the publication of the English translation of Yitzhak Baer's influential *A History of the Jews in Christian Spain*,[22] began to take on new resonance with the emergence of Soviet Jewry— "the Jews of silence"—as a major issue of Jewish concern. Perhaps not surprisingly, therefore, one still finds references to *Kol Nidre* as a Marrano prayer, even though there is no evidence to suggest that it was.[23]

⟨๛⟩

The Magic of the Moment

KOL NIDRE IN PROGRESSIVE JUDAISM

Dr. Annette M. Boeckler

O n Passover in what the Bible calls the first month of the Jewish year, Jews recall their freedom from slavery and the birth of the Jewish people; half a year later at the beginning of the new year according to the Rabbis, Jews reflect their freedom from sin and a new beginning as Jewish individuals. But the Day of Atonement, Yom Kippur, although being celebrated right at the beginning of the Rabbinic new year, has no narrative comparable to the story of the Exodus out of Egypt. Its opening formula, *Kol Nidre*, has become the emotional substitute for the missing liberation narrative. It especially attracted people's feelings after being outfitted with the familiar Ashkenazi[1] melody, somewhere in medieval times, and many Sephardim too, since then, have adapted melodies of incomparable beauty. Most Jews do not understand the Aramaic, and the translation—if it is even in the prayer book—may not be all that revealing, but the *Kol Nidre* melody is enough to evoke, for many, such intense feelings as probably no other Jewish prayer does. Above all, this melody triggers memories: of the

Dr. Annette M. Boeckler is head librarian and lecturer for Jewish biblical interpretation and Jewish liturgy at Leo Baeck College in London. She has a PhD in Bible and studied *chazanut*, both privately (with cantor Marcel Lang, *z"l*) and at the Levisson Instituut in Amsterdam.

year just past, of people who have died, of eras long gone, of Jewish martyrs through the ages. Its peculiar power to awaken Jewish identity comes through the well-known story of Franz Rosenzweig, who, upon hearing *Kol Nidre*, abandoned a plan to convert to Christianity in favor of reclaiming his Jewish heritage.

The *Kol Nidre* melody can also evoke uncertainty of the future and make the listener shiver. Yearnings, fears, and sorrows deep down within are set free. For many Jews, *Kol Nidre* provides the sound of atonement that is the core experience of Yom Kippur and that could not otherwise be put adequately into words.

Nevertheless, progressive Judaism, which began in nineteenth-century Germany, started overwhelmingly without *Kol Nidre*. As we shall see, the tune remained, but without the familiar words, which were reintroduced only with the American prayer book *Gates of Repentance* in 1978.[2]

Classical Reform of the nineteenth and early twentieth century sought to justify Judaism to modern Jews and to the society in which they lived. It was deemed important to say only those prayers that could be recited honestly, without offending the enlightened, rational, scientific mind. The entire notion of annulling vows was anathema to modern ethical consciousness. In addition, the Ashkenazi version of *Kol Nidre* requests freedom from vows that might potentially be made in the year to come, not those already made in the year just ending—a notion that makes little sense logically. It had come into being as a halakhic response to the Talmudic objection against a wholesale annulment of vows in the past, but Reform Jews questioned the domination of halakhah. So morally, logically, and theologically, the text of *Kol Nidre* seemed objectionable to Reform Jews, who sought, therefore, to eliminate it.

There was also a more immediate problem. Since medieval times and even in the nineteenth century itself,[3] *Kol Nidre* had nurtured anti-Semitic misunderstandings. Because of *Kol Nidre*, Christians accused Jews of not keeping their promises.[4] The Christian suspicions finally led to special rituals—an oath that Jews had to take in a public courtroom, guaranteeing the trustworthiness of Jewish testimony generally. The concrete details of the ritual varied from region to region, but generally, in the presence of ten adult male Jews, the Jew called to testify would appear wearing *t'fillin*, head covering, and *tallit*. He would hold and then kiss a Torah scroll taken from a synagogue. He then had to face eastward and declare loyalty to the political head of the country, assuring the court that this oath would not be annulled by *Kol Nidre*. All Jews called to court had to undergo this procedure, even if they were not religious at all. Only then were they allowed to take the usual juridical oath necessary for a normal lawsuit.[5]

Reform Jews in the nineteenth century, who strove so hard to be common German citizens, were appalled by discriminatory rituals such as this. When the assembly of progressive rabbis gathered in their first rabbinical conference in 1844, therefore, they voted to omit *Kol Nidre* from the service. They saw no reason even to provide a liturgical replacement, as they knew it to be a relatively late (post-Talmudic) addition to the liturgy and, therefore, hardly an essential part of it. As they saw it, *Kol Nidre* provided nothing positive, while just causing problems in the non-Jewish world.[6]

Classical Reform Judaism, however, did not succeed in this effort to abolish *Kol Nidre*. Faced with its obvious popularity, the rabbis sought means of including some form of it, while obviating the difficulties caused by the difficult text with which they had no sympathy. In the two hundred years of progressive Jewish liturgy, eight different ways of dealing with the problematic *Kol Nidre* ritual have been developed. They are not all mutually incompatible—sometimes several of them were followed simultaneously.[7]

1. *New text for reading:* New introductory passages were written, but meant to be read, not chanted.
2. *New hymn:* A new hymn was composed to lead into the mood of the day.
3. *Free "interpretive "translation":* An interpretative free "translation" of the traditional *Kol Nidre* was printed in the prayer book. This translation was apologetic, so that the text would not be misunderstood.
4. *Traditional melody, alternative text:* An alternative text was created to the traditional melody of *Kol Nidre*, expressing with words the emotions of the traditional tune.
5. *Traditional melody, imitative Hebrew text:* A new prayer was written in Hebrew imitating the sound of the words of *Kol Nidre*, but with a different message—for example, about annulling our sins, not our vows, or pleading that our vows to return to God may reach God.

6. *Traditional melody, a text from Psalms:* A psalm was sung to the melody of *Kol Nidre*, the most prominent one being Psalm 130, "Out of the depths I call unto You, O God."

7. *Traditional melody without words appearing in the prayer book:* The *Kol Nidre* tune was played on an instrument without words or chanted by the cantor without any words appearing in the prayer book. It was just announced in the prayer book as "The Kol Nidre Chant."

8. *Traditional melody and traditional text, but with apologetic explanation:* The traditional *Kol Nidre* was used, but the text was explained by a sermon in advance, by commentaries printed in the prayer book next to it, and/or by an interpretative free, politically correct translation.

Of all these solutions, the ones that required the composition of substitute texts are especially important, as the texts selected reveal how progressive Judaism has interpreted the theological meaning of the *Kol Nidre* moment.

Interestingly, enough, it was not just progressive communities that were troubled by *Kol Nidre*.[8] Orthodox prayer books too include free interpretative translations or exculpatory commentaries explaining the meaning of *Kol Nidre* in apologetic tones. But the Reform struggle was more universal and provides the broadest variety of alternative texts with theological import.

In what follows, I present the sources in historical sequence. In each case, I provide (a) an introduction; (b) the original source itself—where necessary, with an English translation; (c) a short textual analysis that offers deeper insight; and (d) a conclusion that summarizes the theological meaning of the *Kol Nidre* moment according to the source just discussed.

1. New Text for Reading: The Early Years I— Berlin 1817

One of the first Reform liturgies was published in Berlin in 1817. It begins the evening service of Yom Kippur with a Hebrew litany, in a style imitating the Bible.[9] The text is actually a patchwork of biblical words and phrases. This choice illustrates Reform Judaism's general trend to prioritize the Bible over Rabbinic sources. The leader reads (!) the three passages in Hebrew, to which the congregation replies with the biblical verse *V'nislach* (Num. 15:26), a verse said traditionally after the recitation of *Kol Nidre* (labeled E in this book, p. 95).

עֵדָה־קְדוֹשָׁה דּוֹרְשֵׁי אֱלֹהִים גֵּרִים וְתוֹשָׁבִים! אַתֶּם הַנִּצָּבִים פֹּה בֵית תְּפִלָּה לִפְנֵי אֱלֹהֵי צְבָאוֹת! הִכּוֹנוּ, הִתְקַדְּשׁוּ, הִטַּהֲרוּ לְיוֹם גָּדוֹל וְנוֹרָא, כִּי־ בַיּוֹם הַזֶּה יְכַפֵּר עֲלֵיכֶם לְטַהֵר אֶתְכֶם:

Holy congregation, seekers of God[10], strangers and sojourners![11] You who are standing here[12] in the house of prayer before the Lord of hosts![13] Prepare yourselves, sanctify yourselves, purify yourselves for the great and awesome day.[14] For on this day shall atonement be made for you, to cleanse you.[15]

וְנִסְלַח לְכָל־עֲדַת בְּנֵי יִשְׂרָאֵל וְלַגֵּר הַגָּר בְּתוֹכָם, כִּי לְכָל־ הָעָם בִּשְׁגָגָה:

Congregation: "And all the congregation of the children of Israel shall be forgiven, and the stranger that sojourneth among them; for in respect of all the people it was done unwittingly."[16]

אֱנוֹשׁ, אֱנוֹשׁ, יֵצֶר לִבּוֹ רַע מִנְּעוּרָיו, לַפֶּתַח חַטָּאת רוֹבֵץ בִּדְרָכָיו כּוֹשֵׁל, קַלּוּ אֲשׁוּרָיו לִמְעֹד, שׁוּבוּ, שׁוּבוּ, הִנָּחֵמוּ! מִכֹּל חַטֹּאתֵיכֶם לִפְנֵי ה' תִּטְהָרוּ:

Man, O man! The imagination of his heart is evil from his youth.[17] Sin coucheth at the door.[18] Man stumbles in his ways.[19] How easily do his steps slide! Turn ye, turn ye,[20] repent yourselves! From all your sins before the Lord shall ye be clean.[21]

וְנִסְלַח לְכָל־עֲדַת בְּנֵי יִשְׂרָאֵל וְלַגֵּר הַגָּר בְּתוֹכָם, כִּי לְכָל־ הָעָם בִּשְׁגָגָה:

Congregation: "And all the congregation...."

שִׂימוּ לְבַבְכֶם עַל־מַעֲשֵׂיכֶם,
חַפְּשׂוּ דַרְכֵיכֶם, קְחוּ עִמָּכֶם
דְבָרִים, קוּמוּ וְשׁוּבוּ עַד ה'
אֱלֹהֵיכֶם
רַחֲצוּ, הִזַּכּוּ, הֵטִיבוּ לִפְנֵי
עֶלְיוֹן שִׁפְכוּ שִׂיחַ, כִּי־בַיּוֹם
הַזֶּה יְכַפֵּר עֲלֵיכֶם לְטַהֵר
אֶתְכֶם, מִכֹּל חַטֹּאתֵיכֶם לִפְנֵי
ה' תִּטְהָרוּ:

Pay attention to your deeds, search your ways![22] Take with you words, arise, and return unto the Lord your God![23] Wash you, make you clean,[24] do the good, pour forth your prayer before the Most High.[25] For on this day shall atonement be made for you, to cleanse you from all your sins before the Lord shall ye be clean.[26]

וְנִסְלַח לְכָל־עֲדַת בְּנֵי יִשְׂרָאֵל
וְלַגֵּר הַגָּר בְּתוֹכָם, כִּי לְכָל־
הָעָם בִּשְׁגָגָה:

Congregation: "And all the congregation...."[27]

This was the only text read in Hebrew during the entire year according to this prayer book. The original German was printed below.

The three parts of this litany correspond to the three times *Kol Nidre* is sung traditionally. The text is built around Leviticus 16:30, "For on this day atonement shall be made for you to cleanse you of all your sins; you shall be clean before Adonai." The first strophe leads to the beginning of this verse, the second to the end, and the third to the whole verse in its entirety.

The lines leading up to this verse explain how such purity can be achieved: "Prepare yourselves!" "Turn ... repent!" "Pay attention to your deeds, search your ways!" The human being must be actively engaged in fulfilling certain tasks.

God, by contrast, is passive, according to these introductory passages, quite the opposite of the traditional *Kol Nidre*, where God is the one resolving our oaths. The passive language in the traditional text ("may they be absolved, released, annulled," etc.) avoids *direct* requests from God. But God is *implicitly* imagined as the one who needs to fulfill the wishes, however "passively" they may be framed. Accenting human responsibility and potential, rather than dependency on God, was an overall part of the nineteenth-century ethos on which Jewish reformers thrived.

With this newfound accent on human action rather than divine response, the *Kol Nidre* moment in the Berlin Reform Congregation is a last chance for the human being to repent. The juridical ritual has become an ethical admonition.

2. New Melody: The Early Years II— Hamburg 1819

Compared to the 1817 Berlin prayer book, the one published two years later in Hamburg was more widely used as a model elsewhere. It too omitted *Kol Nidre*. Two Torah scrolls were to be taken out of the ark—an attempt to retain the solemn atmosphere of *Kol Nidre* as a juridical formula. But *Kol Nidre* is missing: the ritual moves directly to the biblical verses traditionally sung *after Kol Nidre*; these were recited responsively between leader and congregation.[28] Before this entire ceremony, however, a German opening hymn was sung from the Hamburg Temple official *Hymnal*.[29]

1. Der Tag erscheint, der Tag voll Freud' und Bangen. Es sammeln sich die frommen Beter hier, Und Alle seh'n mit kindlichem Verlangen, Gott, liebevoller Vater! auf zu dir.	1. The day has come, the day of joy and fear. Pious worshipers are gathered here And they all look with childlike desire God, loving Father, upwards to you.
2. Du willst nach deiner gränzenlosen Güte Den Kindern gern die Missethat verzeih'n; Dies richtet auf ihr trauerndes Gemüthe, Daß sie auf's Neue sich der Tugend weih'n.	2. According to your boundless goodness You will forgive your children's sin. Upwards to you their mourning minds they raise, To dedicate themselves to virtue anew.
3. Gott! denken wir an unsrer Sünden Menge,	3. God, thinking of the multitude of our sins,

Wie wagt's der Blick, empor zu dir zu schaun!	How dare our eyes looking upwards to you!
Das Herz schlägt bange, jede Brust wird enge;	The heart is afraid, each breast feels narrow;
Nur deiner Gnade dürfen wir vertrau'n.	Only in your grace we may trust.
4. Gott! sieh' auf deine Kinder mit Erbarmen,	4. God, look upon your children with compassion,
Wir haben gegenseitig uns verzieh'n;	We have forgiven one another;
Vergieb, vergieb den reuevollen Armen,	Forgive, forgive the afflicted repentant;
Wir wollen fürder jede Sünde flieh'n!	We will henceforth flee away from every sin![30]

The German text was sung to the following melody[31] (accompanied by an organ), which imitates the style of German Protestant church hymns:[32]

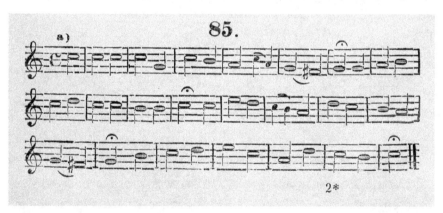

Musical notation, Hamburg hymn.

The opening theme in this hymn is the Day of God, seen by the biblical prophets as a day of severe punishment for human disobedience before the divine (e.g., Amos 5:18–20; Zephaniah 1:15–18). The accent is corporate; the whole community will suffer. The prophet Malachi, however, adds aspects of hope for individuals who have kept God's laws (Malachi 3:16–17; 3:23–24) despite whatever society at large may have done, and this Hamburg hymn draws its power from Malachi's vision. The hymn is reminiscent of a medieval *r'shut*, an introductory poem that requests permission to pray regardless of one's own personal unworthiness. Humans take a passive role in this hymn; their main activity is to trust in God. The last strophe, however, reveals that they have forgiven each other before the moment of this song. The stressing of our mutual commitments may be an apologetic note against the anti-Semitic misunderstanding of the traditional *Kol Nidre* as nullification of Jewish obligations.

The *Kol Nidre* moment here is understood as an opening prayer to get into contact with God—spiritual preparation for Yom Kippur.

3. New Hymn: Leopold Stein (1810–82)— The Hymn "O Tag des Herrn" (O Day of God)

When Rabbi Leopold Stein, who also became famous as a poet,[33] wanted to abolish *Kol Nidre* in his Frankfurt congregation, faithful to the decisions of the rabbinic conference in Braunschweig, "his congregation was reluctant to dispense with the melody; he had therefore to promise that he would compose a poem which could be set to the same music."[34] He explains:

> I, therefore, requested my cantor, Herr J. M. Ochs of Altenkundstadt, to provide me with the simple musical setting of the *Kol Nidré*. This he soon produced, omitting all of the traditional embellishments. I then sought to feel myself into the tune, and to clothe in words the pious feeling of the original composer. In the musical setting before me I found the expression of a threefold feeling: at first, an anxiety at the approach of the solemn day; then a daring rising towards the Divine Pardoner; and, finally, a sincere plea before the throne of the All-Merciful One.... Later on, I composed two further stanzas to follow the first one. In the second stanza, I tried to express the idea of reconciliation with our fellow-men; and, in the third stanza, reconciliation with our own selves, that is to say, the sanctification of our soul through the transcendence of our sensual nature.[35]

In 1866 Isaac Mayer Wise published an English translation, which is added below next to the original German text.[36]

1. O Tag des Herrn! du nahst, —
   Und das Herz erbebt,
   Und Schauer fassen die Seele.

   Sie gedenket ihre Missethat,
   Sie gedenket, daß ihr Richter
   naht—und zittert.
   Sie bangt, sie zagt; sie weint, sie
   klagt
   Und vergeht in Thränen.

   Fasse Muth, o belastet
   Herz!
   Schau' du nur trostvoll himmel-
   wärts!
   Gütig ist dein Herr:
   Gern giebt er Gewähr,
   Naht, sich auszusöhnen.

   Herr! Gott! sieh', sieh' meines
   Herzens Wehen,
   Und neig Dein Ohr!
   Herr, vernimm, vernimm mein
   heißes Flehen,
   Oeffn' uns Dein Thor!
   Nimm weg die Missethat,
   Oeffn' uns das Thor der Gnad',
   Und zieh uns empor.

2. Horch! die Stimme des
   Herrn!—Er ruft
   Mit des Abends Wehen,
   Und Andacht waltet und Stille.
   Brüder, hört, wie mild die
   Stimme tönt!
   Menschen, ruft sie, Kinder, o
   versöhnt—
   versöhnt euch!

1. O Day of God—Thou'rt nigh—
   And my heart is awed—
   And terror seizeth my spirit—

   It remembers its iniquity—
   It remembers that its Judge is
   nigh,—and trembles—
   with fear and grief without
   relief—
   Tears of woe are flowing.

   Cheer thee up, thou heart
   oppressed,—
   Heavenward turn with comfort
   blessed.—
   Merciful is He—
   Forgives iniquity—
   comes in peace to meet us.

   Lord, behold—my heart's pro-
   found contrition—
   Oh, lend Thine ear,—
   Lord, accept—accept my fer-
   vent prayer,—
   As I stand here,—
   Do Thou our guilt remove,—
   and thro' the gate of love—
   Bring to Thee us near.

2. Hark, the voice of the Lord,—
   He calls—
   Thro' the zephyr's whisper—
   Devotion reigneth and stillness—
   Brethren hark, how sweet the
   voice and mild:—
   "Mortals, children, Oh, be rec-
   onciled,—
   Forgive ye,

O folgt dem Ruf!
  o gebt Gehör!
Trocknet alle Thränen.

Brüder, kommt, o
  kommt heran,
Schließet, schließet euch
  liebend an!
Herz soll morgen rein,
rein vom Hasse sein;
Eilt, euch auszusöhnen.

Horch, wer weint? Es weinen
  gekränkte Freunde:—
Schließt neu das Band!
Horch, wer klagt? Es klagen ver-
  folgte Feinde:—
Haß sei verbannt!
O liebt, wie Gott euch liebt;
Vergebt, wie Er vergiebt!
Reicht euch treu die Hand.

3. Nun, Tag des Herrn! So nah!
  Und fülle die Herzen
  Und fülle mit Wonne die
    Seelen!
  Von dem Abend bis zum
    Abend hin
  Heiliget vor Gott den
    Erdensinn—und betet!
  Empor zu Gott, zu
    Gott empor
  Schwingt euch, Erdensöhne!

Stimmet an Gebet, Gesang!
Folget, folget dem
  Himmelsdrang!

Oh, heed that call—obey that
  voice—
Dry all tears of anguish."

Brethren, come, approach
  God's shrine,—
come and join us in love
  benign,
From your hearts efface—
Ev'ry hatred base—
Haste, be conciliated.

Hark—who weeps? Thy friend
  by thee distressed—
The bond renew.
Hark, who wails? Thy foe, by
  thee oppressed—
All wrath eschew,—
Oh, grant, as God above,—
Forgiveness, mercy love,—
show ye friendship true.

3. Now, Day of God,—Draw nigh,—
  And fill thou our spirits,—
  and fill thou our hearts with
    rejoicing.—
  While from eve to eve to God
    ye pray,—
  Banish ev'ry worldly thought
    away—Implore Him,—
  On high to God, to God on
    high,—
  Soar ye up, ye mortals!

Prayer now begin and song,—
Come, O come, after heaven
  long,

Schwinget euch empor!	up to God aspire,
In der Engel Chor	with the angel's choir—
Stimmen unsre Lieder.	now our praises mingle.
Tag des Herrn, o sei ein treuer	Day of God,—Thy faithful
Bote!	guidance lending,—
Führ' uns zurück!	Back do us show,—
Tag des Herrn, komm mit dem	Day of God,—On ev'nings
Abendrothe,	wings descending—
Hell strahl' dein Blick!	Thine eye let glow,—
Bis wieder Abend naht,	When we shall re-appear,—
Führst Du auf lichtem Pfad	On paths of lustre clear,—
Uns zu Heil und Glück.	Bliss dost thou bestow.[37]

Although we cannot know for sure, it is likely that Stein knew the Hamburg hymn and patterned his own composition after its ideas. Like that hymn, Stein's composition too considers the prophetic Day of God in the positive way described in Malachi 3. The second strophe is based on various verses from Isaiah, mainly chapter 40 (especially 40:1–5 and 40:26) intermingled with motives of the purity of the heart (Psalm 24:4) and forgiveness toward each other. The third stanza uses a motif from the *piyyut* sung traditionally on the evening of Yom Kippur *Ya'aleh tacha-nuneinu*, "O let our prayer ascend … may our cry come in to Thee … from eventime … till eventime," and combines it with themes from the *K'dushah*, a text that imagines human beings on earth joining in praise with the angels in heaven.

Stein's hymn found its way into many German (and some American) prayer books throughout the nineteenth and early twentieth centuries.[38] The text and music of the original melody are printed in Abraham Baer's handbook for cantors, *The Practical Prayer Leader* (*Der practische Vorbeter*).[39] In 1882 the famous Berlin cantor Louis Lewandowksi published his own composition for organ, solo, and four-part choir.[40]

The American *Union Prayer Book* created an English hymn to be sung to the *Kol Nidre* Melody[41] by combining the beginning of Stein's third strophe (Day of God / O, come!) with the end of the first (Lord! God! See):

Day of God
O, come!
And fill all our spirits
with peace and with gladness from Heaven.
From the eventide to eventide
Let all earthly thoughts be sanctified
In prayer!
Upward to God, upward to God,
Sons of earth, together!
Lift the voice of prayer and song,
Heavenward born on the current strong,
Upward all aspire!
In the angel choir
Blend our prayers and praises.
Lord! God! See,—
See Thou our heart's contrition,
and bow Thine ear!
Hear, O hear the voice of my petition.
Banish our fear!
Blot out our evil ways,
Open the door of grace,
Bid us enter there![42]

The *Kol Nidre* moment according to Leopold Stein's hymn is about preparing ourselves for God's presence. It is important to remember that Stein drew his inspiration for the moment from the atmosphere of the *Kol Nidre* tune alone (probably inspired by the Hamburg hymn), not from the meaning of the traditional text.

4. Free Interpretative Translation: Ludwig Philippson (1811–89)—A Free Translation Only

In his *New Israelite Prayerbook* (*Neues Israelitisches Gebetbuch*, Berlin, 1864), Ludwig Philippson offered no Aramaic text version at all, but just a German "translation" of the traditional *Kol Nidre*. Hardly a literal translation, however, it is better described as a very free interpretation.[43]

Alle Gelübde, die wir im verflosse-
nen Jahre leichtfertig gelobet und
nicht erfüllt, alle Versicherungen, die
wir leichtfertig gegeben und sie
wichen von der Wahrheit, aller
Gebrauch seines heiligen Namens in
leichtfertiger Weise, wo es nicht
nöthig, sie seien uns vergeben, sie
seien wie nicht gethan und nicht
ausgesprochen!

All vows, which we lightly made
during the year gone by and
have not kept, all promises,
which we gave easily and they
departed from the truth, all
usage of his holy name unnec-
essarily in a frivolous manner,
may it be forgiven, may it be as
not done and as never said.

This "translation" transforms *Kol Nidre* to an open plea for forgiveness
of promises that should not have been made in the first place. It bears
an apologetic tone, confirming the understanding that the formula only
applies to vows made foolishly or too eagerly, to promises that departed
from the truth, and to abuses of God's name. It thereby directly con-
fronts the anti-Semitic stereotype of Jews who won't feel bound by
juridical oaths, and it corrects the misapprehension that *Kol Nidre*
annuls promises between human beings, rather than those made just to
God. Whether forgiveness is actually granted remains an open question.

5. Traditional Melody, Alternative Text: Abraham Geiger (1810–74)—A New Hebrew Text

The first to replace the *Kol Nidre* text with a modern Hebrew version imitating the traditional *Kol Nidre* was Abraham Geiger in his *Israelite
Prayerbook* (*Israelitisches Gebetbuch*, Breslau, 1854).[44]

All my transgressions, and the transgressions of this congregation, and the
transgressions of all Thy people
Israel—blot them out and make them
to pass away from before Thine eyes;
and purify our hearts from this Day of
Atonement, may it come to us for
good. Our heart is broken, our spirit is

כָּל־פְּשָׁעַי וּפִשְׁעֵי הַקָּהָל הַזֶּה
וּפִשְׁעֵי כָל־עַמְּךָ יִשְׂרָאֵל מְחֵם
וְהַעֲבִירֵם מִנֶּגֶד עֵינֶיךָ וְטַהֵר
לִבֵּנוּ מִיּוֹם כִּפּוּרִים זֶה עַד
יוֹם כִּפּוּרִים הַבָּא עָלֵינוּ
לְטוֹבָה לִבֵּנוּ נִשְׁבָּר רוּחֵנוּ

humbled, we have no works. We rely on Thy love alone. O Merciful, do not forsake us, for we are but dust. Requite us not according to our iniquities.[45]

נִדְכָּאָה מַעֲשִׂים אֵין אִתָּנוּ
בְּצִדְקָתְךָ נִשְׁעַנּוּ נָא רַחוּם
אַל תַּעַזְבֵנוּ כִּי עָפָר אֲנָחְנוּ
כַּעֲוֹנוֹתֵינוּ נָא אַל תִּגְמֹל:

Geiger's text centers around a single quotation from *Kol Nidre*, the phrase "purify our hearts from this Day of Atonement to the next, may it come to us for good." The last lines describe the humble nature of human beings, whose "heart is broken" and "spirit ... humbled." Because "we have no works," we rely solely on God's mercy to "requite us not according to our iniquities." By replacing "vows" with "transgressions," Geiger cleverly transforms a release from vows into a confession of sins.

Many others took up the idea of newly creating a singable Hebrew text, sometimes making it sound more similar to *Kol Nidre*, by starting (for example) with *kol sitre* ("all secrets"). All these trials, as Abraham Geiger's own one, copy the style of biblical Hebrew.[46] A text used in Hanover in 1870, however, uses liturgical language. It became widely known because of a note in a famous Jewish weekly journal. It quotes mostly phrases from the *Sh'ma* and Its Blessings, but also from other core Jewish prayers or psalms used in the liturgy. Not surprisingly it starts with quoting the two most important liturgical words themselves, *kol nidre*, but then continues differently: *Kol nidre b'nei Yisrael asher hemah nodrim l'cha* ... "All the vows that the children of Israel made to You [God]." The text was sung to the traditional *Kol Nidre* melody.

(1) All the vows of the children of Israel which they vow unto Thee, O our King, to keep the words of Thy Torah and Thy testimonies, not to depart from the commandments either to the right or to the left, from this Day of Atonement unto

כָּל נִדְרֵי בְּנֵי יִשְׂרָאֵל אֲשֶׁר
הֵמָּה נוֹדְרִים לְךָ מַלְכֵּנוּ לִשְׁמֹר
אֶת דִּבְרֵי תּוֹרָתְךָ וְעֵדוֹתֶיךָ
וּלְבִלְתִּי סוּר מִן הַמִּצְוָה יָמִין
וּשְׂמֹאל מִיּוֹם כִּפּוּרִים זֶה עַד

the next Day of Atonement, may it come to us for good, yea, may all of them ascend and come and be accepted before Thee for mercy. And put it in their heart to love and to fear Thy great and awesome name; and may they never be put to shame.

יוֹם כִּפּוּרִים הַבָּא עָלֵינוּ לְטוֹבָה כֻּלָּם יַעֲלוּ וְיָבֹאוּ וְיַגִּיעוּ וְיֵרָאוּ לְפָנֶיךָ לְרַחֲמִים וְתֵן בְּלִבְּכֶם לְאַהֲבָה וּלְיִרְאָה אֶת שְׁמֶךָ הַגָּדוֹל וְהַנּוֹרָא וְלֹא וְלֹא יֵבוֹשׁוּ לְעוֹלָם:

(2) All the vows of the children of Israel which they vow unto Thee, O our Father, to walk in the ways of justice and loving-kindness and mercy, and not to harden their heart against their brothers, from this Day of Atonement unto the next Day of Atonement, may it come to us for good, yea, may all of them ascend and come and be accepted before Thee for mercy. And bend their inclination, and subdue their stiff-neckedness, so that they may stretch out a hand to those who transgress against them. And may they be cleansed from their sin.

כָּל נִדְרֵי בְּנֵי יִשְׂרָאֵל אֲשֶׁר הֵמָּה נֹדְרִים לְךָ אָבִינוּ לָלֶכֶת בְּדַרְכֵי הַצְּדָקָה וְהַחֶסֶד וְהָרַחֲמִים וּלְבִלְתִּי אַמֵּץ אֶת לְבָבָם מֵאֲחֵיהֶם מִיּוֹם כִּפּוּרִים זֶה עַד יוֹם כִּפּוּרִים הַבָּא עָלֵינוּ לְטוֹבָה כֻּלָּם יַעֲלוּ וְיָבֹאוּ וְיַגִּיעוּ וְיֵרָאוּ לְפָנֶיךָ לְרַחֲמִים וְכֹף אֶת יִצְרָם וְהַכְנַע אֶת עָרְפָּם לָתֵת יָד לְפֹשְׁעִים נֶגְדָּם וּמֵחַטָּאתָם יִטְהָרוּ:

(3) All the vows of the children of Israel which they vow unto Thee, O our Lord, lifting up their eyes unto Thee, O Thou that dwellest in the heavens, to return unto Thee with all their heart and with all their soul, from this Day of Atonement unto the next Day of Atonement,

כָּל נִדְרֵי בְּנֵי יִשְׂרָאֵל אֲשֶׁר הֵמָּה נֹדְרִים לְךָ אֲדוֹנֵנוּ בְּנָשְׂאָם עֵינֵיהֶם אֵלֶיךָ הַיּשְׁבִי בַשָּׁמַיִם לָשׁוּב אֵלֶיךָ בְּכָל לְבָבָם וּבְכָל נַפְשָׁם מִיּוֹם כִּפּוּרִים זֶה עַד יוֹם כִּפּוּרִים

may it come to us for good, yea, may all of them ascend and come and be accepted before Thee for mercy. And renew a steadfast spirit within them, that they may depart from their evil way, and not return unto their folly.[47]

הַבָּא עָלֵינוּ לְטוֹבָה כֻּלָּם יַעֲלוּ וְיָבֹאוּ וְיַגִּיעוּ וְיֵרָאוּ לְפָנֶיךָ לְרַחֲמִים וְחַדֵּשׁ רוּחַ נָכוֹן בְּקִרְבָּם לְמַעַן יָסוּרוּ מִדַּרְכָּם הָרָעָה וְאַל יָשׁוּבוּ לְכִסְלָם:

Alle Gelübde der Kinder Israels, durch welche sie Dir, unserm Könige, geloben, die Worte Deiner Lehre und Deiner Zeugnisse zu befolgen und von Deinen Geboten nicht rechts noch links abzuweichen, von diesem Versöhnungstage an bis zum nächsten uns zum Heile kommenden: mögen sie alle zu Dir emporsteigen und von Dir in Gnaden aufgenommen werden. Sende Du ihnen in's Herz, daß sie Deinen großen gewaltigen Namen lieben und ehrfürchten—damit sie nie zu Schanden werden.

Alle Gelübde der Kinder Israels, durch welche sie Dir unserm Vater, geloben, in den Wegen der Gerechtigkeit, der Liebe und des Erbarmens zu wandeln und ihr Herz nicht zu verhärten gegen ihre Brüder, von diesem Versöhnungstage an bis zum nächsten uns zum Heile kommenden: mögen sie alle zu Dir emporsteigen und von Dir in Gnaden aufgenommen werden. Zwinge Du ihren Sinn, beuge Du ihre Hartnäckigkeit, daß sie zur Versöhnung die Hand reichen denen, welche sich gegen sie vergangen—auf daß sie von ihren Sünden rein werden.

Alle Gelübde der Kinder Israels, durch welche sie Dir unserm Herrn, geloben—indem sie ihre Augen zu Dir erheben, der Du im Himmel thronst—reuig zu Dir zurückzukehren aus vollem Herzen und mit ganzer Seele, von diesem Versöhnungstage an bis zum nächsten uns zum Heile kommenden: mögen sie alle zu Dir emporsteigen und von Dir in Gnaden aufgenommen werden. Erneure Du einen festen Geist in ihnen, auf daß sie von ihrem bösen Wandel ablassen und nie wieder zur Thorheit zurückkehren.

This new text specifies the vows positively: the traditional Ashkenazi reference to the future is retained, but the vows in question are the ones we make today and in the future to keep the Torah. The three stanzas honor the tradition of chanting *Kol Nidre* three times. All stanzas display the same structure with the central thought repeated: "from this Yom Kippur to the next." To avoid total repetition, however, the strophes address God differently: first, *malkenu* ("our king"); then, *avinu* ("our father"); and finally, *adonenu* ("our lord")—three epithets typical for the High Holy Days. Israel's commitment to God receives three expressions also: "to keep the words of your Torah," "to walk in the ways of justice, loving-kindness, and mercy," and "to lift up their eyes to You." The core message of this new *Kol Nidre* is that God may accept our vows to keep the Jewish way of life.

Kol Nidre has been changed into a version of *Ya'aleh v'yavo* ("may they [memories of our ancestors and their piety] ascend and come [and be accepted before you"], a prayer usually inserted into the *Amidah* on the Pilgrimage Festivals and Rosh Chodesh, wishing that God may bless us on the specific festival. The Hanover prayer book thus created a *Ya'aleh v'yavo* for the Day of Atonement, transferred from its usual place in the *Amidah* to an opening prayer for the evening service.

The new text contains a double apologetic note: it stipulates vows between humans and God, not other human beings; and it expresses the sincere wish to indeed keep our promises, thereby rejecting the anti-Semitic charge that Jews cannot be trusted.

The Hebrew *Kol Nidre* version, however, that became most quoted in the years to come[48] was first published in 1899 in Munich. It is the third stanza of the Hanover version, with the only exception that God is not addressed as *adonenu* ("our lord"), as in the third strophe in Hanover, but as *avinu* ("our father"), as in the second. *Avinu* is the way to address God in confessions of sin and is thus the epithet most fitting to the Day of Atonement.

All the vows of the children of Israel which they vow to You, our Father, lifting up their eyes to You,[49] who dwells in the heavens,[50] to return to You[51] with all their heart and with all their	כָּל נִדְרֵי בְּנֵי יִשְׂרָאֵל אֲשֶׁר הֵמָּה נֹדְרִים לְךָ אָבִינוּ בְּנָשְׂאָם עֵינֵיהֶם אֵלֶיךָ הַיּשְׁבִי בַשָּׁמַיִם לָשׁוּב אֵלֶיךָ בְּכָל־לְבָבָם וּבְכָל־נַפְשָׁם מִיּוֹם

soul,[52] from this Day of
Atonement to the next Day of
Atonement, may it come to us for
good,[53] may all of them ascend
and come and be accepted before
You[54] to mercy. And renew a
steadfast spirit in them[55] that they
may depart from their evil way,[56]
and not return to their folly.[57]

כִּפּוּרִים זֶה עַד יוֹם כִּפּוּרִים
הַבָּא עָלֵינוּ לְטוֹבָה כֻּלָּם יַעֲלוּ
וְיָבֹאוּ וְיַגִּיעוּ וְיֵרָאוּ לְפָנֶיךָ
לְרַחֲמִים וְתַחֲדֵשׁ רוּחַ נָכוֹן
בְּקִרְבָּם לְמַעַן יָסוּרוּ מִדַּרְכָּם
הָרָעָה וְאַל יָשׁוּבוּ לְכִסְלָם:

The Hebrew alternative texts that are used nowadays in progressive congregations in the Netherlands, Great Britain, Germany, and elsewhere are mostly based on the Munich version.[58] But the British Liberal prayer book *Machzor Ruach Chadashah* (2003) offers an interesting new variant:[59]

Source of our being, accept the
vows of the Children of Israel that
they will turn from sin and evil, and
walk in the ways of Your Law of
righteousness and justice, from this
Day of Atonement until the next—
may we reach it in peace. We
come to seek Your pardon and forgiveness. Help us to return to You
with a whole heart, and give us
strength to overcome our faults, so
that through us Your great and holy
name may become sanctified.

כָּל־נִדְרֵי בְּנֵי יִשְׂרָאֵל אֲשֶׁר
הֵם נֹדְרִים לְךָ אָבִינוּ, לָסוּר
מֵחֵטְא, מֵאַשְׁמָה וָרֶשַׁע, וְלָלֶכֶת
בְּדַרְכֵי תוֹרָתֶךָ, בְּאוֹרַח צְדָקָה
וּמִשְׁפָּט, מִיּוֹם־כִּפּוּרִים זֶה עַד
יוֹם־כִּפּוּרִים הַבָּא עָלֵינוּ
לְטוֹבָה, כֻּלָּם יֵרָצוּ לְפָנֶיךָ.
אָתָנוּ לְבַקֵּשׁ מִמְּךָ מְחִילָה
וְכַפָּרָה, הַחֲזִירֵנוּ בִּתְשׁוּבָה
שְׁלֵמָה אֵלֶיךָ, וְאַמְּצֵנוּ לְתַקֵּן
אֵת אֲשֶׁר הֶעֱוִינוּ, וְיִתְקַדֵּשׁ
בָּנוּ שִׁמְךָ הַגָּדוֹל וְהַנּוֹרָא.

The text is meant to be sung to the traditional melody of *Kol Nidre*. Below it is a note explaining that the traditional Aramaic version can be found at the end of the book. Congregations may choose which version to use.

According to the editors of *Machzor Ruach Chadashah* itself, this text was inspired by the Hanover 1870 version.[60] In fact it contains major changes. Only the structure of the text is based on Hanover. The most important change is the omission of the core phrase *ya'aleh v'yavo* ("may they ascend and come and be accepted before you"), thus making the prayer a mere wish that our vows be acceptable to God (*kulam yirtzu l'fanekha*)—a wish in the Hebrew that finds no direct translation in the English! Hebrew and English agree, however, that our main plea for the day is that God may help us to return to God.

The meaning of the *Kol Nidre* moment according to these new Hebrew text versions is asking for God's support when we try to change our lives.

6. Traditional Melody, a Text from Psalms: Psalm 130 ("Out of the Depths I Call You")

Some nineteenth-century Reform prayer books began Yom Kippur evening as they did other evening services—with a psalm,[61] often Psalm 84,[62] Psalm 103 (*Bar'khi nafshi*, "Bless Adonai, O my soul"), sung in Hebrew to the melody of *Kol Nidre*,[63] or, most famously, Psalm 130,[64] which Louis Lewandowski arranged so that it could be sung to the melody of the *Kol Nidre*.[65] He used a translation by Rabbi Michael Sachs, which was widely known because it had been published in the Bible edited by Leopold Zunz (Berlin, 1838). This *Kol Nidre* alternative became very famous, especially in the Berlin congregations. It is sung slowly (*andante con moto*) with much expression (*con molto espressione*).[66] The cantor—in Lewandowski's time a man, usually a tenor voice—begins; the organ only supports his melody with no extra motives. Choosing a soloist for verses 1–3 underlines the loneliness of the individual approaching God. With the full choir sound, however, God's forgiveness is affirmed. The composition repeats some lines that stress our search for God, a reflection of nineteenth-century romanticism, which considered the feelings of our souls more important than theological statements about God.

VORBETER MIT ORGEL:	CANTOR WITH ORGAN:
Aus den Tiefen ruf' ich Dich, o Ew'ger!	Out of the depths I call You, O Eternal One!
Herr, erhöre meine Stimme, möge dein Ohr aufhorchen	Lord, answer my voice, may your ear hark

bei meines Flehens Stimme,
bei meines Flehens Stimme.
Wenn die Schuld Du aufbe-
wahrest, Jah!
Herr, wer koennte bestehen?

CHOR:
Aber, aber bei Dir ist die Vergebung,
auf dass Du gefürchtet werdest.
Ich hoffe, Ewiger, es hofft meine
Seele
und auf dein Wort harre ich.
Meine Seele harret auf den
Herrn,
mehr als Wächter auf den
Morgen,
Meine Seele harret auf den
Herrn,
mehr als Wächter auf den
Morgen.
Harre Israel, harre auf den
Ewigen,
denn bei dem Ewigen,
bei dem Ewigen ist die Huld,
und reichlich bei ihm Erlösung.
Und er wird Israel,
Israel erlösen
von all seiner Schuld.

to my voice's plead,
to my voice's plead.
If you would keep the sin,
Yah!
Lord, who could stand?

CHOIR:
But, but with You is forgiveness,
so that You may be feared.
I hope, Eternal One, my soul
hopes
and your word I await.
My soul waits for the Lord
more than watchmen for the
morning,
My soul waits for the Lord
more than watchmen for the
morning.
Wait Israel, wait for the Eternal
One,
for with the Eternal One,
with the Eternal One is steadfast love
and a lot of redemption is with
Him.
and Israel,
and Israel He will redeem
from all its iniquities.

Psalm 130 is one of the fifteen psalms that the Bible labels *shir hama'alot* ("song of ascents"), study texts traditionally read on Shabbat afternoon. Lewandowski's rendition, however, skips the heading and begins immediately with the appeal to God. By this the psalm loses its character as a biblical study text and becomes a personal supplication valid any time. Conveniently, Psalm 130 is of similar length to *Kol Nidre*, and a plea for forgiveness besides, beginning "Adonai, listen to my cry for mercy" (verse

2), and assuring us, "He will redeem Israel from all their iniquities" (verse 8). The psalm furthermore contains no references to animal sacrifice, the priesthood, or the ancient Temple cult—themes that classical Reform rejected.

Additionally, since the sixth century, Psalm 130 (*De profundis*, as it is known in Latin) has been one of seven penitential psalms read in Christian churches as a Good Friday call for repentance. Psalm 130 thus replaced a controversial post-Talmudic legal formula with a biblical study text converted into a personal prayer that Jews and Christians share.

7. Traditional Melody without Words Appearing in the Prayer Book: The *Kol Nidre* Tune without Words

Following its earlier precedents, the 1948 newly revised version of the American *Union Prayer Book* has no *Kol Nidre* text, but it adds instructions to include "The Kol Nidre Chant." In similar fashion, the British Liberal *machzor Gates of Repentance* (from 1973) offers a "Silent Meditation" about God's creation and revelation and our sin, but then suggests, "During this the Kol Nidrey Music may be played."[67] The traditional music is thereby preserved, while the free flow of thoughts that people may have while listening to it is focused by the message of the accompanying printed meditation.

The history of the *Kol Nidre* melody is given elsewhere in this volume (see Mark Kligman, pp. 67–70). Suffice it to say here that it is often said to belong to the so-called *misinai tunes* that originated in southwestern Germany between the eleventh and fifteenth centuries CE, the time when Western European music began to develop strict rules of harmony. The oldest actual witness for it is from the sixteenth century. The *Kol Nidre* tune is not a composed melody in the usual sense; it is rather a collection of certain fixed motifs in the general musical style of the High Holy Days, which can be ornamented and performed in many different ways. Already in the eleventh century[68] it had became customary to repeat *Kol Nidre* three times, first very softly, the second time a bit louder, and the third time loud and firm.[69]

The tune became so widely anticipated within Ashkenazi Jewry that it would feel very wrong to begin Yom Kippur without it—hence the custom, even today, to listen to the *Kol Nidre* melody without the problematic words of its Aramaic text. Some congregations perform German composer Max Bruch's arrangement of *Kol Nidre*, op. 47, Adagio on Hebrew Melodies for Violoncello and Orchestra at the beginning of the *Yom Kippur* evening service. Bruch himself explained:

> Already as a young man, namely in the years 1861–63, I studied folksongs of all nations with great enthusiasm, because the folksong is the source of all true melodics.... So lay the study of Jewish ethnic music on my path.... I became acquainted with *Kol Nidre* ... in Berlin through the Lichtenstein family, who befriended me. Even though I am a Protestant, as an artist I deeply felt the outstanding beauty of these melodies and therefore I gladly spread them through my arrangement."[70]

Bruch saw his composition as merely an arrangement of one of the many folk tunes of the world, not something intended for liturgical usage. Bruch was not even Jewish. Cantors therefore debate the extent to which Bruch's setting counts as a *Kol Nidre* alternative: must liturgically used music be composed as such, or can a non-Jewish, non-liturgical piece be taken to replace a problematic liturgical text?[71] Congregations who use it obviously think the sound is quite sufficient to provide the necessary Jewish meaning.

8. Traditional Melody and Traditional Text, but with Apologetic Explanation: The Traditional *Kol Nidre* Text in Progressive Prayer Books

Since 1978 the traditional *Kol Nidre* has returned to American Reform Judaism.[72] European progressive prayer books followed suit: the Reform Synagogues of Great Britain in 1985 (the traditional text appears beside a new Hebrew version in the tradition of Abraham Geiger),[73] Germany in 1997 (the liberal congregation adapted the British Reform *machzor* for use in German congregations),[74] Switzerland in 2002,[75] and Liberal Judaism in the United Kingdom in 2003 (the text appears only in the appendix).[76]

9. The Special Case of British Jewry: Reform Judaism with Sephardic Origins

The British Reform Movement has its own unique history. It does not share the German roots of progressive Judaism in the United States, Europe in general, and (since 1902) Liberal Judaism in the United Kingdom. The issue at the outset was not so much philosophical as it was practical. A growing number of Jews had moved west from London's East End and needed a synagogue in their area. It seemed opportune to use the move as the occasion to make the service more accessible, that is, shorter and scheduled at more convenient times. The West London Synagogue of British Jews was therefore founded in 1840, by nineteen Sephardim coming from the Spanish and Portuguese Synagogue Bevis Marks and five Ashkenazim.[77] They described it as "a Synagogue in the Western part of the Metropolis, where a Revised Service may be performed at hours more suited to our habits, and in a manner more calculated to inspire feelings of Devotion."[78]

The Sephardic tradition does not know any specific beautiful melody for *Kol Nidre*, although especially of late, a variety of melodies have proliferated. Traditionally, it is chanted in the usual Sephardi style, not unlike the melody of other opening parts of the service.[79] *Kol Nidre* could therefore be omitted without being missed.[80]

In the first edition of the West London Synagogue Yom Kippur prayer book, published in 1843, the service begins with Psalm 5:8, "In the greatness of thy benevolence, I enter thy house; in reverence of thee, I bow down towards the temple of thy Holiness!"[81] From handwritten notes in a warden's copy of the second edition (1866) we know that the congregation stood during this verse.

The Day of Atonement according to the Sephardic tradition does not start immediately with *Kol Nidre*, but with a poem (*piyyut*), *Sh'ma koli*, "Hear my voice, O thou, who hearest every voice." Its twenty-nine verses depict how God heard the patriarchs, the generation of the Exodus, the prophets, Ezra, and the just and pious in every age.[82] The West London Synagogue starts similarly with a poem, albeit a shorter and simpler one, read by the minister (according to a handwritten note in a copy of the fourth edition [1890]):

Almighty God, faithful King, omnipotent, most merciful God,
    I approach thee to supplicate on behalf of thy people Israel,
    who have deputed me.
O sole God! Judge of righteousness,
    who can be pure before thee,
    and who can be purified in thy judgement?
Yet do I beseech thee,
    most merciful and gracious,
    that I may find favour in thy sight,
    and that thine ears may be open to the prayer and supplication which I pour out before thee,
    for myself, for my household, and for my congregation.
Behold us here assembled,
    and as one man, with one heart and in one language,
    seeking mercy from thee, our Father in Heaven.
O God, beneficent and forgiving,
    hear our supplications and pardon our iniquities;
    for in thy Holy Law it is written,
    that thou, O God, wilt not despise a humble and contrite heart.[83]
And it is said:
    he that confesseth his sins and forsaketh his evil ways shall find mercy.[84]
May the words of my mouth and the meditations of my heart be acceptable before thee, O God, my Rock and my Redeemer![85]

This text is actually a version of the traditional opening prayer for *Musaf* of the High Holy Days, *Hin'ni* ("Here I stand [poor in deeds]"), technically a *r'shut*, "[a quest for] permission" to pray on behalf of the congregation that the leader presents to God, all the while confessing his own spiritual poverty that he fears may disqualify him from such a sacred task).

    This revised *Hin'ni* is followed by the last four verses of the Sephardic "Hear my voice." According to handwritten notes in the fourth edition of *Forms of Prayer*, volume 4 (1890), this was sung by the choir.

O answer thy afflicted people,
the humblest of the humble.
Forgive their sins,
O thou, who deignest to accept prayers!
Prolong their life through thine abundant mercy,
and grant the completion of all their requests.
O may their prayers be accounted as incense before thee,
as sacrifices and as burnt offerings.
O God, who deignest to receive supplications,
O hearken to my voice,
thou, who hearest every voice![86]

Then follows *Chatzi Kaddish* and Psalm 38, "O Lord, rebuke me not in thy wrath: neither chasten me in thy hot displeasure...." The use of this psalm in the Yom Kippur liturgy is unique to the British Reform tradition. The opening part finally concludes with Numbers 14:19–20, "Forgive the sin of this people" (p. 95 in this volume) and *Shehecheyanu*. *Kol Nidre* simply does not exist in the tradition of British Reform Jewry.

This order of opening the Day of Atonement remains in all the subsequent seven editions of *Forms of Prayer*. The massive immigration of Jews from Germany after 1938, however, led to a radical change of the order in the eighth edition, which is in use today.

Already in a copy of the sixth edition (in use 1929–53) an alternative Hebrew version of *Kol Nidre* is inserted at the beginning, with the handwritten note that it was to be read in English. The version originates in the *Hamburg Temple Prayer Book* (sixth edition, 1904). It is basically the same as the Munich 1899 version, with some small omissions and additions. Psalm 38 was omitted, according to the same handwritten notes. A copy of the succeeding edition (1953) has the same modern Hebrew alternative text stuck over the text of Psalm 38, which has thus become unreadable. A copy of the seventh edition, used in North Western Reform Synagogue at Alyth Gardens, contains a typeset multiplied sheet of paper according to which the Yom Kippur evening service began as follows:

(The congregation will stand)
Rabbi:
In this hour all Israel stands before God, the judge and the forgiver. In His presence let us all examine our ways, our

deeds, and what we have failed to do. Where we transgressed, let us openly confess: "We have sinned!" and, determined to return to God, let us pray: "Forgive us." We stand before our God. We have trust in our faith and in our future. Who made known to the world the mystery of the Eternal, the One God? Who imparted to the world the comprehension of purity of conduct and purity of family life? Who taught the world respect for man, created in the image of God? Who spoke of the commandment of righteousness, of social justice? In all this were seen manifest the spirit of the prophets, the divine revelation to the Jewish people. It grew out of our Judaism and is still growing. We stand before our God. On Him we rely. From Him issues the truth and the glory of our history, our fortitude amidst all change of fortune, our endurance in distress. Our history is a history of nobility of soul, of human dignity. It is history we have recourse to when attack and grievous wrong are directed against us, when affliction and calamity befall us. God has led our fathers from generation to generation. He will guide us and our children through these days. We stand before our God, strengthened by His commandment that we fulfill. We bow to Him and stand erect before men. We worship Him and remain firm in all vicissitudes. Humbly we trust in Him and our path lies clear before us; we see our future. All Israel stands before her God in this hour. In our prayers, in our hope in our confession, we are one with all Jews on earth. We look upon each other and know who we are; we look up to our God and know what shall abide. "Behold, He that keepeth Israel doth neither slumber nor sleep." "May He who makes peace in His heights bring peace upon us and upon all Israel."

Then follows the full traditional Ashkenazi *Kol Nidre* ceremony, as replicated in this volume, from "In the academy on high" to *Shehecheyanu*.[87]

The introductory prayer is especially interesting, as it is an English translation of a German text that was distributed in 1935 by the head of German Jewry, Rabbi Dr. Leo Baeck (1873–1956), to be read in Berlin synagogues before *Kol Nidre*.[88] In 1945, Baeck came to London and became an influential member not only of the West London Synagogue but of British Reform Jewry in general. It is because of him and the many other German refugee rabbis[89] that the traditional chanted *Kol Nidre* entered British Reform services, alongside the Hebrew alternative from Hamburg that was already there.[90] Today's eighth edition of *Forms of Prayer* offers the full *Kol Nidre* ceremony and the option, "One of the two following versions of the *Kol Nidre*"; version I is the traditional Aramaic text with a free, interpretative translation, and version II is the Hamburg Temple Hebrew text. All original typical features of the West London Synagogue tradition (the opening prayer, Psalm 38) are gone.

Summary

What does the moment of *Kol Nidre* mean? For classical Reform Jews the question had to be answered in two ways: externally (its meaning to the non-Jewish society) and internally (its meaning to Jews). Externally speaking, they created alternatives that would not prove embarrassing in an open society. But by creating substitutes to speak more positively externally, they inevitably changed the meaning of the moment internally. The special moment that resulted was variously:

- An ethical admonition (as in the Berlin litany from 1817)
- A meditation about our unworthiness (as in the Hamburg hymn)
- A spiritual preparation for the encounter of God's presence (as in Leopold Stein's song)
- A confession of sins (as in Abraham Geiger's new Hebrew text)
- A plea that God may listen to our wish to return to God (as in the Munich *machzor* from 1899)
- A time to study the relationship between God and Israel (as in Psalm 130)
- A personal meditative moment open to thoughts of all kind, gently guided by an emotional tune

All these alternatives have left their traces, so that prayer books nowadays may offer not just one but several. In all progressive Jewish congregations, however, the Askhenazi *Kol Nidre* tune can be heard—with its traditional words, with different Hebrew words, or as just a tune.

ⓒⴺⴺⴺⴺⵙ

The Music of *Kol Nidre*

Dr. Mark Kligman

B ehind the music of *Kol Nidre* lies a fascinating story. More specifically, it is the story behind the Ashkenazi melody that is so compelling. Sephardi and Mizrachi congregations too sing *Kol Nidre*, but there it is generally chanted like the rest of the service. In Ashkenazi congregations, by contrast, *Kol Nidre* has been outfitted with a tune that has come to be recognizable by Jews—and even by non-Jews—who otherwise know little or nothing about Jewish liturgy and its music.

To appreciate the uniqueness of the *Kol Nidre* musical story, we need to keep two background points in mind.

First, the recorded documentation of Jewish liturgical music is quite limited. Prior to 1750, there exist only twenty documents with written musical notation. From a variety of written sources and pictorial evidence, we do know that song has long been a part of Jewish worship; we just do not know what was sung.

Second, even though our knowledge of Jewish music is extremely limited, the oldest melodies about which we have any certain information are from the High Holy Days. Some of these tunes we still sing today. These include *Alenu*, the High Holy Day evening chant, and *Kol Nidre*. A term that is used to describe these old melodies is *misinai niggunim* ("melodies from Mount Sinai"). That does not mean, of course, that they

---

Dr. Mark Kligman is professor of Jewish musicology at Hebrew Union College–Jewish Institute of Religion in New York, where he teaches in the School of Sacred Music. He specializes in the liturgical traditions of Middle Eastern Jewish communities and various areas of popular Jewish music. His publications on the liturgical music of Syrian Jews in Brooklyn have appeared in journals and in his book, *Maqām and Liturgy: Ritual, Music and Aesthetics of Syrian Jews in Brooklyn*.

actually go back to Sinai, or even that they are ancient in any way, but they are the oldest songs of which we have any record. If one looks at late eighteenth-century musical manuscripts with melodies from various European cities, the *misinai* tunes are already there. The chant we hear today for *Kol Nidre* is among them, making it one of the oldest in the Jewish tradition. But how old is it?

To answer this question we have to follow the trail staked out by a variety of historical sources, beginning with *Machzor Vitry*, an eleventh-century document composed in France by Simchah of Vitry (hence its title), a prominent disciple in the school of Rashi. Simchah refers to the custom of singing *Kol Nidre* three times (as we do today), each time with a change in musical inflection:

> The first time he [the *hazzan*] must utter it very softly, like one who hesitates to enter the palace of the king to ask a gift of Him whom he fears to approach; the second time he may speak somewhat louder; and the third time more loudly still, as one who is accustomed to dwell at court and to approach his sovereign as a friend

The next important report on *Kol Nidre* comes from the Maharil (1356–1427), an acronym for Moreinu HaRav Yaakov haLevi on Mainz, one of the most outstanding rabbis in all of Ashkenazi history. The Maharil describes prolonging the melody for *Kol Nidre* so that latecomers can be assured they will hear it.

A little over a century later, Ashkenazi Jewish life had moved eastward into the current-day Czech Republic and Poland, where information on *Kol Nidre* reaches us through the great Talmudist Mordecai Jaffe of Prague and, later, Lublin (1530–1612). In his rabbinical code of Jewish law, entitled the *L'vush* (chap. 619), he discusses a fixed tune of high quality, of which he approves; but he complains that in spite of his efforts to correct certain errors in the text, the *hazzanim* were "unable to incorporate the changes in the course of their chanting because they are too attracted to the old melody that fits the familiar text."

What we can deduce from this historical evidence is that a *Kol Nidre* melody was commonplace in the sixteenth century, and so closely connected to the text that no change in it was possible. We cannot be certain, of course, but we assume that Jaffe was referring to the melody we know today. If so, our melody goes back at least to the sixteenth century, making it one of the oldest melodies in the Ashkenazi tradition.

The first written evidence of the *Kol Nidre* melody is by Aron Beer in 1765. The shape of the melody is quite similar to the version we know today, but there are some differences in rhythm and some places where the melody is more ornate. Some nineteenth-century manuscripts repeat the melody with changes that make it more in keeping with the version that is most common today. In 1871 Louis Lewandowski, a synagogue music director and composer in Berlin, published a version of *Kol Nidre* for voice and organ that has become standard ever since.

Kol Nidre is widely known because year after year, audiences of Jews attend Yom Kippur services specifically to hear it. Even Jews who go to little else attend the *Kol Nidre* service, and whatever else they may or may not carry home with them, *Kol Nidre* seems destined to move them. So popular was it, however, that it also became a favorite among cantors who toured synagogues and concert halls in America during the Golden Age of *Hazzanut,* a consequence of the great migration of Eastern European Jews here from 1881 to 1924. Dozens of them recorded *Kol Nidre* on the new technology of the time, 78-rpm recordings. The most famous (and prolific) of this era was Yossele Rosenblatt (1882–1933).

A curious note about the *Kol Nidre* melody is its appeal beyond the Jewish community. In 1826, Beethoven himself incorporated the *Kol Nidre* opening motive into the sixth movement of his String Quartet in C-sharp Minor, op. 131. The entire *Kol Nidre* was set by Max Bruch (1838–1920), who composed a concert for cello and orchestra op. 37 to the *Kol Nidre* melody in 1881. Bruch was not Jewish himself but was introduced to *Kol Nidre* by Cantor Abraham Jacob Lichtenstein, the cantor of the major synagogue in Berlin.

Interest in *Kol Nidre* continued into the twentieth century, and in 1938 Arnold Schoenberg (1874–1951) wrote *Kol Nidre* op. 39 for speaker, choir, and orchestra. We should see Schoenberg's composition as a statement on his evolving Jewish identity. He had been born Jewish but converted to Christianity in the late nineteenth century in order to gain wider acceptance into German culture (a common practice for Jews in Western Europe at the time). He then pioneered an avant-garde school of music using a twelve-tone scale and frequently described, simply, as "atonal." He was highly enough regarded in German culture to be appointed to the faculty of the Prussian Academy of Arts in Berlin, but because of the rising racism in Germany, he was seen as a Jew despite his conversion. When Hitler came to power in 1933, he was vacationing in France. Warned that return to Germany would be dangerous, he reclaimed his Judaism, moved to America, and composed *Kol Nidre* as a way to mark his reentry to Judaism.

Kol Nidre has also found its way into American popular culture. The first talkie, *The Jazz Singer* (1927), features *Kol Nidre* as a musical symbol for the film's message as a whole. Al Jolson was featured as Jakie Rabinowitz, a cantor's son, who disappoints his father by abandoning the world of synagogue music to become a jazz singer. At the film's end, Jakie must choose the world to which his heart belongs. When his father becomes too ill to sing *Kol Nidre* in the synagogue, Jakie cancels his jazz performance to fill in for him. *The Jazz Singer* had an enormous impact on Jewish moviegoers, who saw in Jakie their own story of the mounting identity conflict between loyalty to their Jewish past on one hand and acculturation into the American future on the other. The haunting strains of *Kol Nidre* symbolized the tug of tradition; Jakie's return to the synagogue in order to sing it assured moviegoers that Jewish tradition would never be abandoned.

The Jazz Singer's success may have been one of the factors that prompted popular recordings of *Kol Nidre* by non-Jews—most notably, Perry Como and Johnny Mathis.

The *Kol Nidre* melody ushers in the most solemn day of the Jewish year. No other melody comes even close in its ability to speak to the Jewish soul. The reverence given to this moment in the liturgy and the emotive quality of the melody that marks it make *Kol Nidre* unique in Jewish worship.

ᏗᎻᏣᎯᎯᎾ

PART II
Kol Nidre and Jewish Law

Kol Nidre:
A Halakhic History and Analysis

Dr. Eliezer Diamond

The dramaturgy surrounding *Kol Nidre* on the eve of Yom Kippur notwithstanding, its chanting is, in the long run, a halakhic act, nothing more nor less than a legal formula annulling vows—either vows made over the past year (as in the original textual version and the one favored by Sephardim to this day) or vows yet to be made (as in the text used by Ashkenazim since the time of Rabbenu Tam, who lived in the eleventh century—more on this later). The purpose of this essay is to provide the halakhic framework necessary to make the purpose and function of *Kol Nidre* intelligible.

It is commonplace for human beings, everywhere and always, to state that we will or will not perform a certain task. Occasionally, either to convince others of our sincerity or to strengthen our own resolve, we commit ourselves by means of a promise. The implication of a promise is that our words are not to be taken lightly; our failure to act upon them will call down opprobrium upon our heads, not just from those we have failed, but from others too, who will hear of it and be less likely to view us

---

Dr. Eliezer Diamond is the Rabbi Judah Nadich Associate Professor of Talmud and Rabbinics at The Jewish Theological Seminary and the author of *Holy Men and Hunger Artists: Fasting and Asceticism in Rabbinic Culture*. He is currently editing a commentary on *Yerushalmi Pesahim* written by the late Professor Louis Ginzberg, as well as a book on prayer.

as trustworthy. We pride ourselves on being true to our word, dismiss others who are not, and shudder at the thought that we might become those others, for whom pledges mean nothing.

For biblical Israel and Rabbinic Judaism, oaths and vows (two different legal categories, as we shall see) are essentially promises, but they carry a great deal more weight.

An oath, or *sh'vu'ah*, is a promise either to perform or to refrain from a certain act. Explicitly or implicitly, it calls down a divine curse upon oneself should one fail to fulfill it. Alternatively, it designates not just oneself, but others, often one's children, as surety that the oath will be fulfilled.

A vow, or *neder*, has both a limited and an extended form. Originally, in its more limited biblical sense, it was a means of designating one's property as belonging to God or to God's sanctuary. Once so designated, the item vowed belonged solely and absolutely to God and could be used only by God's representatives on earth, the priests. By implication, intentional use of that property for the personal needs of the person taking the vow (a particularly heinous form of theft called *m'ilah*) resulted in the divine punishment of death. Such a vow dedicates a person's property to God and is called a *dedicatory vow*.

Rabbinic sources extend that usage, to arrive at a variant form of *neder*, a *prohibitory vow*.[1] A vow of this type involves rendering something forbidden as if it had been sanctified for Temple use. One can forbid one's own property to oneself or to others (or the belongings of others to oneself) in this way. A variety of legal formulas have the legal impact of prohibiting usage, but a common form states, "Let any X that I might use be considered *korban* or *konam* ['a sacrifice']"; from the latter we get the Aramaic plural *konamei*, which is found in *Kol Nidre*.

It may be that a prohibitive vow is actually a dedicatory vow, which, paradoxically, takes effect only when it is violated. Thus, when one says, "If I eat this food let it be considered *korban*," that is, "consecrated," he means his statement as an implicit promise not to eat the food at all. The instant he does so, it becomes dedicated to God retroactively back to the point at which the oath was made, and he will have violated the prohibition against profaning the holy.

Such a vow might be taken as a safer alternative to an oath of self-restraint (a *sh'vu'ah*), which accomplishes the same thing, because it is not automatically associated with an actual curse. That is, rather than calling down a curse upon oneself if one fails to observe the restraints to which one is bound by an oath, one simply forbids certain items to oneself using a *neder* (a vow). Breaking the *neder* would constitute misappropriation of something set aside as sacred, a serious matter, but it would not generate a divine curse.

Imagine someone, Mr. A, in a fit of anger, enraged by Mr. B. He could take an oath (a *sh'vu'ah*) in God's name that he will never allow B to use anything that belongs to him. If he changes his mind, he is subject to a divine curse. So instead, he makes a vow (a *neder*) to the same effect, by declaring that anything he owns becomes sanctified if and when B partakes of it.[2]

In sum, both vows (*n'darim*) and oaths (*sh'vu'ot*) should be taken only after careful consideration—oaths especially so, since one may end up changing one's mind. Either one, for example, may result in an unanticipated negative consequence—what the Mishnah calls a *nolad*, a "newborn" or newly arisen situation (from the Hebrew root meaning "to give birth"). Alternatively, one's state of mind may shift such that an oath or vow that seemed well-advised at the time no longer appears to have been a wise decision. One might experience *charatah*, "regret," for having taken it.

Despite the potential pitfalls of oaths and vows, it appears that in biblical times once taken they could not be revoked. A seeming exception to the rule is the fact that the Torah allows a father or husband to cancel a woman's vow on the day on which he becomes aware of it,[3] but this is really just a consequence of the authority that these men inherently have, in biblical law, over the women making the vows; such vows are considered inherently provisional. Never does the Torah suggest that the person taking the vow himself has the option of annulling it. Such a vow would be self-contradictory and meaningless.

The strongest biblical evidence for the inviolability of vows is the narrative of Jephthah and his daughter. In Judges 11, we are told that the chieftain Jephthah takes a vow obligating him to offer to God the first living being to greet him if and when he returns from war victorious. When his daughter hurries out first, he tears his clothes in anguish, for he now must sacrifice her to fulfill his vow.[4] At no point is the possibility of annulling his vow mentioned.

However, sometime during the Second Temple period two means of annulling vows were apparently adopted, at least in some circles. The first is alluded to by the first-century Jewish historian Josephus: declaring a vow or oath mistaken if it had been made out of anger or ignorance of the circumstances.[5] The Mishnah expands this category to include vows made for the purpose of bargaining, vows of gross exaggeration, vows based on misinformation, and vows that cannot be fulfilled due to constraint.

The second is mentioned by the first-century Alexandrian Jew Philo,[6] and referred to thereafter in Rabbinic literature as *hatarat n'darim*, the "loosening" or "unbinding of vows"—the annulment of a vow by a third party, a priest or a sage. The annulment took one of two forms. In the first, the priest, acting on behalf of the Temple—that is, God—simply refuses to accept the dedicated property. The second was to declare that God had been propitiated without the property being transferred to the Temple treasury and therefore there was no longer any need to do so. The notion that a vow can be annulled is a radical departure from the attitude of the Bible. For this reason the Rabbinic sages describe *hatarat n'darim* as "hovering in the air,"[7] by which they mean that it has no scriptural basis.

By the first and second centuries, a fundamental disagreement arose as to the power of sages to annul vows. Could they annul any and all vows regardless of circumstances? Or could they could do so only if there was reason to argue that the vow was fundamentally unsound from the moment of its implementation? The position ultimately adopted by the Talmud was that some basis, called a *petach* ("opening"), was required to allow a sage to annul a vow, but over time the range of acceptable grounds expanded considerably—indeed, some would say, *ad absurdum*.[8]

While *hatarat n'darim* had the salutary effect of extricating people from the negative effects of their oaths and vows, it had its own unintended and undesirable fallout, namely, vows could now be taken frivolously or thoughtlessly. As the Mishnah indicates, it had already become common to vow in moments of anger or as part of a wager. The post-Mishnaic (that is, Talmudic) expansion of the grounds for annulment only increased the likelihood that people would think nothing of taking a vow casually. In effect, moreover, vows became useless, since their validity was now undermined in the eyes of the populace. To make matters worse, the retrospective annulling of an oath made in God's name rendered it a use of God's name in vain.

It was for these reasons, among others, that the post-Talmudic leaders of Judaism known as the *geonim* (flourishing in Babylonia, currently Iraq, seventh or eighth to eleventh century) discouraged the taking of vows and, to the extent possible, avoided involving themselves with *hatarat n'darim*. Indeed, the eighth-century head of the Sura academy, Yehudai

Gaon, relates that in his academy Tractate Nedarim, the volume of the Talmud that discusses vows and their annulment, was not even studied.[9]

However, at some point in the sixth or seventh century[10] a general formula of *hatarat n'darim* was created outside the official Rabbinic world of the Babylonian *geonim*, probably in Palestine.[11] The new formula enabled the wholesale nullification of all vows made in a given period of time; contrary to Talmudic law, it was not necessary to specify the vow in question. This annulment was originally formulated in Hebrew, but it eventually was translated into Aramaic, the language in which it appears in most rites today. In some locales, it became the popular practice to recite this formula at the beginning of services on the night of Yom Kippur. It probably symbolized the possibility of obtaining forgiveness for all of the past year's sins and beginning anew.

The *geonim* responded in a variety of ways. Not surprisingly, many resisted its inclusion altogether. Others tried to reformulate it as a prayer, not a legal formula. Saadiah Gaon argued that the *Kol Nidre* formula could be employed, but only for vows made mistakenly or under duress by the community as a whole.[12] Ultimately, however, the *vox populi* prevailed; by the middle of the eleventh century, despite continued geonic opposition, *Kol Nidre* had become a part of the Yom Kippur service in most communities.[13]

The late eleventh century brought with it a further development. Rabbi Meir ben Samuel, a son-in-law of Rashi, objected to the recitation of *Kol Nidre* as a form of *hatarat n'darim*. His son Jacob, known as Rabbenu Tam, explained his father's objections in detail, pointing out that *Kol Nidre* failed to satisfy at least four of the basic halakhic requirements of that process:

1. Unless an expert is available, *hatarat n'darim* requires a court of three. Neither is the case with *Kol Nidre*.
2. Vows can be annulled only if the person who took the vow expresses regret for having done so for specific reasons. *Kol Nidre* stipulates no reasons why regret might occur.
3. In order for vows to be annulled, their content has to be specified. *Kol Nidre* is a blanket annulment that stipulates the content of none of the vows being annulled.
4. One cannot annul one's own vows, in any event. *Kol Nidre* is precisely that: an annulment of one's own vows.[14]

These requirements, however, applied only to annulments of vows already made. Meir ben Samuel had apparently proposed, therefore, that *Kol Nidre* be reformulated as a *moda'ah*, an anticipatory annulment in advance of all vows that one might take during the coming year.[15] His basis for this notion was a passage in the Babylonian Talmud: "If one wishes to ensure that one's vows for the coming year will not be binding, one should say the following at the beginning of the year: 'Any vow that I vow in the future shall be null and void'" (Nedarim 23b).

The result was a change in the wording of *Kol Nidre*. Rather than the annulment applying "from last Yom Kippur to this one," it became a nullification of vows "from this Yom Kippur until the next." But Meir ben Samuel was an Ashkenazi authority, and his ruling held only for Ashkenazi Jews. Other communities retained the original version referring only to the past, while still others adopted a hybrid formula that included references both to the previous Yom Kippur and to the coming one.[16]

In light of all of the above historical and halakhic information, let us turn to the form of *Kol Nidre* commonly used in Ashkenazi communities and clarify its meaning while also highlighting its problematic nature from both a linguistic and halakhic perspective. The following is a translation and a line-by-line explanation of the most common Ashkenazi version of *Kol Nidre*:

> All vows, *esarei, charamei, konamei,* substitute formulae, *kinusei,* and oaths that we have vowed, sworn, and declared *cherem* and prohibited upon ourselves from this Yom Kippur until the following one—may it come upon us for good—all of these we regret. [They all shall be] permitted, abandoned, put to rest, voided and made void, invalidated and made nonexistent. Our vows are not vows, our *esarei* are not *esarei,* and our oaths are not oaths.

"All vows, *esarei, charamei* ... and oaths that we have vowed ... upon ourselves": Like any thorough legal formula, *Kol Nidre* lists all the possible types of oaths and vows that a person might make so as to be sure to include them in the annulment process. Each term has its own enormously complex legal history, the details of which is beyond the scope of this presentation;[17] suffice it to say that any type of valid vow or oath enunciated in any linguistic formula whatsoever is enumerated here.

"... from this Yom Kippur until the following one—may it come upon us for good—all of these we regret": As mentioned above, given the function of *Kol Nidre* as annulment of vows taken in the past, and given also the use of the past tense in its opening lines, it would be more appropriate to refer back to the period "from last Yom Kippur until this one." The present formula, however, reflects the attempt of Rashi's son-in-law (Meir ben Samuel), grandson (Rabbenu Tam), and their adherents to transform *Kol Nidre* from a retroactive annulment into an anticipatory one. The phrase "all of these we regret" reflects the view that vows can be annulled through a generalized regret (*charatah*), unaccompanied, however, by any statement of the specific grounds for that regret.[18]

"[They all shall be] permitted, abandoned.... Our vows are not vows, our *esarei* are not *esarei*, and our oaths are not oaths": It has been suggested that until this point, we have the statement that an individual would have been made before the tribunal requesting release from vows. Now we get the tribunal's response: the declaration that the annulment is in force.[19] But the use of the first person ("our vows") instead of the second person ("your vows") or the definite plural alone ("the vows") does not comport with that theory; it reflects, instead, the use of *Kol Nidre* as a *pro forma* communal recitation, in which no distinction was made any more between the request for annulment and the granting of it. Since the community just recited the entire formula—as we do now—the person was changed to be in accord with the nouns in *Kol Nidre's* first section.

In sum, then, what is for many one of Yom Kippur's highlights is, in most of its present formulations, a less than coherent legal formula of questionable efficacy. Its inclusion in our liturgy owes more to the mood it creates of generally erasing the errors of the past and beginning anew than it does to its halakhic importance. One could choose, I suppose, to laugh up one's sleeve at the dissonance between, on the one hand, the central importance granted *Kol Nidre* and the confused and questionable nature of its actual content, on the other. Wiser heads, I would argue, would do well to remember the observation attributed to Hillel: if the people of Israel are not prophets, they are nonetheless the children of prophets. The Jewish community correctly intuited that no ceremony could better inaugurate the Day of Atonement than one representing release from failures past and looking forward to a new, hopeful future, a luminescent *tabula rasa* awaiting inscription with words, and deeds, of righteousness and sanctity.

Choice, Commitment, Cancellation

VOWS AND OATHS IN JEWISH LAW

Rabbi Daniel Landes

The dramatic spiritual power of *Kol Nidre* is directly related to the strength and solidity of the commitments that it seeks to release, permit, and cancel. In its core construction, *Kol Nidre* is a variation of a legal device known as *hatarat n'darim ush'vu'ot,* "the release of vows and oaths." *Hatarat n'darim* (for short) is the process by which an individual seeks a grant of release from a major legal authority or from a court of (at least) somewhat educated laypeople. But despite this well-trod process, halakhah worries about this release, admitting that "[the rules about] release from vows hover in the air and have naught to support them" (Mishnah Hagigah 1:8, Danby translation). *Kol Nidre*'s impressive ritual

---

Rabbi Daniel Landes is the director and *rosh hayeshivah* of the Pardes Institute of Jewish Studies in Jerusalem. Pardes brings together men and women of all backgrounds to study classical Jewish texts and contemporary Jewish issues in a rigorous, challenging, and open-minded environment. Rabbi Landes is also a contributor to the *My People's Prayer Book: Traditional Prayers, Modern Commentaries* series, winner of the National Jewish Book Award; *My People's Passover Haggadah: Traditional Texts, Modern Commentaries,* a finalist for the National Jewish Book Award; and *Who by Fire, Who by Water—Un'taneh Tokef* (all Jewish Lights).

communal version of this legal device is startling, for the commitments made in vows and oaths are meant to be kept. Reflecting on these forms of commitment as explicated classically and with an eye to modern theological speculation will reveal much about halakhah's understanding of the role played by choice: first, in making commitments, and second, in canceling them.

Of the many articulated commitments that halakhah regulates, the two that stand out today as singularly relevant to the list contained in *Kol Nidre* list are the *neder* (plural: *n'darim*) and the *sh'vu'ah* (plural: *sh'vu'ot*). The others on the list are conceptual offshoots of these two and/or represent a past reality, applicable to Temple times only. Both *neder* and *sh'vuah* are complex in their legal implications, and the two maintain a dialectical relationship to one another.

The *sh'vu'ah* ("oath") is either an affirmation of a matter of fact or a commitment regarding an action, evoking a direct or indirect mention of the holy name of God. There are four types of *sh'vu'ot*. The first, *sh'vu'at bitu'i* ("an oath of expression"), denotes either an act in the past or in the future that a person has or has not done or will or will not do: one swears, for example (evoking the divine name), that on a certain day one has or has not eaten porridge, thrown a rock, fasted, or done one's homework or that one will or will not do any of these things at a stipulated time to come. If a person makes such an oath and the truth is (or turns out to be) the opposite, this *sh'vu'at bitu'i* is labeled a *sh'vu'at sheker* ("a lying oath"), violating Leviticus 19:12: "Do not swear by my name lyingly, so as to profane the name of your God. I am Adonai." The penalty for knowingly (*mezid*) swearing this way is flogging; the inadvertent lying oath (*shogeg*) is punished by a sacrifice dependent on a person's economic status.

The second category is *sh'vu'at shav* ("a vain oath"). There are three possibilities here, all of which use God's name and thereby take God's name in vain:

- One swears that what is truthfully and commonly known to be true is, in fact, true (that a stone in the backyard is indeed a stone, or that two is two).
- One swears that one will void a *mitzvah* (e.g., not to sit in the sukkah on the holiday of Sukkot).
- One swears that one will do something that is not in one's power to do ("I won't sleep at all for three days straight").

Purposefully taking God's name in vain through any of these examples of a *sh'vu'at shav* is punishable by flogging; an inadvertent breach occasions no punishment but demands repentance for carelessness.

The third form of *sh'vu'ah* is *sh'vu'at pikadon* ("oath of deposit"). Here one swears that something of value that one has (as it were) "on deposit" from another person is not owed to that person. The object may have been deposited for safekeeping (as when I ask you to hold something for me temporarily), or it may be given as a loan (you ask me to loan you money). In either case, denying the debt is outright theft. Other cases too come to mind—for example, denying that one has found a lost object belonging to someone else, or money obtained by cheating, or even a denial of wages—all cases of theft as well, in effect. In all such cases, the violater must repay the principal with an added penalty of a fifth of what was stolen (20 percent) and then offer an *asham vada'i* ("sin offering"). If one really didn't know at all what one was saying when taking the oath, then, in certain circumstances, one is free from paying the added 20 percent and the sacrifice.

The fourth and the last form is the *sh'vu'at edut* ("oath of testimony"), in which those in receipt of information regarding a monetary suit deny on oath that they have testimony to offer. Such an oath, denying testimony, is another instance also of a *sh'vu'at sheker* ("a lying oath"), for which one is liable to a sacrifice dependent upon one's economic status.

In a sense, there is also a fifth form of oath, *sh'vu'at hadayanim* ("an oath imposed by judges [in court]"). Generally, this is an oath by which a person charged with a monetary crime takes an oath of being in debt, so as to be free of incurring further monetary responsibility that would accrue through the penalty imposed on account of the crime. Such an oath remains a technical possibility, but given the severe nature of the possible profanation of God's name, the Sages mostly eliminated evoking the name in this procedure.

A brief review of our categories of *sh'vuot* ("oaths") shows that categories 2, 3, and 4 are all severe violations and are proscribed. The use of halakhic analysis here is to educate us to avoid these wrongful declarations. Even the first category, *sh'vu'at bitu'i* ("oath of expression"), is a certain violation if one lies about the past. It is the swearing about a possible future that becomes questionable, for one may or may not do or restrain oneself from a sworn action or inaction (eating or not eating a certain item, for instance, or investing or not investing in a certain company). Violation— in the future—desecrates God's name. Does *Kol Nidre* offer a way out?

We shall return to that question, but first we must consider the *neder* ("vow").

The *neder* ("vow") is a personal decision not to do something or to derive benefit from someone. In Temple times, it could also refer to a commitment to bring a voluntary sacrifice, but that is not relevant in our days. A *neder* is, therefore, a negative declaration to forbid oneself from something that otherwise would have been permitted (Numbers 30:3). One might, for instance, take a *neder* not to eat certain fruit from a certain fruit stand that one might otherwise patronize. The *neder* differs from the positively articulated *sh'vu'ah* in that the *neder* does not invoke God's name. All one need do is declare that a particular item or practice is forbidden (*assur*) to oneself. Numbers 30:3 continues, *lo yachel d'varo*, generally interpreted, "he should not break his word," literally, "he should not profane his word."

A *neder* is most commonly used to ensure a religious discipline— refraining from sitting during the chanting of the Torah, for example, out of respect. Such a practice, if articulated verbally as a *neder*, or even if just practiced for a certain period of time, becomes a vow that needs to be continued. The strength of such a *neder* has been explained by Rav Kook (Rabbi Abraham Isaac Hakohen Kook, 1865–1935, Latvia and Israel):

> The *neder* ["vow"] represents the depth of natural revelation of the faith instinct that manifests itself in thought, in expression (*bitu'i*), and in action.
>
> "One should not profane one's word. One should do according to all that leaves one's mouth" (Numbers 30:3). The *neder* is the boundary line that protects an individual's personal belief from being overwhelmed by the flow of the great light of codified obligation given from on high, from the mouth of the supreme God, the universal inheritance to the entire congregation of Jacob.[1]

Rav Kook posits two orders to the moral-spiritual life. The first is Torah: divine and compelling, it is imposed upon us from without even while it elevates us. The second is self-legislating, the natural morality or a "natural revelation" that we obtain from within ourselves as we seek through a sense of personal inner obligation to advance to an even higher ethical-spiritual level. This is where the *neder* fits in. It is purely personal, an added obligation that goes beyond the formal codified requirements of Torah, but given its own elevated status by that very codified halakhah that it surpasses. Halakhah, in general, is universal to the entire Jewish people. The *neder* is specific, "custom tailored," by the individual for one's own ethical-spiritual needs. But it is validated and given full worth by halakhah alongside divine revelation itself.

For Rav Kook, then, the *neder* is a source of moral-spiritual strengthening beyond, as it were, the letter of the law. By extension, so too is the *sh'vu'ah*. Both signify higher human commitment and, as such, may not be renounced.

There is, however, an intrinsic difference between a *neder* and a *sh'vu'ah* that has implications for the general category of *hatarat n'darim ush'vu'ot* ("releasing of vows and oaths") as found in the *Kol Nidre* today. According to the classical halakhah, one can actually make a *neder* forbidding certain ritual requirements: "If a person says eating matzah on Pesach, sitting in the sukkah on Sukkot, or putting on *t'fillin* is forbidden to him, then these are forbidden to him. If such a person then ate matzah, sat in the sukkah, or put on *t'fillin*, he is flogged [for breaking his *neder*]" (Moses Maimonides [1135–1204, Spain and Fustat, Egypt])[2] If this ruling is not puzzling enough, Maimonides simultaneously rules, apparently to the contrary, that *sh'vu'ot* attempting to cancel one's performance of a *mitzvah* have no effect. So we have a double problem: Can a *neder* really cancel a *mitzvah*? And if it can, why is the same benefit not extended to a *sh'vu'ah*? The *sh'vu'ah* and *neder* are obviously different. But how?

The difference lies in the fact that the object of the *sh'vu'ah* is the person making the oath. Technically, one makes a *sh'vu'ah* about oneself, not about the object or mitzvah to which one relates. By contrast, the force of a *neder* does not fall on the subject making the *neder*, but on the object or other person forbidden. In addition, a general rule of thumb comes into play differently. In the case of a *sh'vu'ah*, one is always constrained by any prior oaths that have been made. Thus, if one has already committed oneself to even a neutral action by an early oath ("I will wear a green shirt on the first Thursday of every month"), one cannot cancel this action through a second oath ("I will not wear a green shirt on the first Thursday of every month"). One has already committed oneself to the first oath. The second is actually a *sh'vu'at shav*—it cannot take effect and is therefore meaningless, or "vain." The implication for *mitzvot* generally is that, in the case of a *mitzvah*, we have a prior (and therefore over-riding) principle that every Jew is already "obligated by oath from the moment of standing at Mount Sinai." One cannot extricate oneself from that commitment.[3] One cannot, therefore, make a *sh'vu'ah* that extricates oneself from halakhic responsibility to fulfill a *mitzvah*. And this is so on two grounds, first, because there is a prior obligation going back to Sinai obligating the person to *mitzvot*; and second (as we said before), because the prior obligation falls on the person, not on the object of relationship, because a *sh'vuah*, as we saw, falls upon the subject, not the object that the *sh'vu'ah* affects.

Why then can a person make a *neder* that effectively obviates a *mitzvah*? The answer is that it is the person who is obliged at Sinai, not the objects of halakhah (the matzah, sukkah, or *t'fillin*) to which the person relates. And as we saw, a *neder* falls on the object, not the person. So "if one forbids a matter [matzah, sukkah, *t'fillin*] through a *neder*, it is the matter that is forbidden, and the matter is not part of the principle of obligated by oath from the moment of standing at Mount Sinai."[4] Halakhah distinguishes between the *subject* making an *oath* (*sh'vu'ah*) and the *object* to which the *vow* (*neder*) is relevant. The *object* is, as it were, already at some distance existentially from oneself; a *neder* is the halakhic means by which one may choose to alienate the object even further.

This distinction is obviously relevant to how contemporary Jews approach the acceptance or rejection of *mitzvot*. If one has embraced Kantian ethics, then one will assume that the only truly ethical position is that which derives independently from one's own developed ethical reasoning and understanding. By contrast, the religious Jew might argue that ethics derive not from ourselves but from an external source, God. Both positions tend toward all or nothing: ethics are entirely self-legislating (Kant) or altogether received from God (Torah).

The halakhah of *neder* and *sh'vu'ah* takes a moderating position. Yes, obligations come from God, but individual understanding is not altogether irrelevant. The actual objects to which we relate through halakhah are just that, objects, and so may very well be alienated from an individual. Thus, while the halakhah *does not want* an individual to make a *neder* that declares matzah, sukkah, or *t'fillin* forbidden, it nonetheless *respects the integrity of such a declaration* once it has been made. But halakhah refuses to allow an individual to remove the prior oath, a *sh'vu'ah*, made at Sinai by him through his ancestors. Halakhah is anguished by, and deeply regrets, the distancing of an aspect of divine command from the individual, but it understands and even validates it. It will not, however, countenance the distancing and canceling of the self from such a command, from the One who commands, and from the community within which the command is heard and preserved.

Halakhah's valuing of human valuing (and subsequent decision making) is real and deep. It permits a wide range of commitments or statements of alienation, even when it comes to *mitzvot*. And then one *must* keep to these commitments. Once legislated, even *self*-legislated, it is law.

But what if the vow or the future-oriented *sh'vu'ah* is onerous? What if the person's imposed spiritual discipline turns out to be something that no longer can be kept? Or what if one could still keep it physically, but psychologically cannot bear being removed from a Jewish practice that once seemed alien but no longer seems so? This is where *Kol Nidre* comes in. The halakhic system finds a way out. Even though that way has no real status in the written Torah,[5] it at least has a tradition associated with the oral law. It is a close reading of the previously mentioned verse: *lo yachel d'varo*, which is strictly interpreted to mean "The one who made the vow cannot make it *chol* ['profane,' i.e., no longer obligatory], *but someone else can*." That someone else is a Torah authority or, in his absence, a small *bet din* or even three ordinary people who are alert and generally knowledgeable.[6] The release occurs the eve of Rosh Hashanah. Additionally, this is done communally with *Kol Nidre*. Both reflect the process of *hatarat n'darim ush'vu'ot*, "releasing vows and oaths." As Rav Kook states it, "The beginning of forgiveness commences with the forgiving of the blemished vows. This accords with the custom of Israel, who victoriously set in order a public release of vows on the night of Yom Kippur and directed individual releases on Rosh Hashanah eve."[7]

PART III
Kol Nidre:
Translation and Commentary

A. Preamble

Light is sown for the righteous, and
  for the upright, gladness[1] (Psalm
  97:11).

אוֹר זָרֻעַ לַצַּדִּיק, וּלְיִשְׁרֵי לֵב
שִׂמְחָה.

[1]Taken from Sephardi practice, but by now, commonplace among many Ashkenazi congregations as well.

Kabbalistically minded congregations see esoteric meaning in the fact that the final letters of the first three Hebrew words (*resh, ayin, kuf*), rearranged and supplied with vowels, spell *kara*, "to rip" or "to tear," a shorthand reference to the High Holy Day hope that any evil decree that awaits us as the verdict of the day be shredded. The same hope occurs in the traditional Rosh Hashanah service around the blowing of the shofar. All but Reform congregations blow the shofar twice on the new year, once in the morning (*Shacharit*) service and once in the additional (*Musaf*) service. The former (the instance that Reform Jews omit) is introduced by biblical verses (Lamentations 3:56 and five verses from Psalms 119 [160, 122, 162, 66, 108]), the first letters of which, taken together, spell *kara satan*, "tear up Satan." Satan is, of course, the personification of evil, but the term also connotes the forces of evil in the universe and the divine attribute of justice that we hope God will deemphasize relative to the attribute of mercy, the idea being that we are all sinners whom the strict application of justice would consign to punishment. We require God's grace (God's mercy, freely given) to survive High Holy Day judgment.

In rabbinic lore, the attribute of mercy was identified with God's four-letter name, *yod, heh, vav, heh*. Kabbalist Isaiah Horowitz (c. 1565–1630) would combine the letters for *kara satan* with this four-letter name, such that the former was bracketed by the latter. During the shofar blasts, he would concentrate on this combination as a means of influencing the attribute of mercy to swallow up the attribute of justice.

In the same way, while reciting *Or zarua latzaddik* ("Light is sown for the righteous"), kabbalistic worshipers were to attend to the esoteric message of *kara*, hoping similarly to influence the erasure of an evil decree.

Each Hebrew letter, moreover, has a numerical equivalent corresponding to where it falls in the alphabet, so that every Hebrew word, or set of words, can be translated into a numerical sum called *gematria*. As it turns out, the *gematria* of the final letters from the last three words in the verse (*yod, vet, heh*) add up to 17 (10 + 2 + 5), which is the same total as the Hebrew word *tov*, "good," the implication being that reciting Psalm 97:11 will erase the evil decree that strict justice would demand and replace it with the good decree that God's mercy offers.

The Sephardi congregations that include Psalm 97:11 generally follow it with a lengthy kabbalistic meditation in Aramaic that focuses on the inner working of the *sefirot* in all of this. For kabbalists, the universe was created by emanations of divine being into space, making God and the universe identical: God, from the perspective of where the process began; the universe, from the perspective of how it ends. Therefore, whatever happens in the universe happens also within the interior landscape of the divine. The most painful feature of reality is the fact of exile, not just geographical exile from our Land, a historical condition brought about when the Temple was destroyed and Jews were thrown into a diaspora, but metaphysical exile, the condition of sin, fragmentation, and alienation from the state of spiritual wholeness. All of religion is the effort to replace that painful state with its opposite—what we call redemption. For the kabbalistic mindset, ever since the Temple's destruction, Jews have been in metaphysical, not just geographical, exile, but so has the rest of the world, and since God and the world are two sides of the same coin, so too is God.

By imagining God as partitioned into separate spheres (called *sefirot*), kabbalists could provide a master metaphor of God too existing in a fragmented state. Seen globally this way, Yom Kippur is more than an appeal for personal pardon; its ultimate aim is universal redemption from sin, evil, hardship, alienation, and fragmentation.

The extra meditation is a complex and technical treatment of the process of redemption as seen from within the inner working of God, the sefirotic parallel to the earthly realm that we human beings inhabit. Its details require an understanding of the various *sefirot* and their symbolic functioning, relative to each other and to Talmudic teaching, which is assumed to apply to them as well as to us. The Talmud (Bava Batra 74a) cites Rabbah bar bar Chanah as visiting Mount Sinai and hearing "a heavenly voice saying, 'Woe is Me [God] for I swore that I would exile my people, and now that I have sworn, who can annul my oath?'" The Talmud chides Bar Chanah as a fool for not knowing that God's oath has already been annulled, and the *Tosafot* to the passage (a commentary from the school of Rashi, eleventh and twelfth centuries) refer us to a discussion elsewhere in which God is assumed to be able to annul God's own vows. For kabbal-

B. Preparation

Blessed are You, Adonai our God,
ruler of the world, who sanctified
us with his commandments and
commanded us to wrap ourselves
with a tasseled garment.[2]

בָּרוּךְ אַתָּה, יְיָ אֱלֹהֵינוּ,
מֶלֶךְ הָעוֹלָם, אֲשֶׁר קִדְּשָׁנוּ
בְּמִצְוֹתָיו וְצִוָּנוּ לְהִתְעַטֵּף
בַּצִּיצִת.

ists, an internal divine process such as this necessarily entails the action of one or more of the *sefirot* upon the others.

When Israel went physically into exile, the Talmud says, the last of the *sefirot*, the *Shekhinah*, accompanied it, as the feminine aspect of God, an immediately present divine mother, if you will. The question, therefore, becomes how the other *sefirot* can end the rash vow that sent her there. The meditation presents the permutations and combinations of sefirotic activity that might go into annulling that vow, but from the perspective of the *sefirot* alone, as if they are a world unto themselves. Two of the *sefirot* are called the upper and lower father and mother, for instance; since parents can annul a vow of children, perhaps they can cancel God's vow to send Israel into exile. Alternatively, three of the *sefirot* are likened to the three patriarchs, who might represent a *bet din* of three, to whom the power to annul vows is given.

The esoteric considerations implicit in Psalm 97:11 followed by the kabbalistic meditation on the sefirotic process of ending the state of exile that afflicts reality as a whole prepare the kabbalistically inclined worshiper for seeing *Kol Nidre* as far more than an opportunity for personal pardon. Rather, it inaugurates a day to confront the fact of universal alienation that Yom Kippur may, in some measure, alleviate.

[2]The *tallit* is normally worn in the morning but not at night, since its usage is explained by the Torah's statement (Numbers 15:39), "You shall look at them [the tassels, or *tzitzit*] and recall all the commandments of Adonai." Being able to look at them (and, presumably, see them) is taken to imply daylight. The sole exception to the rule is the evening of Yom Kippur. The custom was debated well into the Middle Ages, some people wearing the *tallit*, some not, and some wearing it but saying no blessing over it. Eventually it was decided to don the *tallit* while it is still day, so that a blessing that entails the obligation to look at *tzitzit* not be said in vain. That is why the *tallit* is put on prior to *Kol Nidre*—not yet Yom Kippur, but still daylight. (See BaCH to Orach Chayim 719.)

C. Introduction

By the authority of the heavenly court and of the earthly court:[3]

With the foreknowledge of the God of time and space and with the agreement of this congregation, we give permission to pray with habitual sinners.

בִּישִׁיבָה שֶׁל מַעְלָה וּבִישִׁיבָה
שֶׁל מַטָּה,
עַל דַּעַת הַמָּקוֹם וְעַל דַּעַת
הַקָּהָל, אָנוּ מַתִּירִין לְהִתְפַּלֵּל
עִם הָעֲבַרְיָנִים.

[3]A medieval addition to the ritual by Meir of Rothenberg (1215–93), perhaps the most influential of all early Ashkenazi rabbis. It establishes the context of the ritual, a court setting in which worshipers are being tried. But more than that, the addition is connected to a Talmudic teaching in the name of Simon Chasida (Keritot 6b), "Any fast that does not include the presence of Jewish sinners is not a fast, as we see from galbanum. It has a terrible odor but Torah included it among the spices that make up the Temple incense." It is not simply the possibility that any one of us might be a sinner (so we need permission to pray together); we actually require the presence of sinners for our communal fast to count. This interpretation is already in the *Tur*, the influential law code composed by Jacob ben Asher (1270–1340), whose father, Asher ben Yechiel, was a student of Meir of Rothenberg.

But this was originally an announcement, not a prayer. Mordecai ben Hillel (1240–98), also a student of Meir's, so a colleague of Asher ben Yechiel, says, "People entered the synagogue and were given permission to pray with any person who had violated a communal ordinance [*g'zerat hakahal*], even if the person involved did not request it." Such people, presumably, would already have been put into *cherem*, declared outside the pale so that no one could have anything to do with them; the Yom Kippur fast was declared an exception to that rule. Yet a third student of Meir's, the Tashbetz (Shimshon bar Tzadok), used to say, "We give permission that if there is any sinner among us, we may pray with them." The wording in our prayer book is the version attributed directly to Meir himself. His disciples used their own variants, apparently, but Meir's own usage eventually became normative.

D. The Request

All vows [*nidrei*],[4] *esarei*,[5] *charamei*,[6] *konamei*,[7] substitute formulae [*kinuyei*],[8] *kinusei*,[9] and oaths [*sh'vu'ot*][10] that we have vowed [declared as a *neder*], sworn [declared as a *sh'vu'ah*], and declared *cherem* and prohibited [as an *issar*] upon ourselves from this Yom Kippur until the following one[11]—may it come upon us for good—all of these we regret. They all shall be permitted, abandoned, put to rest, voided and made void, invalidated and made nonexistent. Our vows are not vows, our *esarei* are not *esarei*, and our oaths are not oaths.

כָּל נִדְרֵי וֶאֱסָרֵי וַחֲרָמֵי,
וְקוֹנָמֵי וְכִנּוּיֵי, וְקִנּוּסֵי וּשְׁבוּעוֹת,
דִּנְדַרְנָא וּדְאִשְׁתַּבַּעְנָא,
וּדְאַחֲרִמְנָא וְדְאָסַרְנָא עַל
נַפְשָׁתָנָא, מִיּוֹם כִּפֻּרִים זֶה עַד
יוֹם כִּפֻּרִים הַבָּא עָלֵינוּ
לְטוֹבָה, כֻּלְּהוֹן אֲחָרַטְנָא בְהוֹן.
כֻּלְּהוֹן יְהוֹן שָׁרָן, שְׁבִיקִין
שְׁבִיתִין, בְּטֵלִין וּמְבֻטָּלִין, לָא
שְׁרִירִין וְלָא קַיָּמִין. נִדְרָנָא
לָא נִדְרֵי, וֶאֱסָרָנָא לָא אֱסָרֵי,
וּשְׁבוּעָתָנָא לָא שְׁבוּעוֹת.

People must have been reticent to accept this permission, however, because Joel Sirkes (the BaCH, Poland, 1560–1640) reports that Maharil (Jacob Moellin of Mainz and Worms, 1365–1427) would personally announce permission "in front of the ark, even before the prayer leader began," and that "it became customary for the most prominent person in every town to do the same thing." Sometimes, the person making the announcement was flanked by two other members of the community, making them into the equivalent of a *bet din* (a court) of three. Ashkenazi custom varied as late as the nineteenth century, but the *Shulchan Arukh* calls for the prayer leader alone to make the announcement, a practice that prevailed and transformed the announcement into the equivalent of a prayer.

[4]A *neder* was originally a *dedicatory vow*, the act of dedicating something to God—in practice, to the Temple—as a sacrifice or as something to be reserved for exclusive use by the priests. One thereby abandoned the right to use it oneself. By extension, it became also a *prohibitive vow*, simply prohibiting the use of something to oneself or to others "as if it were a sacrificial offering" (*k'korban*).

[5]An *issar* was originally a subcategory of a *sh'vu'ah*, an "oath" (see below), with the connotation of "being bound" either positively or negatively, to do or not to do something. Eventually, it was interpreted as an independent entity in and of itself: an oath without recourse to the normative oath formula, such as an oath to fast, for example. Of all the terms listed here, *issar* is the least specific and substantive, but it is included anyway, in an attempt to make the list comprehensive.

[6]*Cherem* nowadays means "excommunication," in the sense of being cut off from the community, being declared beyond the pale. But originally (in the Bible) it denoted a dedicatory vow made by entire communities to render spoils of war or of the fight against idolatry beyond the use of anyone and given over, instead, as a sacrifice to God. In general, the items declared *cherem* were utterly destroyed. Eventually, the limitation to issues of war and idolatry disappeared, and the term functioned more generally as a particularly stringent type of vow, entailing destruction of the item vowed. A person might even declare one's own self *cherem*, a conditional vow to let oneself be killed should one fail to satisfy a promise.

[7]A term borrowed from the Greek and used as a substitute for the Hebrew *korban*, "sacrifice." Instead of dedicating an item as *korban* ("a Temple offering"), one would dedicate it as *konam*.

[8]Instead of *sh'vu'ah*, *korban*, and the like, various substitute formulas for vows and oaths were customary. The most common of them, *konam and konas*, are specified here, although *konasei* has been altered to *kinusei* under the influence of the preceding *kinuyei*. *Kinuyei* (singular: *kinuy*), meaning, simply, "epithets" or "titles" for something, denotes substitute formulas in general and is intended to cover all technical terms not otherwise expressly mentioned.

[9]*Konas* (here, pronounced *kinus*; see n. 8 above) is a variant form of *konam*, a term borrowed from the Greek and used in place of *korban*, "sacrifice."

[10]A *sh'vu'ah* ("oath") is the most serious type of sacred promise, since it entails, explicitly or implicitly, swearing in God's name. Oaths could be *assertory* (asserting that such and such is true, as when bearing testimony in a court of law) or *promissory* (guaranteeing that one will or will not do something in the future). The *promissory oath* (*sh'vu'ah*) was generally

E. The Response[12]

The whole Israelite community and the stranger residing among them shall be forgiven, for it happened to the entire people through error (Numbers 15:26).

וְנִסְלַח לְכָל עֲדַת בְּנֵי יִשְׂרָאֵל וְלַגֵּר הַגָּר בְּתוֹכָם, כִּי לְכָל הָעָם בִּשְׁגָגָה.

Pardon, I pray, the iniquity of this people according to your great kindness, as You have forgiven this people ever since Egypt (Numbers 14:19).

סְלַח נָא לַעֲוֹן הָעָם הַזֶּה כְּגֹדֶל חַסְדֶּךָ, וְכַאֲשֶׁר נָשָׂאתָה לָעָם הַזֶּה מִמִּצְרַיִם וְעַד הֵנָּה.

As it says ... And Adonai said: I have pardoned as you asked (Numbers 14:20).

וְשָׁם נֶאֱמַר: וַיֹּאמֶר יְהוָה סָלַחְתִּי כִּדְבָרֶךָ.

replaced by a *prohibitive vow* (*neder*), which accomplished the same thing without, however, using God's name.

[11]The formula designating vows and oaths of the year beginning. The original texts of *Kol Nidre* stipulated vows and oaths of the year just past. Reference to the future instead of the past derives from a halakhic mandate traced to Rashi's son-in-law (Meir ben Samuel) and grandson (Rabbenu Tam), a response to the fact that halakhah allows annulment of past vows and oaths only under certain circumstances, none of which are satisfied by *Kol Nidre*. By stipulating vows and oaths not yet made, *Kol Nidre* no longer violates this express halakhic prohibition.

[12]The "Response" is a combination of two biblical units, Numbers 15:26 and 14:19–20. Numbers 15:26 is the biblical guarantee that God will pardon sins done unwittingly. Its presence here suggests that *all* sins may be treated by God *as if* they are done unwittingly, the assumption being, perhaps (as in Plato), that no one would rationally sin voluntarily, so that even if sins appear to be purposive, God understands them to arise out of an irrationally skewed psyche and will pardon them as if they were done in error. The second part (Numbers 14:19–20) comes from the story of the scouts dispatched in advance to spy out the Land of Israel.

F. Postscript

Blessed are You, Adonai our God,
ruler of the world, who has kept us
alive, sustained us, and brought us
to this time of year.

בָּרוּךְ אַתָּה, יְיָ אֱלֹהֵינוּ,
מֶלֶךְ הָעוֹלָם, שֶׁהֶחֱיָנוּ וְקִיְּמָנוּ
וְהִגִּיעָנוּ לַזְּמַן הַזֶּה.

When all but two of them despair of victory (13:11–33), the people conclude that it would have been preferable to die in the wilderness than to
push on to certain disaster (14:23). Angered over the people's loss of faith,
God threatens to disown them (14:12). But Moses pleads for forgiveness
and receives a guarantee that God has indeed pardoned the people, just as
Moses has asked. That plea and guarantee (14:19–20) are included here,
not solely for what they represent in themselves, but also because they follow verse 18, the classic statement of God's attributes of mercy, known as
"the thirteen attributes." The entire High Holy Day liturgy is predicated
on these attributes ("Adonai, Adonai, God merciful and forgiving"),
which the Talmud describes as constituting their own covenant with the
divine (Rosh Hashanah 17b). When Israel sins, God tells Moses, let them
wrap themselves in a *tallit* and recite these attributes; pardon will be
forthcoming. The final lines of the Response do not cite the thirteen
attributes, but they assume them, as backdrop for Moses's request
("Pardon, I pray ...") and God's response ("I have pardoned as you
asked").

PART IV

Kol Nidre and the Testimony of Prayer-Book Editors

Kol Nidre from *Union Prayer Book* to *Gates of Repentance*

Rabbi Lawrence A. Hoffman, PhD

Unlike other essays in part 4, this one does not describe a current debate on *Kol Nidre*. That is because the North American Reform Movement has yet to publish its newest liturgy for the High Holy Days. In relatively recent decades, we have seen two eras in prayer-book formation among progressive Jewish communities worldwide, the first running (roughly) throughout the 1970s and 1980s, and the second occurring in the 1990s and 2000s. North American Reform was one of the first to publish a new High Holy Day volume in the first era; it is one of the last to do so for the second era. Instead, it deliberated for over a decade on its

Rabbi Lawrence A. Hoffman, PhD, has served for more than three decades as professor of liturgy at Hebrew Union College–Jewish Institute of Religion in New York. He is a world-renowned liturgist and holder of the Stephen and Barbara Friedman Chair in Liturgy, Worship and Ritual. He has written and edited many books, including *My People's Prayer Book: Traditional Prayers, Modern Commentaries,* winner of the National Jewish Book Award; *Who by Fire, Who by Water—Un'taneh Tokef,* the first volume in the Prayers of Awe series; and he is coeditor of *My People's Passover Haggadah: Traditional Texts, Modern Commentaries,* a finalist for the National Jewish Book Award. He is a developer of Synagogue 3000, a transdenominational project designed to envision and implement the ideal synagogue of the spirit for the twenty-first century.

daily, Shabbat, and festival liturgy (*Mishkan T'filah*), which emerged only in 2007. A committee is now working on the High Holy Day follow-up, which is still probably several years away from publication.

We can, however, look at the High Holy Day *machzor* in use now: *Gates of Repentance*, published in 1978. It marked a significant shift from prior North American Reform practice, the *Union Prayer Book*, volume 2, which had defined classical Reform in 1894 and remained in use through two revisions, a "Revised Version" of 1923 and a "Newly Revised Version" of 1945. The last is especially fascinating, because it illustrates so well the way prayer books are composed, and because it demonstrates the degree to which the later *Gates of Repentance* symbolized a break from Reform's classical past. In addition, we are fortunate in having the correspondence of the committee editor in 1945, Rabbi Solomon Freehof, from which we can reconstruct for the first time the fascinating backroom tale of the debate within the committee over what to do with *Kol Nidre*.

As Annette M. Boeckler explains (see pp. 39–66), progressive Jews throughout Europe had adopted all sorts of ways to do without *Kol Nidre*, replacing it (among other things) with a psalm, a newly composed text, or just instrumental music without cantorial solo. In part, *Kol Nidre* had proved to be an impediment to Jewish civil rights in modern societies; in part, the text seemed legal and aspiritual—hardly what congregants flocked to Yom Kippur to consider; and in part, the prayer seemed objectionable on moral, theological, and even halakhic grounds. Some progressive synagogues did, however, allow it to be sung (preferably with a substitute text), since people loved the music enough that without it, it hardly seemed like Yom Kippur.

The *Union Prayer Book (UPB)* of 1894 followed these precedents, omitting the text entirely and going so far as not even to mention that the music might be sung (or at least played on an instrument). It was perfectly conceivable that Reform Jews could experience *Kol Nidre* eve without *Kol Nidre*. The conclusion of the *Kol Nidre* ritual was there: the three biblical verses promising pardon (see p. 95) and *Shehecheyanu*. But instead of *Kol Nidre* itself, worshipers got Psalm 130, a common substitute in Europe as well, since it began with the apt reminder, "Out of the depths I cry unto Thee O Lord," and concluded with the promise that God would "redeem Israel from all his iniquities." In addition, the *UPB* included the third verse of "Day of God," originally a German hymn by Rabbi Leopold Stein (1810–82) in Frankfurt. Isaac M. Wise, the founder of North American

Reform, had translated it, and the *UPB* included the last verse, which asked God to "fill all our spirits with peace and gladness," not (interestingly) the first one, which proclaimed, "My heart is awed and terror seizeth my spirit." "Peace and gladness," yes; "terror," no. The whole thing began with a two-page silent meditation asking God to exchange "the anxieties that often consume our strength" with "pardon ... peace and grace" despite the "sense of our unworthiness."

The 1924 revision was essentially the same thing, except that the meditation had been rewritten to reflect a harsher view of human nature. The problem was not simply "the sense of our unworthiness," but our "wickedness ... selfishness ... unrighteousness ... and abasement." There is still no mention of *Kol Nidre*, which was noticeable, if at all, only by its continued absence.

Both the original *Union Prayer Book* and its 1924 replacement were responses to the influx of Eastern European immigrants from 1881 to 1924. Reform Jews who had arrived earlier from Central Europe had worked hard to demonstrate their commitment to Western culture and modernity. More recent arrivals, "the Russian Jews," had no such sensitivities: they valued the folk Judaism of the Jewish people. By 1945, however, when the newly revised edition of the *Union Prayer Book* was being discussed, many Eastern European arrivals, now grown to adulthood, had joined Reform synagogues. Representing their voice, some members of the 1945 committee championed the restoration of *Kol Nidre*; others felt just as strongly about continuing the long-standing Reform custom of excluding it.

Moderating the debate was Solomon Freehof (1892–1990), the rabbi of Congregation Rodef Shalom in Pittsburgh. Letters back and forth between Freehof and members of his committee give us an insider's view of the committee's struggle over what to do with the troublesome prayer.[1]

Although born in London, Freehof was a descendant of the Alter Rebbe, one of the founders of a major Hasidic dynasty in Poland. As an acknowledged expert in rabbinic law, he had emerged as the Reform Movement's primary interpreter of halakhah. From his responsa, and from his two-volume summary of *Reform Jewish Practice*,[2] we can see that he was by no means anxious to reverse the rationalism that governed Reform Judaism's approach to Jewish ritual generally. Nor, he says (as we shall see), did he want to restore *Kol Nidre*. But somehow, *Kol Nidre* was inserted into the final manuscript so that when the prayer book came out in early April 1945, there it was for all to see.

This was an era without ready air travel and inexpensive phone communication. People took overnight trains to attend meetings, which were necessarily few and far between. Business was done by ordinary mail or, for emergencies, telegrams. On April 6, therefore, Freehof received a telegram from Rabbi Samuel Cohon, the professor of theology at the Hebrew Union College in Cincinnati and a member of the committee. Cohon had received what must have been an advance copy of the prayer book and found several mistakes in it, not the least being the inclusion of *Kol Nidre*. He asked that the book be withheld from further circulation while the committee decided what to do.

But the book was already in print. So that very day, Freehof wired Isaac E. Marcuson, the rabbi in Macon, Georgia, since 1894 and the committee member charged with seeing the book through the printing process, and urged him to stop production. In a follow-up letter, Freehof elaborated his suggestion: Hold up further production, make necessary minor changes, then reassemble the book with the new pages, rather than scrap the entire print run and start over again, thereby "losing tens of thousands of dollars and the entire edition."

The same day (April 6), he responded to Cohon, saying, "You will recall that I opposed having the *Kol Nidre* text altogether. Are you under the opinion that the committee accepted your text? I believe the committee accepted the traditional text (over my objection). I am going to ask Marcuson to look it up." Marcuson was also the committee secretary who kept the minutes. Freehof assumed that production would be held up long enough for Marcuson to clarify the situation.

On April 8, Cohon received Freehof's reassurance and wrote back saying that he was "greatly relieved" to know that it was not too late to undo the damage. He attributed the misunderstanding to "the hardships connected to printing under wartime conditions" (it was exactly a month before Victory in Europe Day and over four months before the war would be concluded with Japan). He regretted whatever cost it would take to correct the errors, but argued, "Whatever the expense, it will be well spent if it will remove *machlokes* [arguments] from the Conference."

By *conference*, Cohon meant the Central Conference of American Rabbis (CCAR), the official organization for the North American Reform rabbinate that had appointed Freehof's committee and to which that committee was ultimately responsible. The use of the Hebrew/Yiddish term *machlokes* gives us some idea of how strongly Cohon felt on the subject.

And he was not alone. In 1930, the CCAR's annual convention, held in Providence that year, had featured an acrimonious debate on *Kol Nidre*. In addition, Cohon had apparently consulted with his colleague at the college, Rabbi Israel Bettan (1889–1957), professor of midrash and homiletics and a member of the Liturgy Committee himself. Bettan, he reported, "was incredulous that the Aramaic *Kol Nidre* has found its way into the book." Since Freehof now said that he too opposed it, Cohon was more certain than ever that the committee as a whole had rejected it, especially since "Goldensohn, Marcuson and Calisch [three other committee members] would not approve of a formula of absolution of vows in our prayerbook."[3]

> You will recall [Freehof goes on], the stormy discussion on the subject at the Providence meeting of the Conference (see *Yearbook*, vol. 40, pp. 101–108) in which not a single argument was advanced in reconciliation of the old formula with Reform Jewish thought. To reawaken the controversy at a time like this when from so many directions, attacks are made on the Conference for temporizing in matters of Reform principle would be a tragic blunder. After all, a century of Reform tradition is against the retention of the text. Even Mordecai Kaplan[4] has dispensed with its use. I would rather have no Hebrew text at all than retain the old one. However, I believe that my substitute solves the problem.

As we see from Freehof's letter to Cohon and from Cohon's letter back, the issue was not simply whether *Kol Nidre* would be reinstated, but whether a substitute text by Cohon was supposed to have been inserted in its place. Cohon had actually composed two prayers, one in English and another in Hebrew, and wanted them both included.

Cohon died in 1959, but his wife, Irma, retained his records and remained his advocate. On September 4, 1973, she wrote to Rabbi John Rayner in London. Rayner had just edited *Gate of Repentance*, the High Holy Day volume for Liberal Jews of Great Britain, and in it, he had included a Hebrew version of *Kol Nidre*. Irma Cohon had not seen the work, but was under the impression that it was the one penned by her late husband, who had not been credited with its composition. Indeed it was, in very large part,[5] and a week later (September 11) Rayner wrote back to apologize, promising that future editions would credit Cohon for his work.

In urging Rayner to correct the record, Cohon's widow sheds further light on the controversy of 1945. "Because of Professor Cohon's characteristic anonymity in all his contributions to the work of the CCAR," she explains, "his name is not recorded as author, and his long struggle with prayerbook revision committees for a meaningful text for the great melody is now forgotten. When the English translation of the lines was accepted, the ritual committee had not the courage to substitute his Hebrew verses for the traditional text." She was right. The committee had accepted his English prayer as a fill-in for the troublesome translation of *Kol Nidre*, but as we saw, the actual *Kol Nidre* had been included as well, and even though objection was raised after the fact about the original's inclusion, no one seems to have argued for Cohon's Hebrew substitute other than Cohon himself. On April 10, Freehof wrote to Cohon telling him so. He agreed to put the matter to the committee a second time, but apparently the vote against Cohon's Hebrew prayer went unchallenged.

Freehof, meanwhile, was having second thoughts about his decision to hold up publication and then patch up the manuscript with some last-minute emendations. The changes Cohon had advocated were becoming too many and too complex for that. In his letter of April 10, therefore, he reviewed the finances, emphasized the money that would be lost if the CCAR were to sacrifice the first printing, and cited Rabbi Felix Levy (1884–1963) of Temple Emmanuel in Chicago, who had seen the book and considered it "a magnificent job," in order to argue that the book was good enough to go forward with, mistakes and all.

> The 30,000 copies of Volume II have been printed and half of them are bound. This cost the Conference somewhat more than $10,000.00. I doubt that we want to throw this money away. In the second printing, which will soon follow, we will make all the changes that we agree upon. Had we not yet printed the edition and the loss would have amounted to two or three thousand dollars, I would have tried to stop it in time. While a number of the changes which you suggest are undoubtedly justified, I assure you that the book is not that bad as to warrant this terrific expense.

Freehof did not even want to yank *Kol Nidre*. After all, he argued, "The *Kol Nidre* in Aramaic or in Hebrew is never recited anyhow, it is sung by the choir. Hence, if we decide to change it [in the second edition], no one will know the difference after a year or so when the first printing gradually is swamped by later printings."

And that is how things remained. On February 7, 1946, Freehof wrote to Rabbi Robert Gordis, president of the Conservative Movement's Rabbinical Assembly of America, and editor of the new Conservative liturgy, which was about to make its appearance. Gordis had sent him an advance copy of a paper that he had written describing his new liturgy and attacking Reform liturgy for, among other things, being driven by political motives rather than ideological purity and for "soft-pedal[ing] the existence of evil and of sin." In his response, Freehof referred also to *Kol Nidre*. "It was inserted," he said, "by a member of the Committee without the knowledge of the rest and was immediately disowned by the other members. While it was too late to withdraw the first printing from circulation, the next printing which appeared only a few weeks later omits this text."

What exactly happened with the second edition?

The *Kol Nidre* ritual there was radically revised from what it had been in 1894 and 1924. Instead of the lengthy two-page meditation (which people probably did not read anyway), "Day of God" was prefaced by a Rabbi's Prayer, in which the rabbi confessed his sinfulness and unworthiness, "to the great task to which I have dedicated my life.... May my people not be put to shame because of me," he prayed, "nor I because of them." The conceptual background for this innovation was a seventeenth-century prayer called *Hin'ni* ("Here am I [poor in deeds]") that began the *Musaf* service and had become a cantorial favorite. For a variety of reasons, Reform Jews had long omitted *Musaf*: it was redundant; it made the service long; and it was focused on the sacrificial cult, even calling for its restoration, a theological principle Reform Jews opposed vigorously. Also, Reform Judaism of the time had exalted the role of the rabbi at the expense of the traditional cantor. So *Hin'ni* was gone. But rabbis loved its message: the spiritual poverty of the prayer leader who dares, nonetheless, to speak to God on behalf of the congregation. The Rabbi's Prayer was a modified version of *Hin'ni*, designed for rabbis to read before a standing congregation as Yom Kippur began.

Then came "Day of God" and Cohon's new prayer in English, based on *Kol Nidre* but an inversion of it: rather than ask that unhonored vows and oaths be annulled, it asked that "all the resolutions we make from this Day of Atonement to the coming Day of Atonement—may they be acceptable before Thee, and may we be given strength to fulfill them." In the first edition, *Kol Nidre* had appeared on the same page. It is missing from the second edition, and in order to avoid repaginating everything, the English prayer is double-spaced so as to fill most of the empty space where *Kol Nidre* had once been. But although absent from the prayer book, *Kol Nidre* is not altogether mssing from the service. Below the double-spaced prayer is the notation in Hebrew, "*Kol Nidre,*" and then, in English, "The Kol Nidre Chant."

Reform Jews growing up with the newly revised version of the *Union Prayer Book* may have concluded that the English version of *Kol Nidre* was deemed so important that it was given an entire page and double-spaced to boot, when, in fact, it was spread out just to take up the space vacated by the missing *Kol Nidre*. *Kol Nidre* was gone, but the chant remained.

Some congregations went farther, however. They bought and used the newly revised edition of the *UPB* but then pasted in a version of *Kol Nidre*, with their own free translation of the words. One such version reads:

> May all the vows and promises before God, which we have left unfulfilled; may all the moral pledges, penalties and other self-imposed obligations we have left undischarged, from last Atonement Day until this Atonement Day now come to us in peace; may they all be forgiven by the Almighty, and be accounted by Him of no moment. We regret having made them, still more we regret having neglected them; may the Almighty Grace strengthen us in the future to keep us from the rash vow, the hastily-imposed self-discipline; and teach us to bear the sufferings of life as they come with patience, and with resignation. Amen.[6]

It was not until the *Union Prayer Book* was retired altogether that *Kol Nidre* returned to the pages of North American Reform Jews, and that was only in *Gates of Repentance*, the 1978 volume that was part of larger liturgical overhaul responding, among other things, to the accent on Jewish particularism and traditionalism that followed the Six-Day War of 1968.

Gates of Repentance was almost entirely the work of Rabbi Chaim Stern (1930–2001), the general editor of the earlier *Gates of Prayer* (1975). Stern was a rabbi in Chappaqua, New York, but had spent a sabbatical in England collaborating with Rabbi John Rayner on producing the liturgy for the Liberal Movement there. Their High Holy Day prayer book, *Gate* [singular] *of Repentance* (1973), served as prototype for the American *Gates* [plural] *of Repentance* five years later. But the British volume did not include the traditional *Kol Nidre*, while the American one did. Stern introduced it from the very beginning, and it passed through the committee with little or no debate. It even included the thirteenth-century Hebrew introduction by Meir of Rothenberg, "By the authority of the heavenly court and of the earthly court ... we give permission to pray with habitual sinners." But it paraphrases these Hebrew words, which are unlikely to resonate with modern worshipers. The proposed English came out very differently! "Kol Nidre: a whisper of wings; heaven and earth embrace; promises are remembered. Saint and sinner alike commune with the Most High. We are at one." The printed version omitted the phrase "heaven and earth embrace."

It was felt, however, that *Kol Nidre* could not simply be restored without some historical explanation that gave it moral credence, at least in its original context. So discussion was held about the purported connection between *Kol Nidre* and the conversos of Spain or other Jews forced to convert to Catholicism in the Middle Ages. As Marc Saperstein reveals (see pp. 31–38), the idea that *Kol Nidre* referred obliquely to Jews whose vows to apostasize had been forced from them goes back only to 1917. The committee discussing *Gates of Repentance* knew better than to believe there was any credence to the claim. But nonetheless, it chose to add a further introduction to *Kol Nidre:*

> Kol Nidre is the prayer of a people not free to make their own decisions, people forced to say what they do not mean. In repeating this prayer, we identify with the agony of our forebears who had to say "yes" when they meant "no."

For good measure, however, it then added a second rationale:

> Kol Nidre is also a confession: we are all transgressors, all exiled from the Highest we know, all in need of the healing of forgiveness and reconciliation. For what we have done, for what we may yet do, we ask pardon; for rash words, broken pledges, insincere assurances, and foolish promises, may we find forgiveness.

Kol Nidre was finally restored to the Reform liturgy of North American Jews, partially as a romanticized identification with Jewish suffering in the past, partially because it is a confession of "rash words, broken pledges, insincere assurances, and foolish promises"; but mostly because Jews have always loved *Kol Nidre* and were saying it anyway. Much of our liturgy fails the test of literalism. *Kol Nidre* is no exception.

⌒〰〰◯

Memories of the Past, Guidelines for the Future

Rabbi Andrew Goldstein, PhD

My first memory of hearing *Kol Nidre* sung was on a record my mother had of Johnny Mathis singing "Jewish songs." Seeing his face on the cover, I wondered if he, like Sammy Davis Jr., was Jewish. Surely he must be if he chose to record this most Jewish of songs, a melody that was used as background music to any documentary on a Jewish theme, even if it was totally inappropriate to the subject of the documentary in question. I still have the record. I cannot listen to it any more, as I don't have an old-fashioned 45-rpm deck, but the cover reminds me of my mother; memory and nostalgia are part of the magic of *Kol Nidre*.

The reason that I have no early recollection of *Kol Nidre* sung in synagogue was that in the days of my childhood it was not sung in most British Liberal synagogues. The "Service for the Evening of the Day of Atonement" in the *Liberal Jewish Prayer Book Volume II*,[1] opened with the instruction "The Ark might be opened for the Silent Prayer," followed by "During the Silent Prayer the *Kol Nidre* music might be played." All very tentative, with no great enthusiasm for the piece that formed the dramatic opening of the service in most other synagogues on that night.

Rabbi Andrew Goldstein, PhD, is chairman of the European Region of the World Union for Progressive Judaism and coeditor of *Machzor Ruach Chadashah*. He contributed to *Who by Fire, Who by Water—Un'taneh Tokef* (Jewish Lights).

The first edition of 1923 choreographed the opening even more tentatively, because it called for the ark to remain shut. After the Silent Prayer, the "Reader" recited a didactic passage by the prayer book's editor, Rabbi Dr. Israel Mattuck, on the theme of the day. The congregation then sat down and only then did the choir sing an English version of Rabbi Leopold Stein's *O Tag des Herrn* (with the rubric "To the music of *Kol Nidre*"):

> Day of God,
> O, come!
> Fill our hearts with peace and gladness.
> Lift the voice of prayer and song,
> Heavenward borne on the current strong,
> Upward all aspire!
> In the angel choir
> Blend our prayer and praises.

The opening sequence of the service was taken from the original *Union Prayer Book,* on which Rabbi Mattuck based (sometimes rather loosely) his British prayer books. Mattuck borrowed from the *Union Prayer Book* the creative idea of following the English hymn with the appropriate Psalm 130, "Out of the depths I have cried unto thee, O Lord. Lord hear my voice...."[2]

As time went on, it must have occurred to many that that there was little reason to downplay *Kol Nidre* when within the popular culture all around us prominent singers like Johnny Mathis (and Perry Como too) were so movingly singing it. Besides, liturgical sensitivity was changing to admit the emotional alongside the rational as perfectly appropriate for communal prayer. As I grew older, therefore, I witnessed the piece gradually reappear in Liberal synagogues. At my first student rabbi assignment in 1965, it was played on a reel-to-reel tape recorder: the ark solemnly opened as the play button was depressed with equal solemnity. I can't recall who the singer was, but it all seemed a little theatrical. As time went by *Kol Nidre* was performed by a solo singer—long before its formal appearance in our 1973 prayer book *Gate of Repentance* (edited by Rabbis John Rayner and Chaim Stern, both of blessed memory). Here it was a Hebrew version, but in the preceding years I recall us singing, though not from our prayer books, the Aramaic original. Elsewhere in this volume,

Dr. Annette M. Boeckler has thoroughly described the various attempts to rewrite the "prayer," often ascribed as the holiest of Jewish prayers, though it is not a prayer at all.[3] I will focus instead on possible reasons why Dr. Mattuck (no doubt influenced by his American upbringing) had such a problem including it and how modern liberal liturgists might deal with it.

Guidelines for the Future

A number of objections have been raised concerning *Kol Nidre*. The first is highlighted by the history of Jewish-Christian relationships.

At the annual conference of the International Council of Christians and Jews held in Berlin in June 2009, a new and significant document was launched: *A Time for Recommitment: Jewish Christian Dialogue 70 Years after War and Shoah*, soon to become known as the "Twelve Points of Berlin."[4] The occasion was introduced by Angela Merkel, the chancellor of the German Federal Republic, who movingly remarked how historic and fitting it was that Jews were back in Berlin regenerating the city that had only seventy years previously been the headquarters of those trying to annihilate them.

In 1947 a much smaller gathering of Christians and Jews meeting in another German town, Seeligsberg, had issued their "Ten Points of Seeligsberg."[5] In the immediate aftermath of the Shoah, it had challenged Christians to remove from their teaching, preaching, and liturgy those anti-Jewish elements that had helped the Nazi ideology cause such devastation.[6] But whereas the Ten Points of Seeligsberg was addressed to Christians, the Twelve Points of Berlin makes demands of the Jews also. One of the four points addressed to Jews is headed "To re-examine Jewish texts and liturgy in the light of Christian reforms ... By addressing the possible re-interpretation, change or omission of parts of Jewish liturgy that treat others in problematic ways."

As an editor of modern Liberal Jewish liturgy myself, I can attest to the discussions held over the need to change the opening paragraph of the *Alenu*, or the place of the *Sh'fokh chamotkha* ("Pour out Your wrath of the nations who knew You not ...") in the Passover Haggadah, or the particularism in a number of prayers in the regular liturgy that pray for the redemption of the Jews, ignoring the plight of the rest of humanity. *Kol Nidre* presents a kindred, albeit different, challenge.

On many an occasion Christian anti-Semites have quoted the *Kol Nidre* as proof that you can't trust a Jew, because every year the Jew recites a formula that cancels out any oaths or agreements made.[7] In the Middle Ages, Jews appearing in court had to take a special oath (the *more judaico*) to declare that any oaths they made there would not be annulled by the recitation of *Kol Nidre*.[8] No wonder Reform Jews attempting early on to be integrated into German society found *Kol Nidre* embarrassing. As Israel Jacobson said at the dedication of the first Reform Temple in Seesen in 1810, "Our ritual is still weighted down with religious customs which must be rightfully offensive to reason as well as to our Christian friends."[9]

Jacobson's second point (prayers offensive to "our Christian friends") is surely unacceptable regarding *Kol Nidre*. We need not bow to the misguided claims of anti-Semites when no anti-gentile sense was ever intended in the prayer nor can it sensibly be construed as such.

But his first objection (prayers "rightfully offensive to reason") is applicable. Going back to the *gaon* Natronai bar Hillel (of Sura, 853–858), many rabbis have objected to the *Kol Nidre* formula. They have declared it contrary to biblical instruction or halakhah but insisted also, at times, that as Natronai's successor Amram (858–871) put it, "The holy academy sent word that this is a foolish custom and it is forbidden to practice it."[10] By "foolish," we may assume that Amram meant "offensive to reason" and, we now know, even rooted in superstition. Indeed, as Rabbi Dalia Marx explains in her essay (see pp. 26–30), parallels to *Kol Nidre* occur in incantation texts on magic bowl inscriptions from ancient Babylon.[11]

But as we have seen, "reason" alone should not define what is acceptable in modern progressive Jewish liturgy. Most of our rituals are based on ancient folk customs and beliefs, and in any event, the fact that some worshipers misunderstand a prayer should not mean its banishment for the majority who are not so misguided.

The *Kol Nidre* found its way back into "official" British Liberal liturgy in 1973 when Rabbis John Rayner and Chaim Stern reinstated it in their *Gate of Repentance*,[12] although they replaced the traditional Aramaic with a Hebrew version based on a Hanover text of 1870. In his American version of this *machzor* five years later, Chaim Stern reverted to the original Aramaic, but with an English paraphrase that sought to overcome the objection against requesting forgiveness in advance for promises we will break in the coming year.[13]

What text then should a modern and honest Liberal or Reform *machzor* use: Aramaic original or Hebrew paraphrase? You could argue that since few really understand the Aramaic words anyway, and since those words do have an incomprehensible, yet mysterious rhythm, they add to the magic of the opening of the Day of Atonement. In *Machzor Ruach Chadashah*,[14] we sat on the liturgical fence with the Hebrew in the text but with a reference to the Aramaic version printed in the appendix.

Anyway, the real power of the *Kol Nidre* belongs not to the words, but to the music. It seems to invoke the past, present, and future of our people and of our own personal lives. John Rayner said of the popularity of the melody that it had three elements: "It has a *plaintive* element which evokes the suffering of our people in ages past.... It has a *penitential* element which expresses our deepest yearnings to be released from the burden of past failures.... Finally, it has a jubilant, *triumphant* element which comes out in its finale. It expresses our highest hopes."[15]

To these three I would add a forth element: *nostalgia*—for all the memories of past Yom Kippur Eves and for those with whom we spend them.

⌒🙰🙰🙰⌒

What If Cleverness Is Foolishness and Righteousness an Illusion?

Rabbi Jonathan Magonet, PhD

My first thoughts on *Kol Nidre*, alas, are somewhat frivolous. I grew up in the British United Synagogue (Orthodox) in the immediate postwar period. The *cheder* teaching was well-intentioned but primitive. Our Jewish learning was limited to bar mitzvah drills, and our experience of synagogue reduced to mind-numbing boredom. If I recall *Kol Nidre* at all, it is mostly of a crowded shul, decorated in white, and some elderly gentlemen standing on the bimah. Sadly, even that may be an invented memory from a time when such events simply did not register.

Kol Nidre only became a reality in my early years as a rabbinic student at Leo Baeck College, conducting services in small, newly created suburban synagogues in London, themselves struggling to find their own *minhag*. Members from similar Orthodox backgrounds seeking a version of their own remembered childhood services mixed uneasily with "classi-

Rabbi Jonathan Magonet, PhD, is emeritus professor of Bible at Leo Baeck College in London, where he was principal (president) from 1985 to 2005. He is coeditor of three volumes of *Forms of Prayer* (the prayer books of the British Movement for Reform Judaism) and editor of the recent eighth edition of the *Daily, Sabbath and Occasional Prayers* volume. He contributed to *Who by Fire, Who by Water—Un'taneh Tokef* (Jewish Lights).

cal" Liberals, former members of the founding synagogue of the movement in St. John's Wood, London. One musical combination put together a *heimische* East End Yiddish-speaking working-class Jew as a part-time hazzan with a retired soprano chorister and organist, trained in the semiclassical musical tradition of anglicized Judaism. Occasionally their styles even met in a musical middle ground.

Some congregations had to contend with the absence of anyone at all who was qualified to lead the singing. In one, we settled for a cellist playing the Bruch *Kol Nidre*—an exquisite opening that completely overshadowed the service that followed. Even more memorable was the congregation that had discovered an old 78-rpm recording of Al Jolson singing *Kol Nidre* in *The Jazz Singer* and asked if it was all right to play it instead. I was in no position to say no and, anyway, was curious to hear it. Jolson sang with charm and a lot of Hollywood emotion, real or manufactured, but only the first sentence, and that repeatedly, while a heavenly choir filled in some of the rest of the opening melody. This also overshadowed the service that followed, though on a different emotional pitch than the Bruch. However, it gave me a lifelong fondness for Jolson.

Frivolity aside, *Kol Nidre* is another of those Jewish prayers of puzzling origin, controversial content (not just for Jews), and tremendous mystique—why else choose that, of all things, for Jolson to sing in the movie!

Part of our problem with the text is simply that the vows it refers to are no longer part of our religious life as once they were in the biblical and Rabbinic periods. In the Bible, they were prominent enough to demand laws to legislate the phenomenon. The danger inherent in vows found its way into biblical narratives—most obviously, Jephthah's vow to sacrifice the first thing to emerge from his house if he returned victorious from battle. In the event, it turned out to be his daughter. Whether she was actually killed is not explicitly stated, and given the overall tenor of the story in Judges 11, it may be that instead she abstained from marriage and having children, which, in that world, amounted to a living death and would have effectively sacrificed Jephthah's dynastic hopes. Whatever the case, the Rabbis were impatient with Jephthah's vow: What if a dog or other animal unfit for sacrifice had emerged to greet him? Worse still, why had he not simply had it annulled by the high priest? Their answer: Jephthah the victorious military leader expected the high priest to come to him, and the high priest expected Jephthah to make the journey. While they preened and defended their honor, a young woman was sacrificed.

Even King David was criticized for an overenthusiastic vow when he told Nathan the prophet of his wish to build a house for God. Nathan, rarely a "yes-man," nevertheless acquiesced until awakened in the middle of the night by God with a contrary message. A physical gap in mid-sentence of the text of 2 Samuel 7:4 allowed the Rabbis to fill in the background. "You know that David is a habitual vower [a *nadran*]," God says, quoting David's oath in Psalm 132:3–4, "I shall not enter the tent of my household, nor go up to my bed, nor give sleep to my eyes, nor slumber to my eyelids, till I have found a place for Adonai." Stop him, says God, before he vows not to eat till he builds it!

Perhaps the last word on biblical vows belongs to Kohelet. He is very circumspect about how to behave with God. So he takes the warning in Deuteronomy 23:22, "When you make a vow to Adonai, do not delay to fulfill it," and adds a rider in his own ironic style: "because He has no desire for fools!" (Ecclesiastes 5:3).

So if vows are no longer a regular part of our spiritual life, and legal contracts are excluded from *Kol Nidre*, we are left with pure metaphor, acted out with all the solemnity and conviction that we can muster. This raises difficult questions about what *Kol Nidre* seeks to achieve and how effective it is.

The early reformers either omitted it or substituted alternative psalm passages or new compositions. I encountered one of these alternative versions, designed to fit the melody, when working on the High Holy Day *machzor* for the British Reform Movement, the first revision in almost a century. One Hebrew "version" was regularly pasted into the reprints of the existing Victorian edition. In an early draft of our new *machzor*, we printed it as the first option and beneath it, as a possible alternative, the traditional Aramaic *Kol Nidre*. Feedback from the congregations indicated a readiness to accept the traditional version, so in the final edition, tradition is given the priority position, with the Hebrew alternative below it, which translates as:

> May all the promises which the children of Israel swear to You, our father, to return to You with all their heart, and walk again in the ways of Your Torah and the path of good deeds and honesty, from this Yom Kippur to the next— may it come to us for good—let these promises ascend and come, be near and seen, be heard and accepted in Your

presence with love. Transform their desires, and in their hearts put the love and fear of Your great and awesome name.[1]

Clearly the intention of our substitute (like the ones that preceded it) was deeply sincere. But it effectively subverts a valuable idea inherent in the original. For beneath the technical legal language about the annulment of vows lies a disturbing truth: that even with the best will in the world, we do not keep our promises, whether to God, to ourselves, or to others. This may not be a matter of bad faith or deliberate deception, but simply evidence of human weakness, witness to a generosity of spirit in all of us that runs up against practical realities, laziness, or simply the changing priorities of a complex and busy life. To acknowledge this truth is to affirm our humanity, to recognize, however briefly, the ways in which we may have let ourselves and others down, and perhaps to encourage us to be a little more responsible with our words in the future. This Reform version, it seems to me in retrospect, comes across rather like a childish promise to do better next time, but with the additional chutzpah of expecting God to let us off the hook whatever we do.

The translation we included was the work of Lionel Blue, flexible enough in the English to speak to today, yet true enough, at least to the intent, of the original.

> May we be absolved from all the vows and obligations we make to God in vain, from this Yom Kippur to the next— may it come to us for good; the duties and the promises we cannot keep, the commitments and undertakings which should never have been made.
>
> We ask to be forgiven and released from our own failings. Though all the promises to our fellowmen stand, may God annul the empty promises we made in our foolishness to Him alone, and shield us from their consequences.
>
> Do not hold us to vows like these!
> Do not hold us to obligations like these!
> Do not hold us to such empty oaths![2]

Like so much of the classical liturgy, this piece too requires a two-way bridge to connect us, on the one hand, with its historical meaning, and on the other, with our contemporary needs that it ought to address. For

me, Ignaz Maybaum, our theology teacher at Leo Baeck College, provided one such bridge, which we included in the meditations before the
service:

> The renouncement of the *Kol Nidre* is an appeal to
> renounce your own point of view. Your wisdom may be
> true wisdom, but in this hour you are asked to abandon it.
> Trust in the wisdom of God alone! Your principles may be
> sound and well-founded, but in this hour you are asked to
> doubt whether they are sound and well-founded. This
> doubt is not one of scepticism but of humility and will
> open your heart to what alone is true and eternal. In this
> hour the *Kol Nidre* asks you to say: I am wrong and God is
> right; my cleverness is foolishness, my righteousness is an
> illusion, my view of the world is false.[3]

❦

Words of Wisdom or Legalese?

Rabbi Charles H. Middleburgh, PhD

As the child of a Liberal Synagogue, born and bred on the south coast of England, I grew up with the words of *Kol Nidre* not even being sung at all on the eve of the holiest day of the year! The scrolls were taken from the ark by three congregational *machers*, but all that happened was that an extract of Max Bruch's sonorous and moving *Kol Nidre* was played on the organ, and the scrolls were then returned to their place without explanation. This peculiar practice informed my synagogue experience until 1973, when the *Liberal Jewish Prayer Book* (*LJPB*) of Israel Mattuck (published in 1937) was replaced by *Gate of Repentance*, edited by the late John D. Rayner and Chaim Stern, *z"l*.

Mattuck's 1937 liturgy had commenced the *Kol Nidre* service with a brief prayer to be read silently, introduced by the suggestion "During the Silent Prayer, the *Kol Nidre* music might be played."[1] It was followed by an English version of the poem *O Tag des Herrn* ("O Day of the Lord"), adorned with the instruction "This Hymn is sung to the music of *Kol Nidre*." The 1973 *Gate of Repentance* substituted the word "may" for "might" and provided a new creative prayer, written by Rayner. Then came the only version of *Kol Nidre* that I knew until I was at university and started looking at Jewish liturgy in a more sustained and forensic manner.

Rabbi Charles H. Middleburgh, PhD, is rabbi to the Reform Jewish Celts of Ireland and Wales; honorary director of studies at Leo Baeck College in London, where he has taught since 1984; and coeditor with Rabbi Andrew Goldstein, PhD, of the Liberal Judaism *Machzor Ruach Chadashah*. He contributed to *Who by Fire, Who by Water—Un'taneh Tokef* (Jewish Lights).

The English translation of the Rayner prayer states:

> Accept, our Father, all the vows of the children of Israel that they will turn from sin and evil, and walk in the ways of Your Law of righteousness and justice, from this Day of Atonement until the next—may we reach it in peace. We come to seek Your pardon and forgiveness. Help us to return to You with a whole heart, and give us strength to overcome our faults, so that through us Your great and holy name may become sanctified.

In his endnotes, one of the crowning jewels of Rayner's legacy to us, Rayner explained the origin and purpose of *Kol Nidre* and then elucidated the origin of the version of the prayer provided in *Gate of Repentance*:

> In most Reform PBs [prayerbooks] it is replaced either by a poem in the vernacular (notably Rabbi Leopold Stein's *O Tag des Herrn*, written in 1840, English versions of which appear in UPB [*Union Prayer Book*], p. 127 and LJPB, p. 68) or by a new Hebrew text, beginning with the words *Kol Nidrey* but going on to ask for God's acceptance of the worshippers' vows of *repentance*.... Our version is similar to one introduced in Hanover in 1870.... It is, of course, intended to be sung to the traditional *Kol Nidrey* tune.[2]

The Hanover *Kol Nidre*, to which Rabbi Rayner, my beloved mentor and teacher, refers, is cited by the late and great liturgical scholar Jakob Petuchowski:[3] it appears in three different versions in the Hanover liturgy because in Hanover, the traditional custom of reciting *Kol Nidre* three times was followed—"with this additional innovation: that each repetition introduced a new element."[4]

As Rayner notes, the inspiration for the *Kol Nidre* that he put into *Gate of Repentance* is the 1870 Hanover version, but it is identical with none of the three that Petuchowski cites. The original *Kol Nidre* had been in Aramaic, of course, and both the Hanover and the Rayner prayers were in Hebrew. But the Rayner version is much more fluent, lyrical, and linguistically compact.

When Rabbi Dr. Andrew Goldstein and I came to coedit the successor to *Gate of Repentance*, *Machzor Ruach Chadashah* (Liberal Judaism,

2003), we debated at some length whether we should continue with the version of *Kol Nidre* familiar to Liberal congregations throughout the United Kingdom since 1973 or whether, following the CCAR's *Gates of Repentance* and the British Reform Movement's *Forms of Prayer*, we should substitute the traditional Aramaic.

Our compromise was to use both: first, the Hebrew with a slightly altered non-gender-specific English translation beginning, "Source of our being" (instead of Rayner's "our Father"); followed by a note saying, "The Aramaic version may be found on page 436." Placing the Aramaic version, with an abridged English translation, at the back of the *machzor* made it less likely that it would be used, but we felt that it was important to give worshipers at least the option of using it—a choice denied previously in the liturgical history of Liberal Judaism.

I am unaware of the number of Liberal synagogues in Britain that use the Aramaic *Kol Nidre*, though I suspect it is very small, and if given the choice, I myself would prefer the Hebrew version with which I have been familiar for most of my adult life. I can enjoy the Aramaic as a piece of text but not as a piece of liturgy: the legalese, the unfamiliar endings of some of the words (which make it a challenge even to read accurately), and the repetitiveness of style conspire against its effectiveness. By contrast, the Hebrew version is expressive and powerful, and its language is wholly consonant with the rest of the service, as well as its principal theme.

And yet, I do have a tiny proviso: the one saving grace of the Aramaic version—a singularly key detail that the Hebrew lacks—relates to the nature of the vows themselves. In the Hebrew version, we ask God to *accept* a particular brand of *well-intentioned* vows we make in the year to come, generally pietistic vows, that is, to turn from sin and evil and walk in the way of God's law of righteousness and justice; by contrast, the Aramaic version asks God to *absolve* us from any and all such vows we may make that turn out to be *problematic* because we failed to keep them. The Hebrew version is a perfectly worthy request, but it seems rather weak to me because God is asked simply to smile upon our righteous intent. The Aramaic parallel has a much more powerful and pertinent resonance, in that it admits human error and asks God to pardon us for our failures.

The Hebrew version is hard to disagree with, but it takes no cognizance of the reality of human life, when the norm for most of us is to start committing sins immediately upon the end of the *N'ilah* service. Even before the last echo of the final *t'ki'ah g'dolah* has died away, we kibbitz about our empty stomachs, critique the clothes worn by our neighbors, judge the rabbi's sermon, and weigh the quality of the singing; but the Aramaic version acknowledges straight away that, human frailty being what it is, no matter what we promise God and ourselves on Yom Kippur we will likely fall short—this is a tendency built into the very human condition, for which we pray that God will forgive us.

For me, the recognition of that condition is crucial, because it allows me to make realistic commitments about the year ahead. I might indeed fail at them, but I might equally succeed, and at least I should try. This is a far cry better than promising the earth on a wave of pious emotion without regard for the human limitations that may trip me up at the very first hurdle.

Perhaps the time has come to re-adapt *Kol Nidre* in a Hebrew form that combines the best of both versions, but in the meantime I shall stick with the existing Hebrew, mindful that it, like most human promises, doesn't quite deliver everything I need.

Two Torah Scrolls and *Kol Nidre*

THE EARTHLY COURT BELOW

Rabbi David A. Teutsch, PhD

For no other service of the year do the members of my *minyan* make such an effort to be on time. *Kol Nidre* is not to be missed. The late afternoon meal before the fast and the rush to arrive in shul on time usually bring me into my seat in the congregation feeling a bit out of focus. But when we all rise and the Torah scrolls come out of the ark, the hush that fills the room reaches in and brings me to stilled attention. Then the haunting music draws me in.

By tradition, the recitation of *Kol Nidre* begins before sunset, because its literary structure mimics a legal release from vows. Such a legal function is barred on a major holy day, so the metaphor results in *Kol Nidre*'s early start. Those honored with the role of holding Torah scrolls (at least two; some congregations bring out all their scrolls) plus the person chanting *Kol Nidre* can be understood as representing the three judges of a *bet din* (Jewish court of law), but I have come to believe that

Rabbi David A. Teutsch, PhD, is the Wiener Professor of Contemporary Jewish Civilization and director of the Center for Jewish Ethics at the Reconstructionist Rabbinical College, where he served as president for nearly a decade. He was editor-in-chief of the seven-volume *Kol Haneshamah* prayer book series. He is the author of *Spiritual Community: The Power to Restore Hope, Commitment and Joy* (Jewish Lights). He contributed to *Who by Fire, Who by Water—Un'taneh Tokef* (Jewish Lights).

the court is actually composed of the two Torahs and of *Kol Nidre* itself. Human judges cannot pronounce God's will in regard to offenses between people and God (*bein adam lamakom*). Indeed, according to tradition, God's judgment hangs in the balance until the end of Yom Kippur, when the judgment is sealed.

What kind of judgment can be pronounced by the words of Torah and *Kol Nidre*? Torah tells us that none of us is so righteous that we have not transgressed (*kol ha'am bishgagah*), and *Kol Nidre* announces early on that *anu matirin l'hitpalel im ha'avaryanim*, "We are permitted to pray with the sinners." But since none of us is wholly innocent, who is the "we," and who are the transgressors? Aren't we all both, at one and the same time? By our presence for *Kol Nidre* we grant each other permission to enter the community of prayer. More difficult is the recognition that I am part of the community gathered in prayer but also an individual isolated by the knowledge of my own personal failings and transgressions. I need to grant myself permission to enter community and to enter prayer; no one knows better than I what is holding me back.

Yom Kippur begins by formally witnessing our individual shortcomings and the potential renewal that can flow from a recommitment to Torah and a re-anchoring in sacred community. We stand together for *Kol Nidre*, affirming our intention to constitute a holy community; as this stirring prayer is chanted, our very presence testifies to our deep desire that Yom Kippur help us confront our flaws and move beyond them.

Striving to make that shift a reality, the Torah scrolls and *Kol Nidre* witness our return to membership in religious community. The scrolls serve as witnesses for the court on high (*yeshivah shel ma'alah*), while *Kol Nidre* uses a formula befitting an earthly court (*yeshivah shel matah*). The familiar music connects the members of the congregation to each other and to memories of earlier generations. I feel the power of the moment.

The release from vows is itself a matter of controversy. Most leading rabbis have consistently discouraged the making of vows altogether: we Jews accord considerable power to words! The Ashkenazi formula for *Kol Nidre* anticipates vows made in the coming year, thereby creating doubt about the reliability of Jewish promises. Perhaps, then, the release aims only at vows made under duress, such as under the Inquisition; or perhaps, the referent is vows that are unintentionally forgotten.

But the words of the release support neither of those explanations, and this failure to explain *Kol Nidre* away has resulted in the development of several *Kol Nidre* variants. Following precedents in Europe and early America, Rabbi Mordecai Kaplan tried to resolve the issue by asking the cantor to substitute the singing of Psalm 130 to the same melody. When his congregation rejected that arrangement, Kaplan moved to a version of the release that covered past vows rather than prospective ones—a return to the original intent, still in use in parts of the Jewish world. That version, still found in Reconstructionist prayer books, is aimed at vows made with good intentions that could not be fulfilled.

The Kaplanian release prepares the way for focusing on the main Yom Kippur theme—atoning for failings that occurred in the previous year. The quotation from Numbers (15:26) that immediately follows the release from vows declares that there will be atonement for all the community of Israel—and for others who are among them—for everyone has gone astray. Then come two verses (Numbers 14:19–20) that ask for God's forgiveness of our people, reminding God of the divine proclamation, *salachti kidvarekha,* "I have forgiven as you asked."

The context of these words in the Torah is the story of the spies' exploration of the Land of Israel. The twelve spies set out at Moses's request. When they return, they describe a rich agricultural land but moan that its occupants are unconquerable giants before whom the spies felt like grasshoppers. The people panic, displaying a lack of trust in God's plan and power, and God becomes very angry. Moses intervenes with God, seeking God's forgiveness, and according to the biblical text, it was only Moses's plea that brought God to say, "I have forgiven as you asked." In the setting of *Kol Nidre,* it is the *sh'liach tzibbur,* the prayer leader, and the congregation who stand in Moses's role and reenact the request that prompts the divine response of forgiveness.

Kol Nidre constitutes us as a holy community of flawed humans seeking to do *t'shuvah,* to navigate our way back onto a good path. It is with gratitude for the community and for the unfolding possibility of returning to wholeness that we conclude the *Kol Nidre* section with *Shehecheyanu,* the blessing that celebrates our reaching this sacred time.

꩜

PART V
Kol Nidre and Interpretations for Today

At Least Credit Me with Being Compassionate

Rabbi Tony Bayfield, CBE, DD

I have a deep sense of Yom Kippur as a day of judgment, as a foretaste of the judgment that will be made at my life's end and, though who can be sure, at history's end as well. I think that's why I respond so strongly to the drama that initiates Yom Kippur so well: three people—the reader with a scroll bearer on either side—representing three *dayanim*, members of a Jewish court, permitting us to pray with sinners.

The history or legend—it doesn't matter which—of medieval Spanish conversos, risking everything to rejoin their sisters and brothers on this most solemn of occasions is awe-some. I use that word despite its debased currency because of its original sense of inspiring reverential fear and wonder. I think of the conversos and know I'm a sinner with far less courage than they. Surely it's the community that is permitted to pray with me, more than me with the community.

Then comes the long stand, as the same difficult passage is repeated three times. I attend to the music, not the words, because even though I can manage the Aramaic, I really don't readily understand it. I was not enthusiastic about being asked to write about *Kol Nidre* altogether.

Rabbi Tony Bayfield, CBE, DD (Lambeth), is president of the Movement for Reform Judaism in the United Kingdom. He teaches personal theology at the Leo Baeck College in London. He contributed to *Who by Fire, Who by Water—Un'taneh Tokef* (Jewish Lights).

Reluctantly, I penciled today into my diary to do it. I had promised it, after all.

Yesterday, January 27, was Holocaust Remembrance Day. This year our central public ceremony was held at the ancient Guildhall in the City of London. I watched the huge screen, transfixed. The first face was that of my beloved friend and teacher Hugo Gryn, *z"l*, who spent the fifteenth year of his life in Auschwitz. The voices were those of his son and his grandson, reading Hugo's testimony.

Then came someone else I know, Holocaust survivor and cellist Anita Laska-Wallfisch. She spoke about the uniqueness of music and the power of the cello, the instrument of her son and grandson. Her son Raphael, one of the great cellists of his generation, began to play Bloch's "Prayer," *From Jewish Life*, no. 1. The atmosphere felt electric, and I was almost certain I was not projecting my own feelings. That great hall was filled with more than two hundred survivors, their families, leaders of the Jewish, Christian, and Muslim communities, and leaders of civic society. I don't know how many of them believe in God or find meaning in religious language—given the audience, altogether British, I suspect a minority, at best. But they—yes, I was sure it wasn't just me—responded to the music, and not just aesthetically. It conveyed the profundity of life that biology cannot wholly explain or define. Andre Schwarz-Bart tells the story of Ernie Levy, *The Last of the Just*, who is murdered in Auschwitz. I was reminded of the closing lines: "Yesterday, as I stood in the street trembling in despair, rooted to the spot, a drop of pity fell from above upon my face: but there was no breeze in the air, no cloud in the sky ... there was only a presence."[1] Another survivor, a real-life Ernie now grown old, spoke about rebuilding life.

Raphael Wallfisch returned, and played *Kol Nidre*—the version by the late nineteenth-century German composer, a Christian, Max Bruch (commissioned by the Jewish community of Liverpool, I believe). I engaged with the moment as I always do.

The origins of *Kol Nidre* are debated, but in concept, it goes back two thousand years to a ceremony of absolution from vows (*hatarat n'darim*) that was attached to Rosh Hashanah. The prayer itself is from the geonic period (circa ninth century). Some add "but from outside Babylon," because many distinguished scholars who accept that tradition as normative (Natronai Gaon, Hai Gaon, Alfasi, Maimonides, Isaac Perfet of Catalonia) objected to it. They despised the idea that Jews might absolve themselves from vows they had not kept or would not keep. History had somehow ignored the memorable Mishnaic warning that absolution applies only to promises made to God, not to fellow human beings.

Liturgist Ismar Elbogen, musicologist Abraham Zevi Idelsohn, and Nobel literary laureate Shmuel Yosef Agnon have all dealt memorably with the prayers of Yom Kippur; they share their discomfort with *Kol Nidre* and detail communities where *Kol Nidre* was banned. But it had gained popularity long before the birth of the melody and was always being reinstituted by popular demand, despite sustained rabbinic objection.

As a compromise, perhaps, Rabbenu Tam, Rashi's grandson, altered the tense of the prayer from past to future: it now requested absolution from vows made to God in the twelve months *after Kol Nidre* is recited. But Agnon, for one, thinks this relatively insignificant and clearly sides with those who blame the *amei ha'aretz*, the ignorant populace, for defying the great rabbinic teachers who would have banned it altogether.

Rabbi Adin Steinsaltz, that remarkable contemporary Israeli sage, still struggles:

> Most of the vows made by a person during the year have little to do with holiness and spiritual elevation; usually they are angry reactions, or attempt to provoke someone. Life is full of aggravated expressions such as "If you do not do this I shall never speak to you again!" or "I shall never set foot in this house again!" Often, such statements are halakhically binding vows. The absolution of vows, and the inner resolution to annul them forever, not only removes obstacles from interpersonal relations but also relieves the spirit of unnecessary burdens, which should be thrown aside, together with all other sins and transgressions.[2]

The late and great Rabbi Louis Jacobs too finds reason to retain *Kol Nidre*. He admits that "Jewish law does not know of the annulment of vows and promises made to others. The *Kol Nidre* has reference only to private vows, to promises affecting the self, e.g., a promise to abstain from food."[3] But, since *Kol Nidre* has been used by Jew haters down the centuries to illustrate the untrustworthiness of the Jew, Jacobs urges us not give *Kol Nidre* up lest it be thought we are tacitly agreeing with our detractors.

For once, I am convinced by neither Steinsaltz nor Jacobs. What is it that has not only sustained *Kol Nidre* for fifteen hundred years but placed it at such a dramatic moment on the most solemn day of the year? Can it really be just popular demand for a quick fix, retrospective or prospective absolution?

I don't know.

I can only ask myself what it means to seek absolution from the promises that I will make to God. For that is what I do as I look up at the reader and elders with their scrolls, permitting me to pray with sinners—and them to pray with me.

Which returns me to yesterday's synchronicity: sitting in the Guildhall listening to Bruch's *Kol Nidre*; being transported to "another place"; aware of a greater reality. But why can't I recapture the feeling? I can remember *that* I felt, but I can scarcely remember *what* I felt, let alone feel it again at will.

I say to myself that it was always that way. The notorious golden calf was made so soon after the revelation at Sinai. "Dear God, why do You make it so extraordinarily difficult, so impossibly difficult?"

"You know very well why. If you could name Me, own Me, capture Me, keep hold of Me and cry, 'Here is God,' I wouldn't be God, would I? Look how people act who think they do own Me, do know Me—for certain.

"I will hold you to every jot of every word of every promise that you make to your fellow human beings. But the next time you know—or think you know—something of Me and make promises to Me, it may well be that you will need to 'be absolved from all vows and obligations you make to God in vain, from this Yom Kippur to the next.' I may be very difficult indeed in your eyes but at least credit Me with being compassionate."

⌀ﾙﾙﾚ

Filling the Void

Dr. Erica Brown

It was late in the afternoon, close to the start of Yom Kippur. Congregants in white began to crowd around the entrance to the synagogue. "Rabbi, why are you standing in front of the doors? We can't get in." Everyone was anxious to find a seat and begin the service.

"I'm sorry. We're full," the rabbi responded. "There's no room for you in the sanctuary." There was a murmur in the group until finally one of the oldest synagogue members spoke up.

"Rabbi, that's not possible. We're all standing out here. I can see through the glass that not one person is in the building."

"Trust me. It's full," the rabbi retorted. "It's so full of promises and vows you made and never kept that there is no room for anything else, even for you."

It is hard to imagine this ever happening, but if we open the ancient pages of the book of Malachi 1:10, we find God uttering a similar complaint to the Israelites: "If only you would lock my doors and not kindle fire on my altar to no purpose! I take no pleasure in you—said Adonai of

---

Dr. Erica Brown is a writer and educator who works as the scholar-in-residence for the Jewish Federation of Greater Washington and consults for the Jewish Agency and other Jewish non-profits. She is an Avi Chai Fellow and the recipient of the Covenant Award. She is the author of *Inspired Jewish Leadership: Practical Approaches to Building Strong Communities*, a National Jewish Book Award finalist; *Spiritual Boredom: Rediscovering the Wonder of Judaism*; *Confronting Scandal: How Jews Can Respond When Jews Do Bad Things* (all Jewish Lights); and *In the Narrow Places*; and coauthor of *The Case for Jewish Peoplehood: Can We Be One?* (Jewish Lights). She contributed to *Who by Fire, Who by Water—Un'taneh Tokef* (Jewish Lights). Her articles have appeared on the *Newsweek/Washington Post* website "On Faith."

hosts—and I will accept no offering from you." By locking the doors to the Temple, God sent the worshipers a message about sincerity: empty words can be tolerated for only so long.

But empty words are sometimes all we have. A year ago, we made promises, we aspired to something, we expected that by this year, things would be different. But here we are again, promises unkept, aspirations unfulfilled, remembering the words we said last year. We will have the chance to utter the same prayerful words all over again this year, this time with new hopes and aspirations, but what about last year's version of those words, the empty version, the words of promise that never came to anything because the promise went unfulfilled? Yom Kippur begins, therefore, with *Kol Nidre*, which opens wide the sanctuary doors for us to leave behind the words of last year before we embark on this year's version. Yom Kippur begins by inviting all of our unsatisfied longings of the past year to stand with us for a few last minutes before we push them into the past and begin to imagine life renewed all over again.

The words of Yom Kippur do not change from year to year—but their context does. We will pour into them all the newfound hopes that another year of life has brought. Before we do, we have the chance to offer up the empty words left over from the year passed, recognizing that we are about to say the same words that we did the year before, albeit attaching to them the new context of another year gone by. *Kol Nidre*, like the other prayers we recite on the day, is an emotional anchor, a centerpiece of prayer for an entire day given over to considering the instability of change: what we actually accomplished, but what might easily disappear; and what we wish we had accomplished, but failed at, in the year gone by.

Despite this opportunity for a clean verbal slate, I have always found *Kol Nidre* the most challenging of services. It is easy to be swept up by the severity and the silence of the moment or the awe created by the Torah scrolls in their white coverings that stand witness against us. The haunting melody of the *Kol Nidre* chant travels through the pews, and you can hear its familiar hum blanketing the congregation. But neither the mood nor the tune can mask *Kol Nidre*'s troublesome language. I am always tripped up by the words. Instead of a meditation on evil or misdirected intentions, *Kol Nidre* is a repetitive Aramaic dirge, an opaque Rabbinic classification of biblical and Talmudic oaths, resembling the most technical of legal contracts in its precision. I can't imagine singing a document that has to be notarized, especially not on the holiest of days.

It is here that translation can obscure meaning rather than enhance it. Better they shouldn't know, I say to myself, what it really means. Those who do not read Aramaic may let the mood and melody suffice. May it carry us all away to a transcendent place.

Just don't leave me behind! I, unfortunately, know the meaning of the words and the Talmudic casuistry behind them. And repeating the declaration three times does little to improve the situation. "Once more with feeling!" just doesn't work for me.

So I concentrate on two expressions in the *Kol Nidre* liturgy that move me: the permission to pray with sinners, and the regret for having made these oaths in the first place. The fact that we are supposed to pray with sinners is derived from the Temple incense offering, which contains many ingredients, including the malodorous spice galbanum. Rabbi Simon Chasida focused on the aggregate nature of the offering, holding that a sacrifice is more compelling because of the diversity of its ingredients. So too with a community. "A public fast where Jewish sinners do not participate is not a fast" (Talmud, Keritot 6b). No convocation of repentance can have meaning without the presence of our human galbanum, our sinners.

"In the presence of sinners"—who are the sinners? It is tempting to read this phrase while throwing sidelong glances at a neighbor or two who *really* should be pounding the chest on this day of forgiveness. These are the people in our communities who have sinned "loudly." Others know. We know. But this permission to pray with sinners is no mere license for *us* to pray with *them*. *I* am the one who is the sinner. *You* are permitted to pray next to *me*. *Please* pray next to me. If you can stand by me when I should have known better but wronged others anyway—perhaps including you—I may just possibly hope to be able to do what is right and good. With you and the others next to me, I may be humbled into appropriate vulnerability. I need you. Even though I have hurt you, you have come. My community gathered around me becomes an insurance policy for the goodness that I cannot accomplish alone.

Kol Nidre is also a time when we battle with regret. It's not only that we have another year behind us. It's that last year too we began with the same optimistic commitment to improve our ways, only to see it all swallowed by realities that got in the way. Our families, friends, and colleagues can either help or hinder us as we seek to achieve our best. We get in our own way all too often. It is a natural thing to regret making the promises that we never fulfilled.

Why then should we promise all over again? If we want to be better parents, children, students, supervisors, and friends this year, must we promise that to anyone to make it so? If we want to lose weight or to refrain from gossip, must we swear that we will? What do words of commitment (that we will probably regret next year) actually do?

I am reminded of Jephthah from the book of Judges. His famous oath to sacrifice the first thing that came through the door if promised victory by God in battle ended with a brutal reality. His virginal daughter came through the door to sing her father's military praises, not realizing that her verbal offering would end up making her a physical offering. Whether the sacrifice ever actually took place is a valid scholarly debate, but irrelevant to the real question of why Jephthah needed an oath at all, and the reminder of at least the unintended consequences that sometimes do occur when we make oaths about the future.

The positive thing about an oath is that it provides an extra kick, or push, to do something that we might otherwise ignore, forget, or avoid. Words have meaning; they construct a verbal reality that establishes expectations upon us. Yet in its multiple tractates that discuss the matter, the Talmud suggests that we refrain from making oaths in the first place. We will inevitably construct these intangible realities with words, because the words have substance only as long as we live up to them. After that, they are nothing but words.

In the ancient world, oaths were taken in God's name. Failure to honor an oath diminished God by taking God's name in vain. Today, few people feel that degree of religious sensitivity. If God's name is invoked at all, it is purely formulaic, not a sign of our commitment to keep true to what we say. But what if it inspired us to live up at least to the divine potential within us? Perhaps the oath's significance lies in the fact that it calls on God to partner with us in helping us live up to our best selves. When we fail to do so, we take God down with us in some small measure.

As *Kol Nidre*'s language of broken vows begins, those of us who struggle with the technical words try to reach beyond them to the language of brokenness, a language of universal pain that even the legal redundancies of the text cannot obscure. At least this one day, we will petition God to help us make words into realities. Aware how we have hurt others, we begin by asking them and God to forgive us for what we could not live up to. We pray they will allow us to try again.

Words Mean Everything, Words Mean Nothing— Both Are True

Rabbi Ruth Durchslag, PsyD

I n my life as a psychologist I rely on words to heal.
In my work as a rabbi I rely on words to inspire.
When I write, I rely on words to communicate.
As a meditator, I have learned that words mean nothing at all.

So what does *Kol Nidre* have to say about words? Its content is troubling and confusing. On this holiest of days we declare that all the vows and promises we make in the coming year will be null and void. Our promises, like soiled tissues, can be discarded at will. No consequences, no costs. How can we make sense of a prayer that trashes the power of words, especially from within a tradition that otherwise extols verbal sanctity?

One way is to look at its origins. It has been suggested that *Kol Nidre* was meant to keep evil demons from twisting our vows and promises and

---

After twelve years as a successful clinical psychologist, Dr. Ruth Durchslag decided to become a rabbi. She is passionate about bringing Judaism to alienated and disaffected Jews who have never found a way into organized Jewish life and reaching out to anyone seeking personal meaning within Jewish tradition. She is also an avid meditator and seeks to create bridges between meditation and Judaism. Toward that end, Rabbi Durchslag is involved in founding the Center for Jewish Mindfulness in Chicago, and works in the federal prison to create interfaith programs for inmates. She contributed to *Who by Fire, Who by Water—Un'taneh Tokef* (Jewish Lights).

using them toward satanic ends. For most of us, however, the idea of the devil as a hovering, active presence in our lives is a bit far-fetched. Though the prayer predates the Spanish Inquisition, some people use the Inquisition as a way of making *Kol Nidre* make sense. Certainly it was a time when Jewish converts needed to know there would be a way to nullify their forced affirmations of faith. Most of us, however, are not forced converts. We are not Spanish. We do not live in 1478. And contrary to the myth that connects it with Spain, *Kol Nidre* had nothing to do with the Spanish Inquisition anyway.

Maybe the way to understand the prayer is in terms of the "New Year's Eve syndrome." We all know it. How many times, high on champagne and possibility, do we proclaim our New Year's vows believing that this year we will really keep them, even though we have never kept them before? *Kol Nidre* understands that we are human and flawed. Even with the best of intentions our promises fall short—to ourselves, to each other, and to God.

A Jewish legal precedent for understanding *Kol Nidre* goes back to our holiest book. In the Torah, in Leviticus 25:10–13, we learn that on the fiftieth, or jubilee, year, all debts and promises are to be annulled. Most of us, who, in any event, know nothing about the jubilee year anyway, would find this appalling. Annul our financial promises and obligations? Give away our possessions and return to each person their ancestral heritage? Highly unlikely. We stopped counting the jubilee year long ago, and were the concept to be resurrected in Congress, it would never pass.

So this Yom Kippur we'll probably do what we have every other year. We'll simply ignore the words of *Kol Nidre*. Enveloping ourselves in memory and music, we'll let the haunting tune take us to a sacred place. Not a bad approach. We are, however, *yisrael*, a people who struggles. Maybe there is even a way to struggle with the words of *Kol Nidre* to make them make sense.

In *Kol Nidre*, we read that all our vows and promises in the coming year will be null and void. Clearly, *Kol Nidre* suggests that our words don't really count. Let us, then, look more closely at what our tradition has to say about the efficacy of words. The Torah emphasizes the importance of the word from its very beginning, when, at the moment of creation, God speaks the cosmos into being. "Let there be light," God says; and there was light. First the words, and only then the light. How much more noteworthy that God chose to speak, given there was no one to listen. Obviously, God believed that words really matter. God understood that words are a powerful, creative force and can be imbued with majesty and meaning. God created the world with words.

Our God is a God who speaks. How often in the Torah do we read, *Vayomer Elohim el Moshe*, "God spoke to Moses"? God talks to the patriarchs, and at the moment of revelation, God uses words to present the Ten Commandments—which, not incidentally, we call in Hebrew *aseret hadibrot*, "the Ten Utterances," and even (in Mishnah Tamid 5:1) *aseret had'varim*, "the Ten Words." Utterances or words—not commandments. How is it that in Hebrew we do not refer to the Ten Commandments as "the Ten *Mitzvot*"?

Jewish mysticism provides a clue. In kabbalistic thought, words are not symbols or representations. Words have a life force of their own. Words are what they mean. Calling the Ten Commandments the "Ten Utterances" reminds us that our moral imperatives are more than a series of symbols. They are actually alive; once spoken, they have a life of their own; we cannot simply take them back. Words have power and cannot easily be annulled.

It is not just God's words, however, that have creative force. Medieval tradition defines human beings precisely as *m'daber*, the species that "speaks," that uses *d'varim*, "words." The Talmud is more precise. In Bava Metzia 58b, the Rabbis compare financial and verbal damages. Rabbi Yochanan considers verbal wrongdoing more serious than cheating a person in business. Rav Shmuel bar Nachmani explains: in commercial damages, restitution is possible; there is no easy restitution for words.

Even our everyday daily liturgy reminds us how much words matter. Three times a day we introduce the *Amidah*, one of our oldest and most central prayers, by chanting, *Adonai, s'fatai tiftach u'fi yagid tehillatekha*, "Open my lips, God, that my mouth may proclaim your glory." I don't know about others, but I can attest that most of my words are not about proclaiming God's glory. Too often I grumble and complain, wasting words on things that don't count (my endless "to do" list, what we are going to have for dinner, and so on) but neglect acknowledging what does. The prelude to the *Amidah* is there because focusing our words on what matters isn't easy. We begin the *Amidah* by reminding ourselves that what we say is critical: in how we live, in how we pray, and in how we relate to the divine and to each other.

Our daily Jewish life is supposed to remind us regularly that words count. Every day we are instructed to say *me'ah b'rakhot*, "one hundred blessings." Not one hundred thoughts. Not one hundred wishes. Not one hundred intentions. One hundred utterances that acknowledge God's greatness and God's bounty in our lives. Only when we *say* words of blessing (not when we just think them) do we actually change our way of being in the world. Thanking and acknowledging God at least one hundred times a day cannot fail to create a lens of gratitude and humility, through which the world will seem a little more miraculous, a little sweeter, a little more awesome. By shifting our verbal relationship to the world, the world shifts. Like God in Genesis, verbally proclaiming reality can make it so.

If even everyday words matter, then our words of promise and avowal should matter even more. How then can we declare our promises null and void on Yom Kippur? How can we be asked to do something so quintessentially "un-Jewish" on one of the holiest day of the year?

Maybe the answer lies in what happens when we take our words away. The point of withdrawing words may not be to annul their impact but to reveal the silence that remains when they are gone. Vladimir Horowitz, the great pianist, once explained his musical genius by saying, "The notes I handle no better than many pianists, but the pauses between the notes—ah! that is where great art resides."

It seems that God too understood the importance of pauses. If God created the world with speech, Shabbat must have been the time for God to remain silent. On Shabbat God simply stopped talking to reflect on what the Divine had said and thereby made. God understood the power of reflecting on our lives from a place of silence. Jews know the creative power of words, but we understand also that quiet is a sacred space.

Rav Kook, the first chief rabbi of Palestine, pointed to the sacredness of silence as worlds beyond words. He was an eloquent writer, an inspirational speaker, and a renowned scholar. But he also sought silence. In his diaries Rav Kook describes how, each day, he quieted his mind so that the "outpouring of the soul could expand without constriction." Rav Kook relied on meditation as a way to access a place of holiness and truth. He wrote, "Speech, when it comes, interferes [with silence] for it appears with its strength to build from the old, from that which is already tottering, tenebrous, limited and cramped."

As a psychologist I share Rav Kook's wariness of words. "Listen to the music and not the words," my supervisor used to say. Freud knew how easy words can divert and deceive. It's why he invented psychoanalysis, a technique that minimizes the influence of the therapist's words. We all know the caricature: the analyst nodding, muttering "hm, hm," and saying as little as possible. Freud called dreams the "royal road to the unconscious"—dreams, not words. Yes, words create realities, but realities may be hurtful, even false. We use words to justify actions even when they are wrong. We weave our life stories with words, never stopping to be amazed at how quickly we become the heroes of our tales.

As a meditator I go each day to a place of quiet to seek my truth. It is not easy: our minds want to fill us with chatter and distract us from the silence that is foreign and frightening. But when I finally achieve silence, the lens of my life shifts. Dead ends open onto paths of possibility, and "no" softens into "yes." From a place of silence, my pronouncements may seem hollow and harsh. I regret commitments I have made or see a way to make commitments that I had not seen before. Often, from this place, I wish I could take my words back. *Kol Nidre* gives me permission to do just that.

This year, the haunting melody of *Kol Nidre* will remind me to honor not just my voice but my silence.

Words mean everything.

Words mean nothing.

Both are true.

☙

"Woe Is Me That I Have Sworn"

THE POWER TO ANNUL GOD'S VOWS

Rachel Farbiarz and Ruth Messinger

O n Yom Kippur we look inward. We delve into our interior spaces and inspect the undersides of our souls. We dig deep. But, as with all our sacred observances, the obligation to look outward is essential here as well. As we home in on our own spiritual blemishes, we are obliged also to focus on the injustices, inequities, and cruelties of the world around us. Our *Kol Nidre* prostrations help initiate us into this demanding and dual-focused process.

Plainly understood, *Kol Nidre* is the recitation of a legal formula for release from our vows—either past due (in the original formula and still today in Sephardi practice) or yet to be made (in the most common formula that has been in use in Ashkenazi congregations since the twelfth century). The prayer, however, can also be understood more esoterically. From a kabbalistic perspective, *Kol Nidre* provides words

Rachel Farbiarz is a writer and artist living in Washington, D.C. As a *D'var Tzedek* Writing Fellow with American Jewish World Service, she has written on issues of social justice and Torah. She formerly worked as a lawyer, focusing on the humane treatment and civil rights of prisoners. Ruth Messinger is the president of American Jewish World Service. She contributed to *Who by Fire, Who by Water—Un'taneh Tokef* (Jewish Lights).

with which God too can renounce harsh vows—the divine oaths that promise destruction, deprivation, illness, and want in the coming year.[1] Thus do we—capricious, imperfect creatures who fail to satisfy our own commitments—dare to suggest that God be included within the "we" of our prayers. *As we release ourselves*, we intone, *"Allow us, O God, to release You!"*

But what kind of infallible, omniscient being would realign the course of history—and the divine will—just because we ask it?

Such a God would have to be one whose infallibility and omniscience coexist with the promise of self-transformation. The "perfection" of this divine being would be characterized not by constancy, but by change. This is the God who vows annihilation but allows the divine hand to be stayed; the God who can be appeased by fasting and sackcloth and appeals to reason and rhetoric.

With pathos, the Talmud relates the encounter of the storyteller-sage Rabbah bar bar Chanah with this regretful being. On one of his many fantastic adventures traveling between Babylonia and Palestine, Bar Chanah walked the wilderness that the Israelites of long ago had wandered. The sage's capable guide led him to no less a miraculous spot than the foot of the holy Mount Sinai itself. There, Bar Chanah was met not by signs and wonders, however, but by a mournful voice, echoing in the wilderness: "Woe is Me that I have sworn [to exile Israel], but now that I have sworn, who can annul it for Me?" (Talmud, Bava Batra 74a).

This is God's voice that haunts Sinai, lamenting the divine oath to exile Israel for its sins. This is a voice neither triumphant nor awesome. It is, instead, a howl in the wilderness, desperate for the undoing of the almighty's terrible commitments.

This is the God for whom we say *Kol Nidre*.

While certainly audacious, our overtures at *Kol Nidre* are neither unwarranted nor unprecedented. God has long made a habit of inviting humans to subvert the divine plan, repeatedly tipping off humanity to imminent, punishing catastrophes. God thus divulges to Abraham that Sodom and Gomorrah are slated for destruction, ruminating, "Shall I hide from Abraham what I am about to do?" (Genesis 18:17). Answering in the negative, this God surely anticipated Abraham's campaign of prayer and negotiation on behalf of the doomed cities.

Likewise do we hear echoes of an invitation to intervene in the aftermath of Israel's own failures. After the sin of the golden calf, God gruffly commands Moses, "Now let Me be alone, and my anger will be kindled against them so that I will annihilate them, and I will make you into a great nation" (Exodus 32:10). Rashi suggests that we understand God's bluster to have "opened a door for [Moses] and informed him that the matter depended upon him: if he were to pray for [Israel], God would not destroy them."[2] Time and again, Moses walks through this door—successfully petitioning to save the errant nation from God's wrath.

And then there is the story of Jonah, a profound meditation on the intimate entanglement of the wills of God and human beings. In Jonah's tale, retold during Yom Kippur's afternoon service, the almighty again solicits human intervention, commanding the prophet to admonish Nineveh to repent and stave off its looming destruction. Shrinking from his task, Jonah tries instead to flee. He is loathe to deliver a prophecy of destruction only to have it undone upon Nineveh's repentance. Jonah, it would seem, would prefer a consistent, wrathful God to one who is moved, changed, and softened by human efforts.

The almighty, however, rejects Jonah's evasion and sends storm, beast, and withering heat to set straight the wayward prophet. Jonah's tale closes with God's rhetorical reproach:

> Should not I care about Nineveh, that great city, in which
> there are more than a hundred and twenty thousand per-
> sons who do not yet know their right hand from their left,
> and many beasts as well! (Jonah 4:11)

God's scheme, Jonah should know, has room within it for reversal and repentance—for human and divine regret. It will not, however, accommodate the prophet's brittle inflexibility. It will not abide Jonah's facile preference for divine consistency above all else.

This is the God for whom we say *Kol Nidre*. The God who begs for human meddling into divine affairs, who beckons us to stanch the flow of promised destructions. As we chant repeatedly over the course of Yom Kippur, this God may be *slow to anger, abundant in mercy*, and *quick to forgive*—but only if we insist upon it.

For this God, we offer up the opportunity to relinquish, renounce, abandon, declare null and void, pronounce neither firm nor established the divine's vows of exile, pledges of destruction, and oaths of suffering. We ask God to subvert the decree whose ink is almost dry.

Through the strains of *Kol Nidre*'s ancient ache we can hear the divine lament that yearns for our response: *Woe is Me that I have sworn* to make suffering, violence, want, and loss essential parts of what it is to be alive! *"Woe is Me that I have sworn, but now that I have sworn, who can annul it for Me?"*

We can. Through the strains of *Kol Nidre* we can listen for what it might mean to relieve God of these vows. Perhaps we cannot hope to completely undo God's terrible commitments. Drought, famine, storm, and plague are, after all, the work of nature's laws, unfolding with relentless indifference. It is incumbent upon us, however, to try to undermine those brutal divine commitments; the God of Abraham, Moses, and Jonah would seem to demand that we do so.

Even if God stops the rain and parches the land, we need not let famine and drought devour the weak. If God forces the water higher and higher, the levees need not break, nor the people be abandoned. If the almighty cracks open the earth, schools and homes need not collapse like piles of twigs; necessities and essential services need not have been already so scarce as to become nonexistent during a crisis. If God lets loose a terrible, preventable illness, it need not be allowed to consume millions unimpeded.

These are, surely, "acts of God," but the extent to which they tumble into unmitigated disaster is significantly in our human hands. Government denial, corruption, and infighting need not have hampered famine and drought relief, as they have in Kenya, one of Africa's most economically successful nations. Want, inequality, and neglect need not have allowed New Orleans to founder and then drown, as it did when the city was hit by a punishing, anticipated storm. Poverty, failed institutions, and a history of exploitation need not have reduced Haiti, as they did, to a country of mass graves when the earth shook below it. And ignorance, stigma, shame, and deprivation need not, as they have, allowed HIV/AIDS to have so devastated communities throughout the world.

Not for nothing does God moan *Woe is Me!* into the wilderness. The almighty cries out so that someone will respond. *Kol Nidre* night asks us to confront God's plea and meet it, to commit ourselves— through *tz'dakah* and compassionate action—to human solutions that relieve the divine's terrible vows. Like the first blood that stained the earth when Cain killed Abel, God's voice "cries out to us" from the ground. On this, holiest of nights, we must vow to answer it.

⊙〜〜〇

The Tyranny of Perfection

Rabbi Edward Feinstein

"**B**y the authority of the heavenly court and of the earthly court: With the foreknowledge of the God of time and space and with the agreement of this congregation, we give permission to pray with habitual sinners [*avaryanim*]."

That last word is intriguing: *avaryanim*, "sinners." Why would we need special permission to pray with sinners? We are all sinners, aren't we? That's why we have come here this Yom Kippur eve.

There is another translation. *Avaryanim* can also mean "Iberians"— the Jews who lived in Spain and Portugal from Roman times until their expulsion in 1492. From 1391 on, a vicious anti-Jewish campaign by the Christian clergy led many Jews to convert to Christianity. It used to be believed that *Kol Nidre* arose specifically to nullify the vow of conversion that those Iberian Jews were forced to take.

To be sure, we now know that *Kol Nidre* came into being long before that era, which had nothing to do with *Kol Nidre* whatever. But the

Rabbi Edward Feinstein is senior rabbi of Valley Beth Shalom in Encino, California. He is an instructor in the Ziegler Rabbinical School of American Jewish University and the Wexner Heritage Program. He is the author of *Tough Questions Jews Ask: A Young Adult's Guide to Building a Jewish Life* (Jewish Lights) and *Capturing the Moon;* and the editor of *Jews and Judaism in the 21st Century: Human Responsibilities, the Presence of God, and the Future of the Covenant* (Jewish Lights). He contributed to *Who by Fire, Who by Water—Un'taneh Tokef* (Jewish Lights).

association between *Kol Nidre* and the Spanish converts (called conversos, or, the older term, Marranos) has remained—partly because of the similar sounding words *avaryanim* and "Iberian" and partly because of the existential lesson for human life in general that the association suggests.

First, the true part of the tale: who were the conversos? Persecution of Jews at the end of the thirteenth century did indeed cause many Jews to accept baptism, some in good faith, others as just a pretext, while practicing Judaism secretly at home. But even the true converts were not accepted fully into Spanish society, and many of them reverted to Judaism in private. The church found itself in the difficult position of telling them apart. Who was the true believer, who the expedient convert, and who the closet Jew?

In 1469, Ferdinand of Aragon married Isabella of Castile, uniting the Christian kingdoms of Spain. They instituted the Inquisition to hunt down all crypto-Jews and kill them. The Inquisition was directed only against lapsed Christians, the people who accepted Christianity, honestly or not, but who then persisted in practicing Judaism anyway. It could not touch Jews who had refused to convert. But on March 31, 1492, the new monarchs issued an edict of Expulsion for them, and on July 31, the last of one hundred thousand Jews left Spain. Those who fled to Portugal were expelled from there in 1496 and 1497.

Left behind were the converts to Christianity, whether in actuality or in pretense. They were encouraged to inform on one another, until eventually no one was safe from the Inquisition's scrutiny and accusation. Over the next generation, thousands of Jews fled Iberia and found their way to North Africa, Turkey, Italy, and Holland, where refugee communities of those who had been expelled had already sprung up.

We get now to the just-so part of the tale—rooted in history but requiring a little imagination. Picture the confrontation between the Jews who had suffered exile out of faithfulness to Judaism and those who had converted to Christianity, professed faith in the Christian God, worshiped publicly in church, and now claimed a place among Jewish people. Does one get a second chance at Judaism?

And imagine further what Ashkenazi Jews must have felt. Unable to tell one Iberian Jew from another, they must have suspected them all of leaving Judaism for convenience and returning only out of necessity. So the Rabbis declared: *Anu matirim l'hitpalel im ha'avaryanim.* We are permitted to pray with these Iberians.

Here's the Yom Kippur lesson from the tale. We are all Iberians—we are all hiding something. We all have secrets. We have all failed at something, betrayed some ideal. We have all found ourselves far from where we planned to be in life. We arrive at *Kol Nidre* seeking a second chance, a second chance to come home, to join the community, to seek God's forgiveness and a new beginning.

Somewhere in the deep recesses of our mind we carry pictures of our expectations, a map for our lives. What happens when we deviate from the map and find ourselves somewhere altogether foreign, outside the pale of what we and others thought we would become?

He was perfectly successful. He lived the perfect life: an exceptional record in school, brilliant career, perfect wife, perfect kids. The whole package. Except it never sat right with him. Maybe because he'd gained it so easily, it felt all too easy to lose. Maybe he felt he hadn't really earned it. Or maybe it just didn't seem to add up to the greatness he'd dreamed of. The inner unrest grew stronger. But there was no one in whom he could confide. His wife was busy with her career and her pursuits. His friends would not have believed him. And besides, men don't easily share these things. So he held it in, and he held it together. He was perfect, and he was perfectly miserable. Welcome to Iberia.

One night at a company party, someone offered him a hit of cocaine. Why not? He never did it in college, too busy earning perfection points. Maybe now it was time to live a little. Moments later he felt remarkable. All the anxiety gone, he was once again at the center of the universe. When the same client visited him days later and offered another hit of the drug, he was eager. Soon after, he contacted the client and asked to buy some of the drug. Another, larger purchase ensued. And another after that. Gradually, the cocaine displaced everything in his life—his work, his friends, his wife and kids. Nothing mattered except the drug. When confronted, he reacted violently and irrationally, denied he had a problem. Piece by piece, he lost it all—the career, the family, respect, love—a perfect tragedy. To support his habit, he resorted to stealing. And then he got caught. In jail, he hit bottom and came to the truth. Slowly, he began to climb up and out and toward *t'shuvah*. Slowly, he made his amends and began again. A true Iberian.

One thing a rabbi knows: Everyone is an Iberian. Everyone has secrets. Everyone has shame. Everyone has moments when life drives us off our map. No one ever planned for a divorce or a disease or a criminal act. No one anticipated an undistinguished career or underachieving child. No one ever expects life to bring failure, to bring disappointment. No matter how good we look on the outside, no one's life is perfect. We all hide, we escape, we deny what's true.

Here is the truth of *Kol Nidre*: There is life after failure. There is treatment for disease. There is rehabilitation after disability. There are new career opportunities. There are healthy new relationships after even the most painful divorce. There are ways to help our kids and to help ourselves. God gives second chances. But only after we let go of the shame, acknowledge what's before us, forgive ourselves, and reach out for help.

Vayomer Adonai, salachti kidvarekha, "And Adonai said: I have pardoned as you asked!"

Kol Nidre night, we are whole again. We are home again. Our failures are forgiven. Our shame is lifted. There is nothing that we must hide; no more secrets. We are finally free.

CANTO

Disruption, Disorientation, and Restarting

THE *KOL NIDRE* ROAD TO RETURN

Rabbi Shoshana Boyd Gelfand

T'shuvah—returning—is not the real challenge; the hard bits are the steps leading up to it. In order to "return," I need first to challenge inertia and stop my current trajectory. Then, I must reorient myself, turning 180 degrees to face the opposite direction. Only then can I take the final step and regain the necessary momentum to begin my journey again, this time on the correct path. Those three steps—stop, turn, and restart—are the prerequisites for *t'shuvah*.

Kol Nidre is a ritual tool that can help us prepare to return. When *Kol Nidre* works, it disrupts our lives by forcing us to pause from our daily

---

Shoshana Boyd Gelfand received her rabbinic ordination in 1993 at The Jewish Theological Seminary in New York. She has served as chief executive of the United Kingdom Movement for Reform Judaism and prior to that was vice president of the Wexner Heritage Foundation in New York. Currently she is director of JHub, a program that incubates Jewish start-up organizations in Europe. She makes her home in London, with her husband, Jonathan Boyd, and their three children.

concerns. It also disorients us by placing us in a liminal state where we experience a form of spiritual vertigo. This vertigo continues throughout Yom Kippur, where over the course of the day, other liturgical tools reorient us to face the right direction. Finally, we are given a push in the right direction, restarting our journey with the *mitzvot* that take place at the close of Yom Kippur, allowing us to fulfill our goal of returning to God in time to celebrate together with God on Sukkot.

Disruption, disorientation, and restarting: liturgy and ritual play an important role in accomplishing all three.

Disruption

Disruption begins well before *Kol Nidre*. It starts each morning in Elul as the shofar is sounded and we recite Psalm 27 to shake up our daily routine. Two days of Rosh Hashanah and the *S'lichot* prayers of the Ten Days of Penitence intensify the disruption. But even if somehow we have managed to remain oblivious to all of that, there is Erev Yom Kippur, which makes it impossible to pretend that life can go on as usual. We eat our evening meal well before sundown, in itself an odd practice that physically jars our bodies. Then we dress in white, avoiding leather or perfume. As we walk into synagogue, we don a *tallit*, the only time in the year that we do so for an evening service.

At this point, we might be forgiven for feeling like one of the questioning children at a Pesach seder. What is going on here? Why is this night different from all other nights? Indeed, the disruption leading up to *Kol Nidre* is at least as powerful as the experience of a looming seder for which we must prepare. Passover disequilibrium is achieved through massive cleaning efforts, washing without a blessing, eating *karpas* instead of bread after washing, and substituting matzah for challah. These variants on the usual Shabbat routine jar us into recognizing that this night is not like all other nights.

It was my teacher Rabbi Saul Berman who drew my attention to the significant parallels between Yom Kippur and Pesach. Both, for example, contain oblique biblical references to Shabbat rest: Pesach is referred to as *mi-mochorat Shabbat* ("from the day after Shabbat," from Leviticus 23:15),[1] and Yom Kippur as *Shabbat Shabbaton* ("Sabbath of Sabbaths," from Leviticus 3:32). The two holidays thereby make us pause to reflect about ourselves as consumers, and not just because they both evoke the image of Sabbath rest, but because both of them limit permission to eat: no *chametz* on Pesach; no food at all on Yom Kippur. Coming almost exactly six months apart in the Jewish calendar, Pesach and Yom Kippur force us to ask essential questions: Am I more than what I consume? How do I relate to others beyond what they consume? How should I relate to God, who is the source of all that I consume? We need to be jarred out of our daily routine of consumption in order to ask ourselves these fundamental questions and reflect on whether or not we like the answers. If not, then we have an opportunity to change, and that is the beginning of *t'shuvah*. Stopping to reflect gets the whole process going.

Disorientation

Stopping, however, is (ironically) just the beginning of the process: stopping to question our lives does not tell us how to change them. Yes, we want to turn, but in what direction, and to do what? The process requires personal disorientation—we must feel shaken enough to be willing to try out alternatives. Professor Ron Heifetz at Harvard sees disequilibrium as essential to human adaptation to change. So long as we remain firmly rooted in our past, we will not be able to do *t'shuvah*. So stopping must give way to something that throws us off balance.

Fasting will do that eventually, but as Yom Kippur gets under way, the physical pinch of hunger and faintness has yet to kick in. So instead of a physical jolt, we are given *Kol Nidre*, a spiritual/emotional one. Everything about *Kol Nidre* is counterintuitive and confusing. Unlike other services during the year, the *Kol Nidre* ritual does not start gently and build to a climax. Rather, we are immediately and dramatically exposed to the *sifrei Torah*, which are removed from the ark at the very beginning of the service. The entire congregation stands, as if preparing to hear the Torah read, yet again we are thrown off guard; we do not read the Torah scrolls. Instead, we invoke a courtroom ambience and chant a legal formula three times, creating an almost meditative trance with the mantra of the *Kol Nidre* melody.

To make matters more confusing, the words themselves make no sense; they constitute an incredibly esoteric legal formula, which annuls vows that have yet to be taken—a legal impossibility. In addition, Jewish tradition provides for the possibility of annulling past vows *before* Rosh Hashanah, thereby creating a sort of liturgical *déjà vu* with *Kol Nidre*.

Even were the words to be legally binding, the medieval melody that has come to be accepted as *misinai* (as if coming from Sinai) overshadows the meaning, as if the legalistic nature of the words is not even the point. The dissonance between the message of the words (legal) and the soulfulness of the music (spiritual) creates a liminal state—a sense of being betwixt and between. What is the purpose of this ritual? What is going on here? One answer is that *Kol Nidre* establishes disequilibrium, an almost intoxicated state of confusion that allows us to explore our souls deeply and discover what we must change about ourselves through confession and *t'shuvah*.

By the beginning of *Musaf* the next day, we have recited the confessional several times, a repetitive reorientation of our inner selves in a new direction. The Martyrology and *Avodah* in *Musaf* invoke historical models, recognizable signposts for us to ground ourselves within the collective narrative of the Jewish people. As we continue reciting the confessional during *Musaf*, we fine-tune our direction and orientation.

During the next service, *Minchah*, we read the book of Jonah, in which everyone and everything change their mind: the non-Jewish sailors, the whale, the king of Nineveh, the people of Nineveh, even God. As the book ends, we are left with the realization that everyone in the story changes and does *t'shuvah*—except, perhaps, Jonah! Has he changed? And what about us? Have we changed during this Yom Kippur reflection? Again we recite the confessional, one more opportunity to make the necessary adjustments that create reorientation.

The final service, *N'ilah*, gives us the ultimate push. Now we are definitely feeling the hunger, the thirst, and the sore back from standing for so long. We recite the confessional one more time, for the gates are closing now; there is little time left to reorient ourselves any more.

Restarting

At the end of *N'ilah*, whatever direction we face is where we will head next; but how to face the right direction? We need be jarred back into reentering the world of the familiar and everyday. So we sound one last blast of the shofar and then, immediately, perform the ritual of *Havdalah*, separating us from the surreal experience of Yom Kippur and projecting us into the world of secular regularity. Our first act of the new day is to recite *Ma'ariv*, a normal daily evening prayer. Even though our bellies are crying for sustenance, we transcend that physical need and focus on regularizing the behavior to which we have committed ourselves. Many even start building their sukkah before breaking their fast, symbolically showing that they have been catapulted into a new trajectory: making their first act one of building a replica of the Tabernacle.

Yom Kippur, when done well, puts us back on the path to God. We get there by allowing *Kol Nidre* to stop us in our tracks and reorient us in a different direction. Then the unfolding rituals of Yom Kippur help us to restart us on the right path so that by the final shofar blast, we have indeed done *t'shuvah*. *T'shuvah* is the easy part—assuming the preparation has been done.

⌘

Lifting the Curtain

THE THEATRICAL *KOL NIDRE*

Rabbi Delphine Horvilleur

The very first words of the *Kol Nidre* announce the greatest liturgical show of the Jewish year, the sacred and collective choreography of the Day of Atonement. It reruns annually to packed houses that gather to begin each new Jewish year on the stage of our synagogues. As such, it is helpful to think of it as a Jewish example of classical dramaturgy, the study of dramatic art that goes back to ancient Greece. Dramaturgy is a heavily codified genre—that is, it follows a set of well-known conventions that were laid down in antiquity and repeated all the way to the eighteenth century. By now, we have a significant body of literature listing the traditional features of a classical play, the ones that make it *kehilkhatah*, "as it should be."

Some of these features are quite universal: the curtain is lifted and the choir starts singing, for example. Others have been subject to emendation and change. Overall, however, the liturgy of Yom Kippur can indeed be seen as a classical play, with *Kol Nidre* as its beginning, the raising, as it were, of the curtain.

Rabbi Delphine Horvilleur is the rabbi of congregation MJLF (Mouvement Juif Libéral de France in Paris). She was ordained at Hebrew Union College–Jewish Institute of Religion in New York in 2008 and became the third woman rabbi in France. She is the creative director of Le Café Biblique, a pluralistic group of Jewish study, and the chief editor of *Tenou'a*, a French magazine of Jewish thought. She contributed to *Who by Fire, Who by Water—Un'taneh Tokef* (Jewish Lights).

In France, every classical play is heralded with the so-called "three strokes." A wooden stick is pounded on the stage floor three times in a row, announcing that the show is about to begin. This custom supposedly dates back to the times when the troupe played before the royal court. It was then the custom to make three strokes as a symbolic salute to the queen, the king, and then the rest of the audience.

Eventually, the three strokes were separated from their court origins but remained as the symbolic opening to the drama anyway. They introduced the changeover in time and place from the everyday environment from which the audience had come to the dramatic time and place in which the drama was being set. These three strokes are echoed in the threefold repetition of *Kol Nidre*, which transports the audience from the everyday to the sacred world of Yom Kippur.

The threefold repetition of *Kol Nidre* is more than just a memory of the court where the three strokes were once invented. The liturgical lines that lead up to the *Kol Nidre* moment return us to the actual court itself: the convergence of two courts, actually, the human court of the justice down below and the godly one, on high, above.

As *Kol Nidre* is sung, the godly court of justice gathers. God is "king" and "judge." Down below, meanwhile, another court is readied to sit in judgment. It is the human *bet din*, symbolized by the Torah scrolls being held aloft. The human court mirrors the divine one, where God is king: appropriately, our tradition calls the Torah a "crown."

The judges then speak and declare: *Biy'shivah shel ma'alah uviy'shivah shel matah*—in effect, "Before the higher and the lower jurisdiction, before the godly court of justice and before the court down below of the Rabbis, the trial can officially begin." The very first words of the *Kol Nidre* ritual, even before the *Kol Nidre* chant itself, is, therefore, a choreographed announcement of a show trial. It suddenly dawns on us that we are both the audience and the accused, facing the divine judge above and a jury of our peers down here below.

"*Qu'en un jour, qu'en un lieu, un seul fait accompli / Tienne jusqu'à la fin le théâtre rempli*": "Let a single complete action, in one place and one day, keep the theater packed to the last." With these words, the eighteenth-century playwright Boileau defined the constraints of classical drama. According to the canon that the French represents, the plot of a classical play must not exceed a day's time. The entire story, from start to end, must take place in no more than twenty-four hours, in a single location, and with a common theme.

Yom Kippur obeys these rules of Greek and classical drama. It unfolds over twenty-four hours with a finale at *N'ilah*. The theme of judgment occurs throughout. And it takes place in the single and singular location of the heavenly and earthly courts, their meeting place, actually, the crowded synagogue.

The décor is there as well—who can doubt that this is a play? The costumes are traditional (we wear the clothes of the high priest). And the curtain falls and rises several times, as we open and close the holy ark throughout the day.

As in classical drama, the audience knows that what is happening on the stage is not a story passively observed but the telling of our most sacred experience in a way that draws us in because it is so obviously our very lives that are being portrayed. Playing out before us from sunset to sunset is the drama of human destiny and the coming to terms with our mortality. This is precisely what theatrical catharsis is all about.

But Yom Kippur theater differs in one important respect from the Greek ideal: Yom Kippur is not a tragedy. The essence of Greek tragedy is the unchangeable fate of the hero. Take Oedipus, for example. There is nothing Oedipus can do to escape the oracle's prediction. His fate is sealed by an irrevocable fatality. In Greek tragedy, the gods call all the shots. With Yom Kippur, however, the fate of the players is not sealed at all, the end has not been written in advance. Yom Kippur reverses the Greek scenario. Every moment of the day reminds us of the absence of fatality in our destinies. That is, in essence, the message of the holiday, made clear at the very outset, in *Kol Nidre*'s very words. *Nidrana la nidrei ... ush'vu'atana la sh'vu'ot*: "Our vows are not vows ... our oaths are not oaths." All the oaths, the promises, the affirmations that we might pronounce can be canceled. All of our declarations, past or future, may well never take place.

How astonishing that conclusion should be to us. We enter the holiday assuming that our oaths and promises must be certainties, that we must have made them presumptuously, not realizing that once made, these promises are set in stone, as definitive and inevitable as an oracle. *Kol Nidre* tells us otherwise. We realize that our words may be called off; there is no more determinism in our words than in our destinies.

The service of Yom Kippur that takes place in front of the divine and the human courts of justice is a celebration of uncertainty and indeterminism. The most sacred day in the Jewish calendar is the opposite of an oracle—what the classical codes of drama would have called an "anti-tragedy."

The etymology of the Greek word for "tragedy" provides a troubling meaning. It is generally believed that the Greek word *tragoidía* derives from the combination of *trágos*, "goat," and *áidô*, "song." In literal terms, "tragedy" is the "song of the goat," the litany that the goat sings as it is about to be sacrificed.

Surprisingly, the same animal plays a key role on Yom Kippur. It is one of the leading actors of the play, as it happens, the goat that was sacrificed in the Temple on that day to atone for the sins of the people. It is the goat that symbolically embodies the human condition, but the goat is the only player that day who won't be able to escape its destiny. We will.

The Yom Kippur drama is no human tragedy but a bestial one, because the oaths, the vows, and the promises that we make are no oaths, vows, and promises (*nidrana la nidrei*). The humility of uncertainty is a protection against the infallibility of the tragic oracle. The judgments and the decrees that we utter are not irrevocable, the ones that we utter no more than the ones that are pronounced against us.

At the heart of our sacred play and in the words of *Kol Nidre*, it is written that … nothing is written.

⌒₪₪〜

"It's Rather Hard to Understand"

APPROACHING GOD THROUGH SOUND, NOT TRANSLATION

Rabbi Elie Kaunfer

When Alice [of Alice in Wonderland] encounters the whiffling and burbling Jabberwock, she remarks: "It seems very pretty, but it's rather hard to understand!" Alice's comment is insightful: such linguistic play is difficult to understand, and that is precisely the point. The idea that words create a meaningful universe is, as a poet said, the "supreme fiction"; language is phantasmal, not transparent to whatever "reality" might be.... God seems to dwell in the making and unmaking of language."

Patricia Cox Miller, "In Praise of Nonsense"

Rabbi Elie Kaunfer is cofounder and executive director of Mechon Hadar (www.mechonhadar.org). He is an Avi Chai Fellow, author of *Empowered Judaism: What Independent Minyanim Can Teach Us about Building Vibrant Jewish Communities* (Jewish Lights), and a contributor to *Who by Fire, Who by Water—Un'taneh Tokef*. *Newsweek* named him one of fifty top rabbis in America.

W hat is it about *Kol Nidre* that is so powerful? Far more important than the cognitive message derived from its translation, this prayer, which is recited only once a year, conjures up images of our annual communal outpouring on Yom Kippur: crowded sanctuaries, introspective worshipers, and haunting music. Perhaps no other Jewish prayer demonstrates so starkly the fact that praying is much more than simply understanding, translating, and saying a prayer's words.

Once when I was in Israel, I visited a first-grade class that was learning the *Amidah*. The prayer book in use provided space under the traditional words for the students to record what the blessing meant to them. I looked at one boy's entry for the blessing asking for a good agricultural year. The boy had written, "I pray that my brother comes home safely from Lebanon." In prayer, words and intentions don't always match.

On the surface, *Kol Nidre* is a technical legal formula, not even really a prayer. Its function is to release us from all kinds of vows made or, depending on the version, yet to be made. But the content of *Kol Nidre* seems almost incidental to the emotional valence of the words that constitute it. Why is that?

One obvious reason is the music, which has the power to transcend the limits of verbal translation.

Much has been written about this music, most especially the powerful melody known to most Ashkenazi worshipers. A. Z. Idelsohn, a leading scholar on the history of Jewish music history (1865–1921), puts it this way: "While the text, a mere renouncement of vows, is devoid of religious emotions, its musical setting is generally accepted as an expression of the deep religious feelings which move the Jewish heart on the eve of the Day of Atonement."[1] Idelsohn is certainly tapping into a widely held sentiment about the power of the music.

But are there no "religious emotions" to *Kol Nidre* other than the music? It has certainly aroused plenty of emotions in its day! It evoked official rabbinic opposition almost since its initial appearance in the liturgy, and the Jews who defended it against its powerful rabbinic opponents predated its haunting Ashkenazi melody by many centuries. Is there something else, then, about the prayer that is so appealing? Something beyond the music, on one hand, and the literal textual meaning on the other?

I believe that the power of *Kol Nidre* does indeed stem from its words—not from their meaning, however, but from their form and sound. It is precisely the strangeness of those words that constitutes its ability to move us so powerfully as we reach toward the divine.

The text of *Kol Nidre* is in Aramaic, a language once familiar to most Jews but now a strange collection of syllables even, in many cases, for native Hebrew speakers. Interestingly, a Hebrew version of *Kol Nidre* once existed. One form of it, at least, is preserved in a manuscript of *Seder Rav Amram Gaon* (ninth century), although many texts there, probably including this one, are interpolations from a later era.[2] A Hebrew version is also attributed to Hai Gaon (d. 1038). But the harder-to-understand Aramaic version is the one that we use today. In any event, finding a modern Hebrew parallel has its own inherent difficulties, since even those who understand Aramaic cannot easily find accurate ways to translate the list of technical synonyms that constitute *Kol Nidre*'s key words.[3] Precisely because the prayer defies easy translation, worshipers tend to dwell on its succession of syllables, not the cognitive meaning of its words, as their main worship experience.

Kol Nidre has the sound and feel of a magical incantation. The magical roots of *Kol Nidre* have long been noticed—ever since the discovery of Aramaic incantations written on ceramic bowls, some mirroring the language in *Kol Nidre* itself.[4] The tradition to say *Kol Nidre* three times also derives from incantation practice.[5]

Incantations are known for their use of language in a nonrational manner. Some incantations, we know, began sensibly enough in their original Greek contexts, but their original meaning was lost even as the words were preserved in a twisted version and used for incantations.[6] Regarding magical names, we are told, "It is their very strangeness which makes them magically potent."[7]

Kol Nidre's overlap with magical spells should not be taken to mean some form of derision or dismissal, as if to say, "Oh, we don't believe in magic anymore." Like it or not, there is a deep power to the words of magical spells, precisely because they force us to confront our inability to understand everything we say.

And this, I would argue, is the central experience of Yom Kippur. First, we recognize that in a world so focused on articulation and expression, deep relationships defy linguistic boundaries. Who could express in words the love of a parent for a child? Or the pain of a husband losing a wife? Stepping into the intensity of Yom Kippur through words that don't "mean" reminds us of the futility of language to capture our emotions.

And second, on a day focused on confronting the divine presence, we can't pretend that all the words we are about to say in the *machzor* will encapsulate or accurately describe God and our potential relationship with God. Reciting something "very pretty" but "rather hard to understand," as Alice in Wonderland puts it, reveals clearly the lie that God can be captured in words.

Kol Nidre allows us to skirt the grooves of our minds that rely so much on expressive language. When you catch yourself drawn in by *Kol Nidre* despite not knowing what it means, allow yourself to remain open to all those noncognitive experiences that make up the deeper human spirit. After all, as the Rabbis themselves recognized, in many ways all prayer is futile; only emotions can penetrate the heavens:

> Rabbi Eleazar said: Since the day the Temple was destroyed, the gates of prayer are locked. But even though the gates of prayer are locked, the gates of tears are not locked. (Talmud, Berakhot 32b)

⚬⟋⟋⟋⟋⟍⟍⟍⚬

The Sound
and Pageantry
WILLINGNESS, ASPIRATION, AND DISCERNMENT

Rabbi Karyn D. Kedar

I n prayer, we often say things we don't believe. The liturgy does not present a mere manifesto of belief, and when we pray it is rarely just to ratify an idea, consider an ideological stance, or express a deeply held belief. Sometimes prayer's purpose is to carry us away, to be a vehicle for transcendence. Sometimes praying draws back a curtain to reveal the complex and elusive world of spiritual stillness, introspection, and contemplation. And sometimes, despite the obscure ideas upon the page, we are transformed, and despite what we say, we are moved beyond words.

Kol Nidre is a dramatic example of the power of prayer despite the words that make it up. It has indeed survived the centuries, but not because it legally releases us from our vows. In fact, at several periods of

---

Rabbi Karyn D. Kedar is the senior rabbi at Congregation B'nai Jehoshua Beth Elohim in Deerfield, Illinois. She is the author of several books, including *The Bridge to Forgiveness: Stories and Prayers for Finding God and Restoring Wholeness; Our Dance with God: Finding Prayer, Perspective and Meaning in the Stories of Our Lives;* and *God Whispers: Stories of the Soul, Lessons of the Heart* (all Jewish Lights). She contributed to *Who by Fire, Who by Water—Un'taneh Tokef* (Jewish Lights).

Jewish history, the rabbis wanted to do away with it; but the people felt the power of the prayer, so it was retained. It is written in Aramaic, the vernacular that the public could understand, but as time went on and Jews learned the vernacular of whatever country they inhabited, Aramaic became a language even more foreign than Hebrew. The meaning of the words was lost, and for most of us, so too was the purpose for which the words had been composed. Yet, the power behind the prayer remained.

And so what is the power of this prayer, if not in the words and ideas? The force of *Kol Nidre* lies beyond the boundaries of intellect and in the realm of spiritual transcendence. The abiding force of the prayer is derived from four converging elements: the spiritual state of willingness, the poetic sounds of music, pageantry, and contextual framing.

Willingness

The stage for *Kol Nidre* is set within a distinct time and place. Just as the evening falls and darkness is about to prevail, Jews gather, as if drawn to some inexplicable moment by the force of tradition. On *Kol Nidre* we come to synagogue knowing somehow that we ought to be there and anticipating something significant that may happen. The call to assemble, the setting, and the anticipation all conspire to create a psychological and spiritual willingness to be vulnerable and open: we come with the expectation of being moved, carried away, changed. We have eaten for the last time for the next twenty-four hours. We dress differently: in white and *tallit* (if we follow tradition) or in new clothes, bought and picked specially for the moment. The physical garb is symbolic of a spiritual readiness for majesty.

The Poetic Sounds of Music and Pageantry

We are asked to rise. For a very long time, unsure of how long it is, we stand at attention. We gaze upon the Torah scrolls cloaked in white, sensing their weightiness in our leaders' arms. As they struggle to hold them, they stand and straighten, shifting and swaying back and forth, causing the scrolls to move slightly, and the silver bells chime softly. We are aware of the great responsibility of holding the Torah and try to remember the penalty for dropping one, as if acknowledging that it is we who have somehow already relinquished the commanding force of the words within.

Then, as the moments go by, we notice our bodies, shifting from one foot to another, feeling our weight, wondering when we can sit down again.

Through it all, we listen to these ancient Aramaic words that we do not comprehend. Somewhere in the centuries, the literal sense of the text—its annulment of vows—has receded into the Jewish collective unconscious, allowing space for a symbolic meaning more profound than any annulment of vows could be. The power of the prayer lies not in its ideas, but rather in the poetic devices of cadence, repetition, and alliteration of the Aramaic text combined with the power of the music. Musical and poetic cadence and measure, the repetition of syllables, emphasized by the melodic lines surpass the limitations of the denotative or connotative meaning of the text. The musical and poetic sounds take over, providing a concise and compact rhythm beyond the words, and luring us into a world beyond language. Meaning is discovered in a flash of a moment, not the extended logic of explicative thought. *Kol Nidre* has become poetry unhindered by thought, a trance created by hypnotic repetition of sounds that are at once ancient, distant, familiar, traditional, personal, and penetrating.

Beyond even the music is the pageantry that the music accompanies. The whiteness of the Torah covering and traditional clothing becomes a metaphor for purity; the newness of the clothes that people wear become a metaphor for a new beginning. The Torah scrolls represent spirals of meaning, the commanding voice of history and morality, of story and ethics, of behavior and belief. We hear the sounds of *Kol Nidre*, feel the weight of the moment, see the possibilities of a life where goodness becomes commonplace because the highest expression of ourselves prevails. We are the pageantry. We are the poem. This is a moment of transcendence.

Aspiration and Discernment as Contextual Framing

Kol Nidre is bracketed by texts that teach two spiritual principles on the way to repentance: aspiration and discernment. Aspiration is the acknowledgment that life can be better. It is the desire to change, to elevate our lives to higher ideals and behaviors. Discernment is the ability to see the path that will lead us to the life that we aspire to.

Kol Nidre's preamble teaches us the spiritual principle of aspiration: "Light is sown for the righteous, and for the upright, gladness" (Psalm

97:11). This brief reference recollects the moment in creation when light first bursts forth upon the universe—not the light of days and seasons, or of moon, sun, and stars, for they are created on the fourth day, but (as Rashi explains) the mystical light of origins that is planted in the soul of every living being; it is the light of all the righteous who are yet to come into the world. As *Kol Nidre* begins, we are to have in mind the core of light and goodness that is our essence. We are to live up to the promise of this light, through deeds of love and kindness, through *mitzvot*, and by living our life's purpose with meaning and conviction. On this holiest of days we need to aspire, to peel away the darkness that surrounds the core of our being.

But the path to righteousness is not clear. The path that we are meant to walk, that leads us to fulfill our purpose, requires discernment. *Kol Nidre* is followed by a reference to the biblical story of the scouts who spy out the Land of Israel before the Israelites enter it:

> The whole Israelite community and the stranger residing among them shall be forgiven, for it happened to the entire people through error [Numbers 15:26].... And Adonai said: I have pardoned as you have asked [Numbers 14:20].

The setting is all-important. Freed from Egyptian bondage, the Israelites have marched not only to the geographical borders of the land but to its spiritual borders as well, where their destiny as a people is about to be fulfilled. Spies are sent. Two return with visions of optimism and abundance—a land flowing with milk and honey. Ten predict doom and disaster—a land that devours its inhabitants; a land filled with giants, before whom we are like grasshoppers. Both accounts are right: it is a land surrounded by foes, harsh and unyielding; but also a land with abundant harvest and promise. God pardons those who succumbed to fear. However wrong, it is an understandable and tempting conclusion.

The paradox of the Land of Israel is the paradox of the human spirit. Will the Israelites find a land flowing with milk and honey? Or a land that devours its inhabitants? And what will we encounter in the new year? With *Kol Nidre*'s moment of spiritual stillness, we part the curtain into our future. Do we see abundance and possibility or mere obstacles that evoke our fear? Here lies the challenge of discernment.

In the context of *Kol Nidre* we find an answer. The spies ask for forgiveness, and forgiveness is granted. Their sin was the lack of discernment. In the landscape of the territory toward which they had been heading ever since Egypt, they saw the possibility of the Jewish people's demise, not the potential for Jewish destiny fulfilled. On this sacred night we look upon the landscape of our souls; are we filled with negative thoughts and behavior, or can we discern the path toward "the light that is sown for the righteous"?

Aspiration begins our sequence, music and pageantry transition us through a moment of transcendence, where we may discern what is possible. And if this liturgical sequence does its magic, then what is left is gratitude. The *Shehecheyanu* is normally a powerful, yet simple, acclamation that God has kept us alive, sustained us, and brought us to this very moment. In the context of *Kol Nidre* it is a moment of grace, where we capture the insight that the way of the past year need not be our way forward from this moment on. The cadence of *Kol Nidre* can become the cadence of our life, creating light where there is darkness, living a life of poetry and symbolism, of deed and goodness. Standing before God and the Jewish people, we can claim our gift of the light that was sown for us, in anticipation of lives filled with goodness and beauty.

☙∞❧

Is *Kol Nidre* Typical?

Dr. Reuven Kimelman

What a peculiar question to ask—whether *Kol Nidre* is typical! Everybody knows how exceptional it is. The moment, the mood, the court scene, the legally charged Aramaic and Hebrew are all out of the ordinary. We stand without shoes, dressed in white, wrapped in *tallit* at night, while chanting a threefold crescending repetition from contrition to rectification to pardon, without mention of God or the division between saint and sinner. Surely these extraordinary factors are enough to explain how this longest-running, off-Broadway drama became an annual, worldwide sellout for over a millennium.

But is it? Or do we need an additional factor: the focus on language and words? That may be the case since the focus on language and words typifies Yom Kippur in particular but is true also of prayer in general. Words are the pith of prayer. Take one look at *Al Chet*, the standard Yom Kippur confessional, and you cannot doubt the power of the word. True, the hardened heart, the supercilious and begrudging eye, the obdurate brow, the stiff and haughty neck, the violent and misplaced hand, the running legs to evil, the light head, all get their due, but nothing stands out more than the tenfold references to the sins of the mouth—vain utterances, gossipy tongue, slanderous speech, false words, deceptive promises, cynical asides, insolent tone, foul language, idle words, and lip-alone confessions.

Dr. Reuven Kimelman is professor of classical Judaica at Brandeis University. He is the author of *The Mystical Meaning of Lekha Dodi and Kabbalat Shabbat* and of the audio books *The Moral Meaning of the Bible* and *The Hidden Poetry of the Jewish Prayerbook*. He contributed to *Who by Fire, Who by Water—Un'taneh Tokef* (Jewish Lights).

Even before Yom Kippur begins we get this all-important emphasis on words. The leitmotif of the pre–Yom Kippur Shabbat Shuvah ("Sabbath of Return") provides these two verses from Hosea 14:2–3:

> Return, O Israel, to Adonai your God,
> for you have fallen because of your sin.
> Take words with you and return to Adonai.
> Say to Him: "Forgive all guilt and accept what is good;
> Instead of bulls we will pay (the offering of) our lips."

Returning to God demands words, for the path of repentance is paved with words. They include, says the prophet, "Forgive all guilt and accept what is good." The meaning of "good" here is debatable: some say it is good deeds, others a good heart, and still others words of contrition. The last fits the alternative rendition of the last line, which has been read as *p'rei s'fateinu*, not *parim s'fateinu*, giving us, "We will pay with the fruit of our lips," that is, "words."

This concern with words in prayer accounts also for that most oft-repeated verse in the liturgy appearing some five times in the daily liturgy alone, namely, Psalm 78:38. It says: "But He, being merciful [*v'hu rachum*], forgave iniquity and would not destroy. He restrained his wrath time and again, and did not give full vent to his fury." God's mercy here should be understood in the light of verse 36 of this psalm, which deals with insincere and deceitful speech: "Yet they deceived Him with their speech, lied to Him with their words." This explains the beginning *vav* of *v'hu rachum*, which is rightly translated as "but," meaning "nonetheless." Even though "they deceived Him with their speech," *nonetheless* God was merciful enough to restrain his wrath.

The repetition of this verse demonstrates the centrality of requesting forgiveness for insincere and deceitful speech. Accordingly, the verse introduces the evening service. It was also common once to start the afternoon service with it, and it opens the *Tachanun* ("Supplications") for Monday and Thursdays. It once began Psalm 145 (*Ashrei*) as well, and even in the medley of psalm verses appended to the morning *Hodu*, it begins the threefold mention of mercy.

The point is that as we start to use words in prayer, we are struck by how words are otherwise used—a recognition that easily induces the request for God's mercy upon us! This same awareness accounts for the prayer appended to the *Amidah*. Although the Talmud provides over ten examples of personal prayers coined by different rabbis after their *Amidah*, the one that was incorporated into the siddur is that of Mar the son of Ravina, *Eloha'i n'tzor l'shoni meira* ("My God, keep my tongue from speaking evil and my lips from speaking deceit").

In sum, it turns out that our liturgy frequently begins with a request for atonement and ends with an appeal to use words for moral elevation, not debasement.

It is therefore not surprising that the Day of Atonement should open with a concern for the use and misuse of language. Explanations for *Kol Nidre* often revert to its historical origins, but (as the essays in part 1 of this book make clear) those origins are shrouded in mystery and rarely what the authors who use history to justify it want it to be. Another way of looking at it is the halakhic perspective of annulling vows, but the halakhic issues involved are too obscure for such a popular prayer. In any case, what is lacking in these explanations is a sustaining reason behind the continuation of the practice through time. Why things originally came about may not be connected to why they are maintained.

The almost universal feeling that Yom Kippur *must* begin with *Kol Nidre* is an existential reflection on what we know about words: to verbalize is to pledge. *Kol Nidre* impresses upon us that when we speak, we inevitably put our lives on the line, uttering promises in the making. Even were we prevented from fulfilling them, the issue is of sufficient gravity as to demand a formal, even legal, as it were, ceremony of nullification.

The consequentiality of words is reinforced by the poetics of *Kol Nidre*. It can be divided into five units:

1. All vows [*nidrei*], esarei, charamei, konamei, substitute formulae [*kinuyei*], kinusei, and oaths [*sh'vu'ot*]": This opening unit features *nidrei* and then six other nouns for "pledges," all joined together, five of which are trisyllabic, marked by hard consonants, and ending with "ei."

2. "That we have vowed [declared as a *neder*], sworn [declared as a *sh'vu'ah*], and declared *cherem* and prohibited [as an *issar*] upon ourselves": This second unit transforms four of the nouns of the first unit into first person verbs. Besides the conjunctives, each has four syllables, opening with a "d" sound and closing with a "na"

sound (*dindarna, d'ishtabana, d'achareimna, di'asarna*). Even the final term, *nafshatana* ("upon ourselves") has four syllables and ends with a "na."

3. "From this Yom Kippur until the following one—may it come upon us for good—all of these we regret": This is the third unit, but I will return to it at the end. For now, note how it does not fit. Unlike the Aramaic of the rest of *Kol Nidre*, it is in the Hebrew save for the last phrase. Were we to skip the Hebrew and continue with the last phrase, *kulhon icharatna v'hon* ("all of these we regret"), we would note that its middle word *icharatna* rhymes with the previous word, *nafshatana*, while the rest of it is alliterative and assonant with the next phrase *kulhon y'hon sharan* ("they all shall be permitted"). The two are linked by the sound "*hon*," which concludes four of the six words.

4. "They all shall be permitted, abandoned, put to rest, voided and made void, invalidated and made nonexistent." As noted, unit four begins with *kulhon y'hon sharan*. The "sh" sound of the last word leads into the eight remaining words of the unit. The first two continue the "sh" sound with the alliterative and assonant pair *sh'vikin sh'vitin* ("abandoned, put to rest") followed by the comparable pair *b'telin um'vutalin* ("voided and made void"). In the wake of these two couplets consisting of four words ending with "in" come two more two-worded couplets, *la sh'ririn v'la kayamin* ("invalidated and made nonexistent"), which start with *la*, and end with the same "in" of the previous four words.

5. "Our vows are not vows, our *esarei* are not *esarei*, and our oaths are not oaths": The last unit displays an even more remarkable rhyme scheme. Its nine words are divided into threes, creating what is almost a pervasive triple rhyme (*nidrana la nidrei, esarana la esarei, sh'vu'atana la sh'vu'ot*). The use of *la* in the middle of the three phrases links it to the *la* of the last two phrases of the previous unit. The first two phrases, *nidrana la nidrei, ve-esarana la esarei* ("our vows are not vows, our *esarei* are not *esarei*"), recall the first two of unit one; the third, *ush'vu'atana la sh'vu'ot* ("and our oaths are not oaths"), recalls the last of unit one. By mentioning the beginning two and the final closing one, all are included. Adding "na" ("our") to the three terms evokes also the second unit with its four terms for oaths ending with "na." The result is seven terms

for promises ending with "ei," seven terms for nullification—six ending with "in," one with "an"—and seven verbs of commitment ending with "na." The drive for seven is already evident in unit one, which, in seeking to be exhaustive, extends the list of synonyms for vows to include technical, vernacular, and even no longer applicable cultic terms. Apparently, seven stands for the total range. In any case, *Kol Nidre* is rung together by the end recapitulating the beginning and sewn together by the threefold use of seven for its major elements.

The linkage of sounds creates a rhetorical pattern where a sound of one unit gets repeated in the next unit tying unit one to two, two to three, three to four, and four to five. This creates a staircase crescendo effect that goes back one step only to jump forward two steps. The concordance of sound enhances the poem's auditory impact through a complex crisscrossing of alliteration and assonance. The result is a starting and stopping that prolongs the articulation, slowing the chanting to *lentissimo*. Each term gets individually heard, savored, and mulled over. As every cantor knows, tone, pitch, and pace give it its dramatic quality. By spanning the vocal range from simple cantillation to full musical figuration with timely sighs and sobs, emotions are brought to a pitch. The incantatory melody spooks us into confronting the year that just slipped through our fingers. By referring to the past year in the Sephardi traditional version or to the coming year in the revised Ashkenazi version, we end up pondering a whole year where, admittedly, our vows were not vows. Quite aware that our past record does not bode well for the future, we fear lest the best of our intentions in the coming year also come to naught.

At the center of *Kol Nidre* is the paradox of the middle unit, to which we said we would return. The Ashkenazi version, "from this Yom Kippur until the next Yom Kippur" no longer mentions the voiding of past vows but prays instead that unfulfilled vows *in the coming year* not be held against us. That assumes, however, that we will be around by next Yom Kippur, an assumption that mitigates the urgency of the entire day! Isn't the whole point of Yom Kippur the possibility that we will not end up being sealed for life after all?

This upbeat assumption to the contrary is strengthened by the ritual response (Numbers 15:26), "The whole Israelite community and the stranger residing among them shall be forgiven, for it happened to the entire people through error." By concluding this way, *Kol Nidre* assures us that whatever vows we cannot fulfill are deemed inadvertent, not deliberate, and susceptible, therefore, to forgiveness. What better way to enter Yom Kippur!

⚮

All Bets Are Off

Rabbi Lawrence Kushner

Context shapes meaning. *When* something is read may determine what it *means* more than what it *says*. Take *Kol Nidre* for example. How the proclamation began, what its author(s) originally intended, or, indeed, even its contemporary translations are superseded and overwhelmed by when it is heard by the Jews.

In the words of a former congregant, "*Kol Nidre* means: All bets are off." For him and, I now suspect, for most Jews, hearing *Kol Nidre* is like the sound of flipping that silent software switch that anyone who has ever fiddled with a computer has discovered with relief and joy: Restore Default Configuration. Go back to zero. Clean slate. Fresh start. You see before you on the screen one simple question: Begin New Game? In other words, everything that has been promised (and everything that might yet be promised), everything that has been said (and everything that might yet be said), everything that has been done (and everything that might yet be done)—they're all erased, null and void. You get a

Rabbi Lawrence Kushner is the Emanu-El Scholar at Congregation Emanu-El of San Francisco and the author of many books on Jewish spirituality and mysticism, including *I'm God; You're Not: Observations on Religion and Other Disguises of the Ego*; *The Way Into Jewish Mystical Tradition*; *Honey from the Rock*; *The Book of Letters: A Mystical Alef-bait* (all Jewish Lights); and his novel, *Kabbalah: A Love Story*. He contributed to all volumes of the *My People's Prayer Book: Traditional Prayers, Modern Commentaries* series, winner of the National Jewish Book Award, as well as to *My People's Passover Haggadah: Traditional Texts, Modern Commentaries,* a finalist for the National Jewish Book Award, and to *Who by Fire, Who by Water—Un'taneh Tokef* (all Jewish Lights).

roomful of people all hoping for that and you have yourself the holiest prayer in the book.

I am reminded here of a curiously and surprisingly similar, but less well-known, liturgical formula initiating the Passover festival almost six months away. We take all the crumbs we collected during the preceding evening's search and set them on fire. Then we recite, *Kol chamira v'chami'a* ... (also in Aramaic), proclaiming null and void "all kinds of leaven" in our possession, whether we have found it or not; even the leaven we didn't find and didn't even know about is magically declared out of existence, "like the dust of the earth." It's the identical and liberating notion that, in order to begin a new time, we must nullify everything from the old time.

In a similar vein, Rabbi Jack Reimer once taught me that, on Yom Kippur, we dress up like our own corpses. We don't eat or drink, perfume or deodorize ourselves, or have sex. We wear white; some even wear their burial costume. In this way, Yom Kippur effectively rehearses not only our own physical deaths but also the death of the old year, the death of the old ego. You want that something new should come from you? Then you must, first, let go of everything you have been or thought you would be: *Kol Nidre*. It squeezes the last crumbs from our collective psyche.

Hasidism elevates this spiritual emptiness, all-bets-are-offness to the level of ontological reality. The dissolving of oneself into the ocean of divine possibility and rebirth is called entering the *Ayin*, the Holy and Ultimate Nothingness. In the words of the Hasidic master Rabbi Dov Baer of Mezritch:

> Nothing can change from one form to another—for example an egg that would hatch into a chick, without first completely nullifying its present form, which is to say, the egg. Only then will another form be able to come forth from it. It is this way with everything in the world: it must attain the level of *Ayin*, Nothingness. Then it will be able to become something else."[1]

In the same way, before we can initiate the process of atonement and returning to God, we must first relinquish everything we have said (or been) and everything we expect to say (or be). We chant the *Kol Nidre*.

I am grateful to Rabbi Dan Shevitz who first brought this story by Elimelekh of Lizhensk to my attention.[2] Once a very wicked man came to the rebbe seeking atonement. The rebbe consented to help him, but only on the condition first, that the man would liquidate all his assets—the jewelry, the real estate, everything—and second, that he put in writing every sin he had ever committed. After months, the man returned with a suitcase filled with cash and a sheaf of papers filled with sins. As the rebbe read the list he was horrified and then repulsed by their depravity. The rebbe moaned; the man fainted. The rebbe revived him and went on with the reading. Again and again, seven times, the rebbe would cry out in sadness and the man would pass out.

When Rabbi Elimelekh had completed reading the list, the man was white as a sheet. The rebbe sighed: "Only death could atone for such a life!"

"I will do whatever you say," said the man.

Now the rebbe turned white, for he realized that he had inadvertently pronounced an irrevocable death sentence. "Very well," said the rebbe. "In such cases, the death sentence is to be carried out by pouring molten lead down the throat."

"I will do whatever you say," replied the penitent, again.

The rebbe instructed the man to take some of the money from the suitcase and buy a ladle, some lead, and some tin for the flux and then to come back with his siddur and a blindfold.

Together Rabbi Elimelekh and the man watched as the metals became liquified over the fire's heat. "Are you sure you want to go through with this?" the rebbe asked.

"Yes."

"Are you sure that all your sins are recorded on the list? God forbid your death should miss a sin."

"Yes."

"And, are you sure that by your death you mean to make atonement for all your sins."

"Yes."

"Very well," said the rebbe. "Then put on the blindfold and recite the words of the *Sh'ma*."

The man did so.

"Now, open your mouth," said the rebbe.

The man opened his mouth.

But then, at the last moment, Rabbi Elimelekh, instead poured a spoonful of marmalade into the man's open mouth.

"Since you have been willing to suffer your own death," said the rebbe, "it is accounted you by heaven as if you had actually died. Here, go take this money. Spend it like a mensch."

☙

The Room with No Back, Only Forward

Rabbi Noa Kushner

I t's so true it's almost cliché: the hardest part of *t'shuvah* (turning, chang-ing, repentance) is admitting, at long last, that there is a problem, and the problem is within *us*. The purpose of *Kol Nidre* is to bring us this unsettling idea, so that we might begin to change.

It is a natural defense instinct: Many of us enter the room on Yom Kippur with the illusion that we are only observers. We don't really imag-ine that the meaning of *our* lives will be decided over the next few hours. We sit toward the back, readying ourselves to be witnesses to the service, distant participants.

But *Kol Nidre* quickly gets personal, through an unflinchingly per-sonal reach that embraces everyone in the room; as it touches and then cap-tures us, one by one, we discover that the room we are in suddenly has no back and no observers. Wherever we are sitting, we are each in the thick of it, all of us the same. Everyone is welcome, and everyone is guilty of something.

Kol Nidre, then, takes us from dispassion to engagement; from the protective stance with which we enter to the self-implication with which we leave: this moment is about "me," not someone else. How does the prayer accomplish this transformation? The way any good counselor would: in stages.

Noa Kushner is founding rabbi of The Kitchen. One part indie-*Shabbat* community, one part San Francisco experiment, and one part tool kit for DYI Jewish practice. The Kitchen is building a connected, spiritually alive Jewish generation and a new resonance approach to religious life. She con-tributed to *Who by Fire, Who by Water—Un'taneh Tokef* (Jewish Lights).

Stage 1: "I am not guilty like those people, but I can still pray with them."

Kol Nidre begins the service. The first three lines place us, without any preparation, before a heavenly court.[1] Although we may prefer to imagine ourselves as the judges, the jury, or even the lawyers, we are actually the defendants, the ones on trial. Immediately, we are presented with the idea that, just by being in the room, maybe just by being alive, we are being judged. What we do matters.

Even with our acceptance that we are on trial, however, we quite naturally continue to imagine our innocence. *Kol Nidre*, we conveniently assume, is a plea provided for all the *others*, the really guilty ones who surround us like defendants on a courtroom bench.

Cleverly, the third line of *Kol Nidre* does not try to disabuse us of this fiction:

> In front of the *yeshivah* of the heavens / and the *yeshivah* below
> In the name of God ("the place") and in the name of the holy community
> *We are permitted to pray with those who have fallen.*[2]

Even by this third line, we have not yet admitted anything. We acknowledge only that if there are *others* in the room who are guilty, we are not forbidden from praying with *them*. In a cunning move, without requiring a single admission of personal guilt, *Kol Nidre* focuses our attention on the possibility of wrongdoing among us. Then, as we pray collectively, our prayers and the prayers of "the guilty" are mingled further. What was once strictly "theirs" has become partly "ours."

Stage 2: "I'm not guilty now but might be in the future."

The beginning of *Kol Nidre* proper lists the many ways that we break our promises, the obvious implication being a jump to the straightforward admission of our guilt. But at this point the ritual refers only explicitly to the future, "from this Yom Kippur to the next," as if those broken promises have not yet happened, but might still occur.

This emphasis on the future softens what might otherwise be a difficult step. Rather than admit to things that are already broken and over, we instead invoke imaginary future promises gone sour and, in the same breath, try to mitigate any consequences. We start not with remorse but with prevention, as if we were protecting a newborn who might get into trouble.

But we have to admit that the preventive urge arises out of our experiential knowledge of our failures, which begin to come more clearly into view. And so, in this convoluted way, without asking us to admit to anything we have done, the prayer has brought us face to face with our own limitations. By praying for a release from what may (we reluctantly admit) become broken vows and unfulfilled oaths, we simultaneously construct a bridge to what we have already done.

In asking us to sign on for a kind of insurance policy against future mess-ups, *Kol Nidre* helps us to acknowledge that mistakes are inevitable and that falling is an integral part of life. Even the most rigid among us would be hard pressed now to ignore the mounting evidence against his or her innocence. Envisioning the future as sure to include our own mistakes, not just those of others, we arrive at the irrefutable conclusion that we do more than sit *among* the guilty; we *are* the guilty—this is part of being human. But being human also includes the possibility of transformation. We remember that once claimed, failure can redeem.

Stage 3: "Forgive Us"

In contrast to *Kol Nidre*'s methodical, legal, and repetitive feel, a function of its redundant Aramaic text that constitutes "the request," the following three pieces of Torah that make up "the response" are quick and to the point. It's as if the prayer wants to convey the immediate reward we can expect from an admission of our guilt. There is no dwelling on what has already happened, or the damage we have done. As we tentatively attempt to inhabit the room where the failures in question are now our own, we are bolstered by a series of promises of complete forgiveness.

The first verse (Numbers 15:26) explicitly denotes the future. We have just asked for relief only from the mistakes we might still make, so this text announces, "The whole Israelite community and the stranger residing among them *will be* forgiven."

If we look closely, we notice a "missing" verb: *ki l'chol ha'am bishga-gah*, "for [*it was done*] by all the people in error."[3] Having no verb in the past tense reinforces the message: we must see beyond the guilt of the past so that we have the strength to seek forgiveness. The emphasis, moreover, is on the collectivity, not the individual; out of twelve words, nine are devoted to the description of the community.

The next two verses (Numbers 14:19–20) occur sequentially in Torah and replay a scene of asking and granting forgiveness in a pivotal moment of Israel's history. These words are the very ones Moses uses to beg for our forgiveness after we sent the spies to scout Israel, rather than trust in God's promises to us. As we consider *t'shuvah* and the possibility of change, this verse reminds us that faith is paramount. We cannot wait for guarantees. It was skeptical fear that caused our ancestors to panic and withdraw from taking possession of their next stage in life: settling the promised Land of Israel; and it is the same skeptical fear that causes us to panic and withdraw from our own next stage of life: settling into the promises that follow *t'shuvah*, "change." We need to trust that speaking our failures will not lead to our demise; quite the contrary, saying them will set us free.

Finally and immediately, upon making the request, it is granted: *Salachti kidvarekha*, "I have forgiven, according to your word." It seems, in fact, not just simultaneous, but anticipatory—by the time we ask for forgiveness, we already have it, for God does not say, "I forgive," but "I have forgiven." And this forgiveness is given as a direct connection with *our* word, *kidvarekha*. At the end, but only at the end, the ritual of *Kol Nidre* turns from the future to the past. Daring finally to look back, we see there was nothing to fear after all; there was and is only divine forgiveness.

꧁꧂

Imagining Nothing

Liz Lerman

My father, a great social activist and an ecstatic Jew, often quoted Torah, though I was never sure how accurate he was. One of his favorites: "The Torah says you change the world one person at a time," as if the scroll were some kind of backup band, adding emphasis to the grand libretto of his life, reciting the words that he sang to my brothers and me every day: change the world, make it better.

In my life as a choreographer I have often needed to hear my father's words lest I take off after bigger audiences and misguided ambitions. I have to believe that changing one person at a time is at least a useful act. But lately I have been musing that it works the other way too; you can change the world one person at a time, or one person can actually change the world, even when they don't know the potential impact of their actions. The history of *Kol Nidre* contains such a person, and that person is the grandson of Rashi, called by many names but for our purpose here, Rabbenu Tam. Why am I curious about him? Rabbenu Tam changed time.

As both a dancer and a choreographer, I care about time. In my world, time's passing is first and foremost a physical thing: the way we

---

Liz Lerman is founding artistic director of the Liz Lerman Dance Exchange. A member of Temple Micah in Washington, D.C., she was the Sally Priesand Visiting Professor at Hebrew Union College–Jewish Institute of Religion. She is the recipient of the National Foundation for Jewish Culture Award in Performing Arts, the American Jewish Congress "Golda" award, and a MacArthur Fellowship. Her latest book is *Hiking the Horizontal.* She contributed to *Who by Fire, Who by Water—Un'taneh Tokef* (Jewish Lights).

actually inhabit our bodies in this business of living from moment to moment. But it is also an emotional and intellectual activity.

The dancer in me combines them all—physical, emotional, and intellectual—responding to timing in countless ways. I might notice it by preparing to be on the next beat correctly along with my ensemble. I might find meaning in its use by the way I engage one arm in a slow passage across the body to cause tension, or stretch. And in order to get that movement right in tone, or dynamics, I might have to pay attention both to the arm and to the way I shift my weight to sustain the slowness—in which case, I have to be aware of both standing leg and moving arm, putting me, as it were, in two places at one and the same moment.

The choreographer in me uses time to communicate: time becomes a fact, a datum of information. The way I manipulate bodies in time carries enormous expressive power to those doing the movement and to those doing the watching.

Time is also history, the unfolding actions of our lives, as well as memory. As I age, my relationship to time changes. The parts of my own history and that of my many communities that I choose to bring forward to the present are involved and evolving. I need help navigating these dilemmas of time and find that law and ritual help me deal with it all. From the American Supreme Court all the way back through the rabbis of the Middle Ages, I find attempts to create systems that allow us to regulate our memories as we live with the passage of time.

So what did Rabbenu Tam do? He changed our relationship to the sense of time. How did he do that? He simply said, that at the moment of *Kol Nidre*, we will stop focusing on what we have done in the past and think instead of what lies ahead in our future.

But how did he do this? What made him think of this idea, of changing the tense of such an important prayer / legal document? And why was it more important than it looks? I imagine a "just so" story, the way it just might have happened.

Let us conjure up the life of Abraham ibn Ezra. He too is a Talmudic scholar, poet, writer, and also something of a scientist. After leaving Spain he traveled for many years and is said to have crossed paths with Rabbenu Tam, with whom he was contemporary.

Imagine then, these two men meeting. What do they do when they meet?

They must start by exchanging Torah, either speaking their words or handing over written copies. And then they walk together, the words coming sideways, and nesting among the trees or the horizon; from time to time, they must stop talking to look down and make sure they do not tumble. I like this on-again, off-again approach. Functional silences allow for space, breath, and reflection on what the other person has said. So they are walking together and discussing "their work."

Ibn Ezra recounts his travels. He says that while in India he has learned of a system of numbers, including a new one: zero. It means many things. In fact they have thirty-three words to describe it. It also means unity, chaos, emptiness, the beginning, or really just before the beginning.

This idea is difficult. Rabbenu Tam shivers a little. "What do you mean before the beginning?"

Ibn Ezra cannot say.

That night, men gather from all around to hear Ibn Ezra, news of whose presence has spread by word of mouth. He discusses Torah but also numbers. His listeners seem uninterested, however, in a numerical system with the complexities of a zero. This, he notices, is true wherever he travels in the Jewish world. They ask him Torah, not numbers. They are not like Rabbenu Tam, who had been such an avid listener earlier in the day.

Ibn Ezra and Rabbenu Tam meet again the next day, and this time Rabbenu Tam begins the conversation. "I have been thinking ... about the zero. The nothing. The empty space. Let me tell you my problem," says Rabbenu Tam. And then he begins to recount the difficulty of the ruptures in his community, the long lines of people waiting to complain about petty things someone said or did. He tells people that maybe these hurtful words and deeds were unintended, and anyway, they are small matters that should not take up so much of a person's life. Imagine life as a "space of time" totally cluttered by hurtful things that fill up all the space, leaving no room for joy, for creativity, for God.

"Zero is also a space," says Ibn Ezra. He means actually a space-, or place-, holder, but in itself, zero is empty.

"Imagine zero, then," thinks Rabbenu Tam, "as a space in life that is empty of complaints and hurtful things said or done." That would make it timeless too, for it is a kind of nothingness, neither past nor future, just an in-between space with nothing in it."

On the third and last day of their visit, the two men are thinking about the Days of Awe that are approaching. "I have a garment that is a sieve," says Ibn Ezra. "I take it out at night and spread it like a tent, and then stars pierce it with their gleams."[1]

Rabbenu Tam laughs, "My community is like that. It surrounds and covers me, yet I can see through it. In fact," he adds, "I had a dream last night in which the sky was my congregation, with lights everywhere, each and every one of them a face, twinkling over me, but also ready to pounce ... to spring into my every pathway with their needs and complaints." He now returns to the idea of a "zero" space in someone's life. What if he could gently move these people to a place of zero, where for the briefest of time there was no history and no future, just the emptiness of a present where everything is possible?

In a creative leap of thought, he imagines telling people that this year they may sit for a moment in between time. This Yom Kippur, they will say *Kol Nidre* differently. Looking ahead, not past, they will be freed from petty thoughts of what has already happened, yet still not be in a place where what is yet to happen has actually occurred. They will be at point zero, ready to begin anew.

If people step out of the past, maybe some of the scars that get ripped open at every opportunity can actually heal. Maybe we could start praying from an empty place of now.

My father also believed we were descended from Rashi. I had always thought this was more metaphor than fact—something about the lineage of the Jewish people and our connection to each other. But on the day I came home to tell him I was going to marry the storyteller Jon Spelman, I saw that this reached well beyond abstract idealism. Dad seemed a little disappointed at the news, as I think he was still worrying about my financial situation due to my chosen profession, dancer and choreographer, and I know he was hoping for a doctor son-in-law. I wasn't sure it would help to tell him that Jon's family had been on the Mayflower, but I told him that historical nugget, hoping he would be assuaged. He wasn't. Instead he stated in a loud and somewhat belligerent voice, "Well, you just go tell that family that you are related to Rashi."

Maybe my father, in the passion of the moment, was telling a lie. Really, it doesn't matter that this virtual oath, "You are related to Rashi," might have been a purposeful transgression, a man hoping that his daughter would be all right in her future. Because every year, whether together in the actual synagogue or separated by the thousand miles between our homes, my father and I would be at *Kol Nidre* occupying a space between past and future, living with the knowledge that at least for the next year we had protection for our passionate frailties and a space to imagine anew.

And I got this protection because a supposed relative of mine, Rabbenu Tam, talked to a traveling mathematician and imagined nothing.

◠◦◠

A Vote of No Confidence

Catherine Madsen

Adonai, we are your people and you are our God, before and after we sin. Bind us not by our intentions, not even by our sworn promises, whose force you annul as the wind scatters the chaff; bind us only by our return to you, naked of honor as we came out of the womb.

What are we without our vows? We become like children or invalids, without anchoring responsibilities. To be released from our vows is to be released from our purpose: unmoored, cut adrift, abandoned. The cancellation of vows—before they are made, no less—is as much a dismay as a relief.

Kol Nidre is not an absolution but a vote of no confidence. It presupposes that we cannot be trusted: we make vows and fail to fulfill them, we make the wrong vows, we are inconstant, faithless, hapless. The prayer is prefaced by a declaration that we are permitted to pray with sinners. Who else is there to pray with?

There is a certain dignity in the list: the enumeration of vows, renunciations, bans, oaths, formulas of obligation, pledges, and promises—and

Catherine Madsen is the author of *The Bones Reassemble: Reconstituting Liturgical Speech*; *In Medias Res: Liturgy for the Estranged*; and a novel, *A Portable Egypt*. She is a lay leader at High Holy Day services at the Jewish Community of Amherst, Massachusetts, and bibliographer at the National Yiddish Book Center. She contributed to *Who by Fire, Who by Water— Un'taneh Tokef* (Jewish Lights).

then their nullifications: undone, repealed, cancelled, voided, annulled, regarded as neither valid nor binding. The prayer tolls. At stroke of midnight God shall win. Then where is dignity?

There is no automatic relationship between making a vow and knowing how to fulfill it. Countless divorced people know this. There can even be an inverse relationship between the public display of taking a vow and the private ability to keep it. To some unmarried couples (including some gay and lesbian couples, not all of whom are desperate to be married), the making of public promises suggests not a need to declare and celebrate the relationship but a need to shore it up: not a triumph of social equality but a doubt of one's attention span. Married couples who "renew their vows" call into question the original vows' validity; they undermine the very principle of performative speech by trying to perform it once more for good measure. Meaning to reinforce the vow, they demonstrate its flimsiness. How can the new vow sustain the relationship if the old vow could not? How can it even signal the shift of understanding that *will* sustain the relationship?

The Torah, and still more the rabbinic mind, is ambivalent about vows. While teasing out the implications of a talmudic discussion on the nazirite vows and the suspected wife's ordeal of the bitter waters, Rabbi Ira Stone concludes that "the vow is a perversion of language" which "undermines the stability of all social relationships" by destroying their voluntary nature. In biblical and rabbinic usage, a vow tends to be something supererogatory, ascetic: one forbids oneself something that is generally permitted. The *nazir* refrains from wine and from haircuts, and avoids all contact with the dead. In the case of a husband who imposes an ascetic vow on his wife, Stone says, "The marriage relationship ... is undermined by vows. How much more so the other relationships of society. How much more so the relationship between the individual and God."[1]

How voluntary, though, is the relationship between the individual and God? Like Jewish marriage, it is essentially not a vow but a contract: our observance of the *mitzvot* will be rewarded with well-being and our dereliction punished with misery. But it is a contract initiated by God, who consistently chooses people against their will. The metaphors of father and king, out of favor at present, are unsettling partly for their accuracy: a father begets us, and a king holds our fate in his hands, whether we like it or not. God chooses us whether we like it or not, and our modest protestations against being singled out do not spare us, any more than reluctance spared Moses or Jeremiah or Jonah. This is God as exigency, interruption, the intrusion of an unopposable will. We are free to abandon religion, but that does not solve the problem; exigency and interruption pursue us, they are in the nature of things. In the end we have to decide—this is the only way to stay sane—to absorb the interruption, to proceed from it, to live deliberately the life we have in place of the life we wanted. To put it in terms of free will and determinism, the only direction in which we can assert our free will is to work voluntarily within a set of conditions we have not determined. ("I accept the universe," said Margaret Fuller. "By God, she'd better!" said Carlyle.)

From the time the Israelites said *Na'aseh v'nishma*, "We will do and we will hear," and then went on to make the golden calf, we have been ambivalent about God. Both the Torah and our history give strong evidence of God's ambivalence toward us. Jacob Taubes suggests that what we experience "latently" in *Kol Nidre* is not the repeal of our own vows, but "a repetition of the primal scene, the suspension of the destruction that was sworn by *God*" after the making of the calf.[2] In this reading, the purpose of Yom Kippur is to annul God's own vow, to "dare to release him from his oath." The traditional liturgy is austere and decorous, and lets this purpose remain a hint. But the hint is supported by our insistence on repeating God's thirteen attributes of mercy (Exodus 34:6–7)—without the attributes of justice in the second half of verse 7—and appending to those thirteen attributes the phrase from Exodus 34:9, *V'salachta la'avoneinu ul'chatateinu un'chaltanu*, "Pardon our iniquity and our sin, and take us for your own." By recalling again and again this all biblical scenes, the liturgy insists that God's vows are and should be as breakable as ours.

The last hundred years have made liturgical subtleties inaudible to thinly educated or altogether secular Jews. In another sense, the last hundred years have made these subtleties both more interesting and more urgent: more interesting because psychological theory has made us alert to the repressed, and more urgent because our trust in God has eroded. What became of God's vows during the European destruction? Were they forgotten? Were they fulfilled perversely? Was the God of the 1930s and '40s the God of Deuteronomy 28:63, who delights in destroying and annihilating—by how many ingenious and surely undeserved cruelties—the disobedient people he had once delighted to build up?[3] Is God helpless against a bureaucratic reign of terror, passively malignant in permitting it, or actively interested in its depravity?

Jews of earlier times, who could not walk away from God, could release him from his oath politely, almost imperceptibly, in the guise of annulling their own oaths and seeking forgiveness. We, who stay under protest or attach ourselves against our better judgment, are not content with the barely perceptible. The proposed liturgical revisions calling God to account in David Blumenthal's *Facing the Abusing God* are raw, earnest, and blatant:

> Our Father, our King, forgive and forbear punishment
> for all our purposeful sins.
> Our Father, our King, ask forgiveness and forbearance
> for all Your purposeful sins....
> Our Father, our King, cause us to do complete repen-
> tance before You.
> Our Father, our King, do complete repentance before us.[4]

An accusing people for an abusing God: if we must absorb *this* exigency, *this* interruption, we will do it on our own terms.

Ritual is emblematic, or if you prefer fictive; it is effectual not in itself but in its effects on us, in its concentration and focusing of our experience. Yom Kippur enacts the circuit of failure, shame, atonement, and resolve we travel all year; it succeeds not because it relieves us of our faults but because it makes our faults present to us. It exposes its own fictiveness in Isaiah's denunciation of unrighteous fasting: it mocks our ritual austerities just as we begin to be strongly aware of hunger and thirst. It pits God's justice and God's mercy against each other as almost mutually annihilating—the mercy winning only by a hair—and puts justice and mercy in our own hands as essentially identical, in the relief of hunger and poverty.

The structure of Yom Kippur is not symmetrical; the vows annulled by *Kol Nidre* are not reaffirmed at *N'ilah*. By the end of the fast we have had practice in another kind of commitment; to last out the day is to know something about voluntary relationship. The vows are permanently annulled; our obligations remain.

ᏫᎻᎮᎧ

Over-Promise, Under-Deliver ... and Then Forgive

Rabbi Rachel Nussbaum

Usually this is a casual community: our Shabbat services often take place on picnic blankets spread out on the ground in parks, and people tend to show up in jeans in T-shirts. But tonight we're dressed more formally, many of us in the white of *kittels* and *tallitot*. Our attention is more focused, too, waiting for the service to begin. We chant *Or zarua latzaddik* ("Light is sown for the righteous") as the Torah is removed from the ark and carried in a slow procession around the room. We stand quietly, as before a *bet din* (a court), and we listen to the three-fold chant of *Kol Nidre*, humming it along under our breaths.

The external trappings and the choreography of the *Kol Nidre* service push us to behave more formally, to step out of our usual selves and inhabit the "higher versions"—the selves we aspire to be. The liturgy, too, forces us to consider the gap between who we are and who we wish we were; it encourages us to set our sights higher.

It is striking just how many words *Kol Nidre* uses for talking about our commitments. There are seven distinct terms: (1) *nidrei*—vows, (2)

Rabbi Rachel Nussbaum is rabbi and executive director of the Kavana Cooperative in Seattle, Washington. She was ordained at The Jewish Theological Seminary of America. She was recently awarded an Avi Chai Fellowship for her innovative approach to Jewish community building. She contributed to *Who by Fire, Who by Water—Un'taneh Tokef* (Jewish Lights).

esarei—restrictions, (3) *charamei*—special pledges, (4) *konamei*—vows of abstinence, (5) *kinuyei*—verbal commitments, (6) *kinusei*—vows carrying penalties, and (7) *sh'vu'ot*—oaths. The sevenfold "redundancy" of terminology signals importance, especially because seven is a key number denoting completion, as the seven days of creation. It is impossible to read *Kol Nidre* and not understand just how seriously we Jews are supposed to take our commitments. The promises we make are real, and of utmost consequence.

But as seriously as the liturgy seems to take vows, the flip side of the coin is our declaration that the vows that we will make in the coming year should not be understood as binding. In fact, we nullify them completely as we declare that our vows are not vows, our restrictions are not restrictions, and our oaths are not oaths. In doing so, we recognize that we are only human, and therefore we cannot possibly be expected to uphold all of our commitments.

At first blush, it seems that we've just walked into quite a paradox. Out of one side of our mouths, we declare that our obligations are central and of utmost importance, while out of the other side, we simultaneously write them off as unattainable. How can we reconcile this tension?

The truth is that we do not. This is a tension that we all know; we live with it day in and day out; Yom Kippur simply highlights it for us. Even if we cannot always achieve what we set out to do, we still need to articulate aspirations for ourselves. The many kinds of vows, pledges, and oaths that *Kol Nidre* denotes refer to this highly aspirational part of human nature. Its point is to signal to us that despite our awareness that we will necessarily fall short, we still should set a high bar for ourselves in advance. This is far preferable to setting mediocre standards and achieving them.

Perhaps this sounds like a trite idea, but rest assured that it is not. A popular business adage would advise us to "under-promise, over-deliver"—in other words, set low standards for what others should expect so that that we can exceed those expectations and seem great in comparison. While there may be practical benefit to living by "under-promise, over-deliver," *Kol Nidre* points us in exactly the opposite direction!

Kol Nidre's directly opposite lesson of "over-promise, under-deliver" has proved particularly relevant to the bonds that guarantee community. When I co-founded the Kavana Cooperative in Seattle in 2006, we drew on preschool and grocery store co-ops for inspiration and settled on a cooperative communal model that requires a very high level of commitment and investment from participants. People who join become "partners" in the cooperative and commit to attending on a regular basis, making a significant financial contribution each year, and taking on a volunteer role.

Last year, a team of partners met to refine the community's mission statement. We spent the greatest amount of time debating whether it was fair to claim that Kavana (among other things) "demands participation in our community." Some felt that this was a stretch: that because we have no mechanism for enforcing such high standards, it was not worth stating them in our mission statement. In the end, it was the other voices in the debate that won out, and ours is now the only mission statement I have read that employs the verb "demand." For decades, many Jewish communal institutions in this country have tried to be more welcoming by lowering the expectations for membership. The example set by our new Jewish community illustrates that, on the contrary, the most compelling models may be the ones that require the most of participants. As the rabbi of this community, I take great pride in the fact that we set our sights so high, even knowing that not all of our community's partners will be able to live up to the high ideal of participation and volunteerism.

Finally, it is worth drawing attention to the fact that *Kol Nidre* proceeds immediately from the annulment of vows to three verses from Numbers that contain the same root word for forgiveness: *v'nislach, s'lach na*, and *salachti*. This progression drives home the point that *Kol Nidre* is not only about setting high standards, but also about offering understanding and forgiveness when people falter. In these verses, it is God who does the pardoning. So by setting a high bar but then forgiving ourselves and others when we fail to reach it, we act in accordance with the concept of *imitatio dei*, emulating the divine.

All of this is a good reason to treat *Kol Nidre* with unusual formality and respect. After all, it is not every day that we have the opportunity to affirm publicly the importance of setting our sights high, even if the goals we set are not totally achievable; and not every day either do we get the chance to guarantee understanding and forgiveness for ourselves and others.

⌘

Courting Inversion
KOL NIDRE AS LEGAL DRAMA
Rabbi Aaron Panken, PhD

L egal dramas are all the rage these days. It is close to impossible to watch late-night television without chancing upon a forensic scientist in a sparklingly white lab coat brilliantly developing damning evidence to put a perpetrator behind bars; or a well-dressed attorney passionately convincing a jury to save his client from a certain death penalty; or a team of good-looking FBI agents protecting a sequestered witness from those out to prevent her from testifying. Not to mention the non-criminal, so-called "reality based" offerings of the Judge Judy ilk. Such is the standard fare endlessly repeated in the dark hours of cable offerings.

But in synagogue? In shul on Yom Kippur, we hardly expect high legal drama in place of our regular sorts of prayer.

By "regular prayer," I refer to the common claim that at its core, Jewish worship comprises three essential forms: praise, petition, and thanksgiving. These three forms, it is imagined, direct the most natural of human reactions toward God, each one reflecting human recognition of the divine presence in concrete and understandable ways. Praise expresses our sense of awe and wonder, particularly prompted by God's overwhelming creation that surrounds us; petition pleads for the initiation, continuation, or expansion of divine benefits, for ourselves and for those

---

Rabbi Aaron Panken, PhD, teaches Rabbinic and Second Temple literature at Hebrew Union College–Jewish Institute of Religion. He contributed to *Who by Fire, Who by Water—Un'taneh Tokef* (Jewish Lights).

we love; while thanksgiving renders an emotional response to the realization of how greatly we are blessed.

These three forms more or less cover the basic "prayer waterfront," but some authors also discern still deeper waters, far from shore, where other forms of prayerful expression may lurk. Some view *talmud Torah*—religious study—as prayer (certainly our prayer book is filled with study, after all). When Abraham Joshua Heschel marched for civil rights in Selma, Alabama, he said he felt as if "his legs were praying"—can stirring acts of social justice also be prayer, then? Some call music, dance, visual art, and sacred architecture independent forms of prayer. Others see praying through yoga, meditation, and divergent forms of enhanced mindfulness as the most meaningful worship possible. Still others advocate nothing more than simple silence to bring the worshiper to new heights of religious understanding.

And yet, in this hefty list of prayer potentialities, *Kol Nidre* is unique. Nowhere else do we find another case quite like it. Creating religious meaning through enacting a communal court proceeding to release vows is simply *sui generis*. Think about it: Would the reading of charges, their disposition, and the penalties affiliated with them in a modern civil or criminal court actually make for moving religious ritual? Can we imagine heading off to observe a jury box or a *bet din* to find spiritual enlightenment? This intentional use of a courtroom setting to create a meaningful prayer ritual is, to my knowledge, unique in Jewish prayer, and unique also to the moment of *Kol Nidre* within it.

With each Yom Kippur's haunting chant of *Kol Nidre*, we are asked to find meaning in this distinctive construct. And what makes *Kol Nidre* so unique is that it represents both the ritualized performance of a court drama and an inversion of that same drama, all rolled into one.

The drama of a courtroom scene implies a tight focus on human accountability that accords well with the other grand themes of Yom Kippur (God as divine judge, inscription for reward or punishment, etc.). The inversion of that scene arrives when the way a court would regularly act is entirely overturned. This mirroring between a court that demands firm justice, and its inversion—a court that dispenses with it—reveals the twin truths that permeate the core ideals of Yom Kippur.

Consider first the court session. It begins with a formal calling into session, an announcement of its source of authority, and a designation of the community it will affect. "In the *yeshivah* above, and the *yeshivah* below; with the knowledge of God and with the knowledge of the congregation; we are hereby permitted to pray with sinners." *Yeshivah*, here, from the root *yashav*, "to sit," represents a technical term—the formal sitting of both heavenly and earthly courts. The process of judgment, here, is duly and dually situated so as to cover the two broad Rabbinic categories of potential sin: "in heaven" for transgressions *bein adam lamakom* (between human beings and God) and "on earth" for transgressions *bein adam lachavero* (between one human being and another). Both God and humanity have thus authorized these legal proceedings, ensuring their complete authority and validity. Court is called to order.

The text next supplies a veritable cornucopia of vow-related terminology worthy of a fine legal thesaurus. This, too, reinforces the formal legal character of the proceedings. Even today, most legal proceedings suffer from an overabundance of what we like to call "legalese"—that hard-to-understand insider jargon that hampers lay comprehension even as it creates a palpable sense of lawyerly authenticity and authority. Legal documents regularly attempt to anticipate all possible variations of a situation by using expansive lists of terms. Take out your copy of a recent lease or mortgage and read all the fine print about what *might* happen, and you will find this tendency at its finest.

This same propensity for detailed technical language now appears in the words of *Kol Nidre*. In reality, many of the terms for vows listed there have long since fallen out of use in regular parlance. But such language heightens the "courtly" feeling and enhances the dramatic tension of the ritual through authentic-sounding legal discourse, creating a strong connection back to our ancient Rabbinic traditions and highlighting the continuity of our collective Jewish story.

Note, as well, that the courtroom scene of *Kol Nidre* utilizes the past tense almost exclusively. This is no surprise, for sitting courts generally do not consider defendants' actions to come—rather they focus on allegations of particular misdeeds the defendants have already committed. But in the contemporary Aramaic text of *Kol Nidre*, we find an odd conflict between the past tense of the vows made and the forward-looking time frame indicated by the words "from this Yom Kippur until the next one." This is a result of the editing of our text over time. *Kol Nidre*, in its original form (before emendation by Rabbi Meir ben Samuel in the eleventh century), released vows taken "from last Yom Kippur until this one," a much more sensible activity for a convened court. This earlier version followed its legal form faithfully, focusing entirely on past vows and releasing them (after all, can one legally release a vow that is not yet made?). Once altered to our current text, "... from this Yom Kippur until the next one," though, *Kol Nidre*'s focus shifted to anticipate vows to come.

How can we resolve this apparent conflict between releasing vows made in the past and addressing future vows as yet unmade? To understand this, a bit of background on the Rabbinic rules of *hatarat nedarim*—the releasing of vows—is helpful. In the Mishnah, Tosefta, and Talmuds,[1] Rabbinic sages had the authority to release individuals from vows. There were divergent opinions, however, as to whether the power to release vows simply inhered in the rabbis themselves, or if they had to locate invalidating errors in the vows themselves to permit their dissolution. Sages often sought problems in intention or formulation that existed at the moment of the origination of the vow. Such problems could include difficulties in the language of the vow, an individual who made a vow while lacking full understanding of the ramifications of his or her statement or the making of a vow lacking true intention to fulfill it, among other possibilities. Any of these problems could be utilized by a Rabbinic sage to invalidate an errant vow.

Here, then, lies the compelling utility of our current version of *Kol Nidre* that speaks mostly in the past tense, yet still anticipates vows made during the coming year. An annual blanket statement that calls into question the formulation or intention of future vows introduces just enough uncertainty to allow the sages (and thus, a court convened before Yom Kippur) to release those vows in the future should the need arise. One opinion in the Babylonian Talmud (Nedarim 23a–b) even suggests that anyone who would wish to release vows in the future ought to make such a comprehensive statement at the beginning of each year (perhaps the *locus classicus* for the entire development of *Kol Nidre*). So, the conflicting past/future temporal structure of *Kol Nidre* actually allows for the creation of a useful uncertainty for future vows, thus generating a preemptive loophole for their subsequent release.

This is where the inverted form of the court scene begins to emerge and where the overall structure starts to make sense. Since vows made previously have presumably had uncertainty injected into them via prior recitations of *Kol Nidre*, a court session can now record their dissolution, thus freeing the individual from his or her past vows. At the same time, the words "from this Yom Kippur until the next one" now create vital precedent for the release of future vows, to be utilized in future recitations of *Kol Nidre*. The inverted part of the court session is, therefore, used to dismiss responsibility for prior actions, as well as prepare for the invalidation of future legal activities. Hardly a normal action for a court.

It is in the penultimate sentence of the prayer where this inversion becomes most evident. In normal Jewish contracts (the *k'tubah*, or marriage contract, for example), we often find the closing words *v'hakol sharir v'kayam*, "and all is valid and binding." In the inverted court system of *Kol Nidre*, all vows and oaths are *la sh'ririn v'la kayamin*, "not valid and not binding." Where we expect a legal statement to verify at its close that all the terms therein are legally in effect, we find precisely the opposite—these vows and oaths are beyond ineffective, for they do not even exist: "The vows we have undertaken are not vows, the restrictions to which we have committed ourselves are not restrictions, and the oaths we have sworn are not oaths."

Through both straightforward and inverted use of Jewish jurisprudential verbiage, then, *Kol Nidre* manages to imbue the moments immediately before Yom Kippur with meaning by addressing both the past and the future. It relies upon the uncertainty it generated in prior years to release individuals from obligations from the past; at the same time, it generates anticipatory uncertainty to allow future releases when their time comes as well. In so doing, *Kol Nidre* becomes the pivot point between the past and the future, between the straightforward and the inverted, and between accountability and release.

It is no accident that in this, the very last moment before Yom Kippur begins, after we have prepared throughout the entire month of Elul and the *Aseret Y'mei T'shuvah* (the Ten Days of Repentance), after we have participated in *tz'dakah*, *t'shuvah*, and *t'fillah*, when we may be wearing white and eschewing leather, and when we are now starting our fast, that we visit the court one last time to do whatever we can to secure a favorable outcome on this ultimate Day of Judgment. These final legal preparations help put the supplicant's house in order before the time of judgment.

In the conclusion of *Kol Nidre* we find the most stunning inversion. In the three final biblical passages the legalistic focus is entirely replaced with an emphasis on forgiveness (*s'lichah*), kindness (*chesed*), and communal cohesion (*l'khol adat b'nei Yisrael*). On Yom Kippur, God is said to move from the seat of judgment to the seat of mercy—converting a judg-

ing sovereign into a loving parent (those two aspects enshrined so beauti-
fully in the *Avinu Malkenu* prayer). Courts, the very seats of justice, normally hear evidence, analyze and apply legal precedent, and render
rational decisions that are fair and just, unaltered by feelings or preju-
dices. Yet in this moment, it is forgiveness and kindness that ultimately
rule the day. Such a conclusion to *Kol Nidre* sends the message that the
ways of judgment on Yom Kippur differ markedly from those of the
everyday—on Yom Kippur, we can be forgiven despite broken vows and
missed obligations, not because we are worthy of being declared innocent, but because God is (and human beings, hopefully, are) merciful.

The ultimate message? If God can invert even the divine court from
justice to mercy at this critical time of year, then, in our judgment of others, so should we.

৩ৠৣৣৣ৩

The *Kol Nidre*
Mirror to Our Soul

Rabbi Sandy Eisenberg Sasso

We call them the Days of Awe. The prayers and the music through-out the liturgy try to capture the solemnity of the season, to lift us up, even if the year has beaten us down. But if we were to choose just a single piece of this liturgical drama that pulls and tugs the hardest at our souls, that draws the most Jews to the synagogue, on time, even if they attend no other day of the year, it would be *Kol Nidre*.

It is as though for a brief moment we are like the figures in a Chagall painting, so very light, floating above the ground, released from the earth's gravitational pull.[1] The ark is opened. Everyone rises. The elders of the congregation, those who sustain the community through service, leadership, and financial contribution, stand holding the Torah scrolls, which are dressed in white. The usual banter ceases. An unaccustomed hush pervades the sacred space.

Then there is music. Some say they come only to hear *Kol Nidre* sung. It is hard to say exactly when it was composed—sixteenth-century Germany is the usual date given—but in any case, the stirring melody so familiar to Ashkenazi Jews has captivated generations. The sounds seem

---

Rabbi Sandy Eisenberg Sasso is senior rabbi of Congregation Beth-El Zedeck in Indianapolis, where she has served since 1977. She is the author of award-winning children's books including *God's Paintbrush* and *Cain and Abel: Finding the Fruits of Peace* (both Jewish Lights). Her first book for adults is *God's Echo: Exploring Scripture with Midrash*. She contributed to *Who by Fire, Who by Water—Un'taneh Tokef* (Jewish Lights).

to come from a deep place in the soul, drawing the community into another, loftier realm.

Upon hearing *Kol Nidre*, Franz Rosenzweig, while on the verge of conversion to Christianity, returned to Judaism and went on to become one of the twentieth century's foremost Jewish philosophers.

A number of years ago, the grandmother of an Indianapolis high school student died. Among the items hidden away in her apartment was a barely used book with a mother-of-pearl cover. It turned out to be a *machzor*—a High Holy Day prayer book; for the first time, the grandson learned that he was Jewish. He was unsure what to do with this newly uncovered family secret, but when he found out what the book actually was, he did know this: he was a cellist and he wanted to learn to play *Kol Nidre*.

But when we look at the words, we have to wonder why the prayer survived, let alone why it commands the attention of the largest Jewish audience of the year. What are we to make of the words? *All the vows, bonds, pledges, obligations, and oaths that we have sworn upon ourselves from this Yom Kippur until next Yom Kippur ... we now request release.... They are not valid nor are they in force. Our personal vows are not vows, our personal bonds are not bonds, our personal oaths are not oaths.*

Originally, the prayer asked for release from promises made, but not honored, in the year just past. In the twelfth century, the prayer was changed in the Ashkenazi liturgy to request release from pledges made from this Yom Kippur to the next. Like it or not, it at least makes sense to ask forgiveness for all those things we pledged in good faith and did not fulfill, but what are we to make of a prayer that virtually guarantees that we will make even more promises and then not keep them? Forgiveness—a priori?

Jewish tradition reminds us that *Kol Nidre* refers only to vows an individual makes to God, not promises made to, or about, other human beings. These vows concerning others are addressed during the Ten Days of Repentance (*t'shuvah*) that precede Yom Kippur, when we seek forgiveness from those we have wronged, and we make amends. The Day of Atonement, by contrast, is the time to make amends to God; it is precisely about us, our personal failings, our inability to be true to ourselves, to God, to the persons we are and hope to become. And yet on this very day, we seem to be saying to God, "Don't count on us. We will likely be untrue to ourselves, to You. We will say what we do not mean; we will promise what we will not keep." But even if only in our relationship to God, it is appropriate to invoke forgiveness—a priori? Isn't that disingenuous, hypocritical?

For this very reason, Rabbi Mordecai Kaplan suggested that we retain the melody and substitute Psalm 130 for the words.[2] (Psalm 130 may have originally opened the Yom Kippur evening service.) He was following a long line of eminent protesters, going back to the eighth century, when rabbinic authorities first heard of the prayer and began condemning it. Rav Amram Gaon, the ninth-century author of our very first comprehensive prayer book, called it *minhag sh'tut*, "a stupid custom"; he, along with other *geonim*, wanted to do away with it.[3] From the early founders of modern Orthodoxy to Reform Judaism, from Rabbi Samson Raphael Hirsch to Rabbi Abraham Geiger, Jewish leaders wanted either to remove the prayer or to change it. But tradition persisted. Over the centuries whenever rabbis, disturbed by the words of *Kol Nidre*, suggested a different text, the community objected. Why?

Kol Nidre begins with these words: "By the authority of the heavenly court and of the earthly court: With the foreknowledge of the God of time and space and with the agreement of this congregation, we give permission to pray with habitual sinners."

Who are those "habitual sinners"?

A Jewish legend associates this prayer with the Jews of Visogothic Spain who were forced to convert to Christianity but who secretly remained Jews. I shall never forget learning the story of one woman who grew up Catholic. Every Friday night she would place two candles on her dinner table and light them. Before kindling the flames, she would turn the picture of Jesus in her dining room to the wall. On the other side of the frame, she had placed a mirror. She did that so that at least once a week she could see who she really was.

That is the power of *Kol Nidre*. To begin the meal before the fast, we place two candles on our dining table and light them. Then we come to the synagogue. *Kol Nidre* is the mirror. At the beginning of Yom Kippur we look in that mirror to see who we really are.

And who are we really? We make promises with every good intention, and we break them without intending. We give our word and mean it, and we take it back without meaning to. We plan to do good and we do—sometimes; but we also do harm without intent. Sometimes we act like fools; sometimes we are hypocrites.

We come together on *Kol Nidre*, and we admit it. We tell the truth. We hold up the mirror and look into it. We make no pretense. We wear no masks. We admit that we are not all that we hope to be. Once a year we acknowledge that we are not always at our best. We are altruistic *and* selfish, kind *and* unkind. We forgive and forget *and* we hold grudges and resent. We excuse ourselves *and* blame others. We think that we can gain control of things. But still we fail. And for once, we do not manufacture excuses. We confess—each of us alone and all of us together.

A Hasidic teaching admonishes us to carry two pieces of paper in our pockets. On one piece we should write the words "For my sake was the world created." The other should read, "I am but dust and ashes." In other words, we are not of one piece. We are created in the divine image, capable of extraordinary things. But despite scientific advances and medical breakthroughs, we remain mortal: our designs are less than grand; they turn to dust and ashes. We are neither as good as the optimist would describe us, nor as bad as the pessimist would imagine us.

We like to think that the rationalists who emphasize human progress are the most realistic; that the religious mind is inclined to flights of fantasy. But the opposite is true. Religion asks us to look in the mirror and to see not just what can be, but what is, to face our less than perfect humanity and our mortality.

In no other service is the liturgy so completely honest. The prayer is so powerful because of the drama, because of the melody, and because it is true. We will make promises about the kind of people we want to be and we will mean them, every one of them, really, this time, this year. Still, we know that we won't always live up to them. The prayer doesn't exonerate us. It holds a mirror up and enables us to see ourselves as we really are. For only when we are honest with ourselves can we change.

Kohelet was wrong. The biblical sage taught, "It is better not to vow ... than to vow and not fulfill" (Ecclesiastes 5:4). For God, says Kohelet, "takes no pleasure in fools" (Ecclesiastes 5:3).

It is better to set high goals and then fall short of them than to promise nothing at all. It doesn't make us fools; it makes us human. *Kol Nidre* knows our human face in the mirror. It asks us to recognize that sometimes we promise to fix things—make the road smoother for our children, take away the pain of disease, the agony of loss, the ache of failure—and we can't always keep that promise.

Life is filled with more than the scrapes and bruises of childhood that require naught but a kiss and hug to make them better. Life's real issues are far more complicated and sometimes intractable. Technology assures us a solution for every problem; medicine promises a pill for every pain. But religion recognizes that we are mortal; we can't fix everything; and *Kol Nidre* reminds us to forgive ourselves for it.

I recently learned that you can trap bees on the bottom of a Mason jar without a lid. The bees fly in for the honey at the bottom of the jar and then they think they are stuck, because they never look up to see that the jar is open. Life weighs us down. Like the bees on the bottom of the Mason jar, we think that there is no way out of our situation, that we are trapped. *Kol Nidre* and the High Holy Days tell us to look up.

Technology is not so forgiving. One of the problems of the Internet is that it does not forget; it keeps all our data—forever. We cannot delete foolish e-mails or unflattering photos that we send in a moment of anger. Our digital past remains indelibly with us. How different is the Book of Life where tradition pictures God recording our good and bad deeds. That record is erasable through *t'shuvah*. If we regret something written in our own life's book, atonement is our delete button. The Rabbis teach that if individuals have repented, we are not allowed to remind them of their past errors (*Mishneh Torah, Hilkhot T'shuvah* 7:8). Our past does not shackle us to the bottom of a Mason jar; we can look up. We can begin again.

And so, at the beginning of the holiest evening of the Jewish year, the divine voice says, "Look up! I pardon, as you have asked [*salachti kidvarekha*]." We are welcomed home with love. We call that love, grace. It is like the unconditional love our parents gave us when we were children that enabled us, no matter how many times we fell down, to get up again. Popular wisdom to the contrary, Christianity didn't invent the idea of grace; it learned it from Judaism. It is what in Hebrew we call *chesed*, "lovingkindness." It is what allows us, despite the face in the mirror that reminds us of life's fragility and past faults, to look up.

And when we know that grace, no matter how many times life knocks us down, no matter how many promises we make and cannot keep, no matter how many times we feel like we have hit bottom, we are able to look up. We escape the earth's hard gravity and we transcend. For a few moments a year, *Kol Nidre* offers us that gift. Like the characters in a Chagall painting, we are able to soar, to begin again.

☙❧

Release beyond Words

KOL NIDRE EVEN ON A VIOLIN

Rabbi Jonathan P. Slater, DMin

Rabbi Menachem Mendel of Kotzk once attended a wedding where he heard a young man playing a violin. He called to the violinist and asked him to play Kol Nidre. *Hearing its somber, moving tones, Rabbi Menachem Mendel said: "It is possible to be moved to do* t'shuvah *even by hearing* Kol Nidre *played on a violin!"*[1]

The Kotzker expresses here something that I think is true for many: the melody of *Kol Nidre* itself calls something out of us. He likely didn't mean that *Kol Nidre* has this effect only because of our many experiences of observing Yom Kippur with family and friends. Rather, the melody has its own intrinsic power to inspire us to self-transformation, a power that stands beyond the literal meaning of the words.

That is a good thing. Many of us have no personal connection to the literal meaning of the words. We are not so concerned about vows we might make to God (or the consequence if we do). Yet, the music, the

---

Rabbi Jonathan P. Slater, DMin, was ordained at The Jewish Theological Seminary of America and has a doctor of ministry degree from the Pacific School of Religion. He is the author of *Mindful Jewish Living: Compassionate Practice* and codirector of programs at the Institute for Jewish Spirituality, as well as an instructor in meditation at the JCC in Manhattan and other venues. He contributed to *Who by Fire, Who by Water—Un'taneh Tokef* (Jewish Lights).

performance of the ritual, and the prayer (regardless of the words) affect us deeply. I believe that Rabbi Shlomo Hakohen Rabinowitz of Radomsk (Poland, 1801–66), in his book *Tiferet Shlomo*, captures more of what we are feeling at that moment:

> From the day that the Temple was destroyed and we went into exile, the holy *Shekhinah* has gone with us, as Jeremiah says: "He [God, the *Shekhinah*] was chained [*asur*] in fetters among the exiles who were exiled from Jerusalem and Judah" (40:1). All of our prayers, ultimately, are for the sake of the *Shekhinah*, that She be saved from exile soon, and we will be saved and experience all good with Her thereby. Thus, before we start the prayers of this mighty and holy day, we begin: "*Kol Nidre* ... the restrictions to which we have committed ourselves are not restrictions [*esarana la esarei*]." We pray that the *Shekhinah* return promptly to her proper place: that our sins no longer create a barrier between us and God, that She no longer be captive [*b'ma'asar*] with us.
>
> Further, we declare, "The oaths we have sworn are not oaths [*ush'vu'atana la sh'vu'ot*]." The Talmud (Ta'anit 85a) teaches that the Holy One swore [*nishba*] that He would not return to the heavenly Jerusalem until the earthly Jerusalem is rebuilt. When we see that the exile has endured so long because of our sins, we pray: while You, God, have sworn [*nishba*] not to return to the heavenly Jerusalem until the earthly one is rebuilt, we release You of that oath [*matirin hash'vu'ah*], saying "the oaths we have sworn are not oaths [*ush'vu'atana la sh'vu'ot*]": the oath that God swore because of us is no longer a binding oath.[2]

Note clearly: Rabbi Shlomo changes the meaning of the words completely! In his reading, *Kol Nidre* is no longer simply a declaration of our desire to be free of the obligations we unintentionally or wrongly take on ourselves. It is instead a declaration of our wish that all exile and alienation be given an end! While he couches this in cosmic terms (praying for the sake of the *Shekhinah*), he really is speaking of our inner experience, of our awareness of the impact of our actions on others.

The way that his teaching makes sense to me is when I understand that to talk about God and the *Shekhinah* is to talk in metaphors. Our relationship to the divine realm is a mirror of our relationships in the human realm. Working on my relationship with God is for the sake of making me a better person here and now. Developing spiritual awareness helps me to know more clearly my emotional/psychic being, to see with greater honesty my relationships with others. The quality of my spiritual life is made evident in how I am in the world.

So, I understand that to "pray for the sake of the *Shekhinah*" is to shift my personal focus from self-concern to other-concern. The suffering of the *Shekhinah* in exile is the suffering of all who are alienated, pained by broken relationships. Similarly, to imagine that God was carried off to Babylon, bound in chains, is to express awareness of how our actions— particularly for ill, but in the end, all of them—constrain others. Everything we do implicates us, and we are accountable for the consequences of our actions.

When we realize that we have made mistakes, we also recognize that our mistakes have had consequences. Others have been hurt by our words or deeds. They are bound up, chained in the exile and alienation our actions have caused. When we seek to make amends for the mistakes— particularly when they have harmed other people—we really are hoping that we can undo, in some manner, what we have done. We are willing to acknowledge our fault, to express our regret, to offer to make compensation. But doing so will not always relieve the other of his or her suffering. Yet, that is really what we want the most: we want the pain that we have caused to be taken away, for the suffering of the other to end. And that is how I understand praying for the release of the *Shekhinah* from exile: that "she" (the other, the one we have harmed, even our own soul) be released from the suffering I have caused her.

When we take stock of our lives (as we do on Yom Kippur, inspired by *Kol Nidre*), we also come to see how our actions shape the behavior of others. When we act selfishly, thoughtlessly, our acts have consequences. People around us respond to our actions. We instruct them, through our deeds, as to what they should expect from us. We bind their future conduct, limit their freedom, by our behavior. They shape their actions according to ours. We make the world in our image, influencing others' response to our behavior. (Of course this works both ways, but we are paying attention now to our responsibility for how we impact others.) When we come to see ourselves clearly, we realize how our mindlessness has warped the lives of those around us. We see how their responses to us are perverse, because we were false. We see how their lives have been warped by our expectations and wish only to free them to live more true to themselves, just as we now strive to live more in line with our true selves. This is how I understand praying that God be released from bondage: I pray to release God and all others from my "vow," the constrained, "chained" behavior they assumed in response to me.

So, when Rabbi Shlomo of Radomsk teaches that at *Kol Nidre* we wish to release the *Shekhinah* from her captivity, we are saying that we want to release others from the pain we have caused them. When we pray to release God from God's vow, we are saying that we want all those constrained by our mistaken actions to be freed, to live at ease, as their true selves. This is the work of *t'shuvah* that happens at *Kol Nidre*, throughout Yom Kippur, and on any day that we wake up—even if it is only to the melody of *Kol Nidre* played on a violin.

CRANO

Night Vision

A GIFT OF SACRED UNCERTAINTY

Rabbi David Stern

*Light is sown for the righteous, and
gladness for the upright in heart.*

Psalm 97:11

Speaks true who speaks shadow.[1]

Paul Celan

Kol Nidre takes place *bein hash'mashot*, in twilight's luminous shadow.
It is an evening service that begins in daylight so we can conduct the
absolution of vows without trespassing on the Sabbath of Sabbaths. Like
twilight, *Kol Nidre* is arrestingly beautiful and disorienting at once. To a
dreamscape melody, we recite a consummately dry legal formula. The text
bends time, speaking of future vows with verbs in the past tense. It raises
ethical questions by granting us advance amnesty for broken promises on
the very day we are supposed to be attending to questions of our moral
reliability. Its language suggests precise distinctions among vows, oaths,
and pledges, but it ends up blurring more distinctions than it creates:
between night and day, sinner and righteous, past and future, heaven and

---

Rabbi David Stern is senior rabbi of Temple Emanu-El in Dallas, Texas. He
contributed to *Who by Fire, Who by Water—Un'taneh Tokef* (Jewish Lights).

earth, penumbra and light; above all, between the plaintive strains of its opening melody and the message of hope and release the ritual aims to convey. Rich in sight and sound, it is brilliantly, somberly, powerfully, unsettling. It breaks our hearts and lifts them at the same time.

We enter the *Kol Nidre* experience wrapped in a *tallit*, a reminder that this is a daytime transaction: from the word *ur'item* ("that you may see") in Numbers 15:39, our tradition concludes that the obligation of *tzitzit* depends upon our ability to see the fringes and therefore applies to daylight hours only. The *tallit* thereby recognizes the workaday nature of the *Kol Nidre*'s quasi-legal text and the declarations we gather to make before nightfall: the release and remission of vows and oaths. This is not the stuff of magic incantations—pages and pages of Tractate Nedarim are dedicated to the mundane circumstances under which vows can be made or annulled.

But then comes the mysterious *Kol Nidre* practice: we keep the *tallit* on even after the daytime work is done. We wear it not only for the *Kol Nidre* chant itself, but throughout the evening service, the only evening service of the year when we do so. The teachers of our tradition have offered up a range of explanations for bringing this daytime custom into the night. Yom Kippur is replete with customs that echo Jewish mourning practice, as our tradition bids us to consider our lives and deeds under the aspect of our mortality; some see the evening *tallit* as evocative of Jewish burial shrouds.[2] Others suggest a connection to a Talmudic passage (Rosh Hashanah 17b) in which God appears wrapped in a *tallit* to reveal the divine attributes to Moses;[3] perhaps we don the *tallit* on *Kol Nidre* to mirror and invoke that revelation of compassion and to remind God and ourselves of the divine image we were created to reflect.

But I think the *tallit* at *Kol Nidre* means more. *Kol Nidre* and Yom Kippur depend upon a sense of removal from our daily lives, and the darkness of *Kol Nidre* night is fundamental to that reflective withdrawal. Yet the darkness fails if it blinds us; the removal is wasted if it serves only as retreat. Yom Kippur practice—fasting, refraining from work and sex and daily dress—is about dying deeply from our daily lives in order to see them more clearly. So as we enter the realm of night and simulated mortality, we bring with us, against all other custom, the *tallit*, our symbol of seeing. We even prepare for the darkness with a Psalms verse about light: *Or zarua latzaddik*— "Light is sown for the righteous." This night, unlike any other, will bring both the freedom of darkness and the capacity for illumination, the urgent insistence upon seeing. And the *tallit* reminds us that as the night takes hold, as our fast progresses through the day and we get a bit hazy, the resolutions we make will eventually need to be brought into the clearer light of visible and tangible commitments. Like the Jacob who awakens from a dream of promises at the foot of a ladder and starts to demand some more mundane proof from his generously promising God, the *Kol Nidre tallit* reminds us that our resolutions are not just dreamy ruminations without consequence, but will need to stand and be seen in the light of day. The *tallit* is a symbol of the opportunities and obligations of night vision, of the challenge and promise that precede *Kol Nidre*'s first word.

Kol Nidre is a ritual of twilight because it insists on subverting expected distinctions. First, we bring the *tallit* of seeing into the darkness and sing of the light sown for the righteous. Rabbi Meir of Rothenberg's introduction to the text of *Kol Nidre* then proceeds through a rhythmic joining of other opposites: "the heavenly court and the earthly court" (*biyshivah shel ma'alah uviyshivah shel matah*); "the foreknowledge of the God of time and space and the agreement of this congregation" (*al da'at hamakom v'al da'at hakahal*); "We give permission to pray with habitual sinners" (*anu matirin l'hitpalel im ha'avaryanim*). Normally separate realms become one: the heavenly court and the earthly court, the consent of God and the consent of the community, ourselves distinguished (supposedly) from habitual sinners.

It serves as perfect prelude to the text of *Kol Nidre* itself, which issues a profoundly compassionate but insistent reminder that "our vows are not vows." On a most basic level, *Kol Nidre* is not a self-justifying release from obligation, but a sobering recognition of our inconstancy: our best intentions are only intentions and are subject to all the vagaries of human weakness and limitation that will leave them unaccomplished.

But *Kol Nidre* as a twilight ritual goes even further. It is a deeply humbling reminder that all of our accustomed certainties, all the clear bright lines we typically draw—between good and evil, between who is right and who is wrong, between what we will surely fulfill and what we will not—are not so clear and bright; they are less distinct and more of the dusk than we think. By recognizing, prospectively and retrospectively, our failures, *Kol Nidre* forces us to acknowledge that not only our vows and oaths, but any rock-ribbed self-assurance, even our most confident commitments and professed certainties, can be misguided, shortsighted, intolerant, incomplete.

That acknowledgment produces a host of questions: What were my hidebound certainties of the past year? Whom and what did they serve? Did they hurt others or exclude their wisdom? Did they advance the values of my tradition, promoting justice and compassion in the world? In its emphasis on humility, *Kol Nidre* provides a corrective to the toxic certainties of the polarized political discourse in America today. What if we approached each other with the humility to recognize that our most confident convictions will always be qualified by the limits of our own knowledge and understanding? In its haunting melody and strangely legalistic language, we begin to sense the twilight truth: our high horses too often stumble, and our soapboxes stand on shaky ground. *Kol Nidre* grants us the gift of sacred uncertainty: the chance to begin this new year with a sense of what we do not know, rather than a narrow certainty about what we do. It's what Buddhists call "beginner's mind." What if every time I were ready to proclaim some self-evident truth, I allowed *Kol Nidre* to whisper in my ear, "Says who?"[4]

As a rabbi standing before the congregation on *Kol Nidre*, I feel my heart beating, pressed against the Torah scroll I hold in my arms as I look out on my community. Many are weeping: moved by memory, by this moment, by the descending and then ascending notes as they begin the hard work of the day ahead. I am inevitably stirred by their courage, by *Kol Nidre* itself, by the vulnerability I feel, by the security of holding the Torah that measures my heartbeat.

But what does it mean to recite a statement of release in the presence of the Torah itself, with all the commitments that Torah demands? Are we absolved of these oaths too, the ones the Torah seeks of us? The *Kol Nidre* answer seems to be yes—this is a Torah *im ha'avaryanim*, a Torah that belongs with those who sin and stray, not a Torah that needs to be protected from our fallibilities and inconsistencies. It stands before all of us as challenge, as anchor, as horizon. And it leaves behind (in many places) an empty and open ark—a coffin-like reminder of the mortal urgency of the day.

"Speaks true who speaks shadow": in its insistence on skepticism about certainties, *Kol Nidre* uncouples the notion of truth from the comfort of absolute clarity. There is great truth to be found in interstice and shadow, in the spaces between confidently held convictions. But if so, then *Kol Nidre* raises, on our day of striving for moral acuity, the question of moral ambiguity. On the one hand, the humbling message seems to be that we should stay flexible in the face of the world's complexity. But at the same time, what is the point of Yom Kippur if not to restore us to our guiding convictions? How do we do both? Similarly, even as *Kol Nidre* grants release from the commitments we fail to keep, we know that chaos would ensue without some sense that we could hold each other accountable.

At the outset of the day when we seek to both confirm our moral horizons and to forgive and be forgiven for moral failings, *Kol Nidre* sets a deep spiritual challenge: to hold our convictions with both strength and compassion, to pursue them with integrity and humility. In the everyday twilight where *Kol Nidre* is inevitably set, we are asked to offer and accept trust; to mean what we say; and in every promise made and every promise accepted, in their fulfillment and in their sometimes failure, to still hear *Kol Nidre*'s haunting, hopeful melody—the poignant sound of our human limitations and God's great forgiveness.

჻

Ritualizing *Kol Nidre*
THE POWER OF THREE

Dr. Ellen M. Umansky

With each year's approach of Rosh Hashanah and Yom Kippur, I find myself, all over again, anticipating *Kol Nidre*. It is more than the haunting melody that moves me; it's the ritual itself. Central to this ritual is a text that I, like so many contemporary Jews, find problematic. Why make religious vows that we hope God will annul and why regret having made them? What is the meaning of religious obligation if we intend in advance to be released from it? Rather than ignore the words of this text or simply view them in their historical context (a difficult task since the precise historical context of this legal formulation is unclear), I have attempted to extract its larger, meta-historical meaning. In so doing, I have come to believe that the key to understanding *Kol Nidre* lies in the words chanted before and after.

The introduction to *Kol Nidre* invokes an image of God as king, sitting on his heavenly throne rendering judgment. While I don't find this metaphorical image to be particularly compelling, I *do* find compelling the subsequent liturgical image of God as existing within "time and space." Here God is invoked, not as the God of the Jewish people, but as an omnipresent being. God is everywhere, seeing and hearing everything.

Dr. Ellen M. Umansky is the Carl and Dorothy Bennett Professor of Judaic Studies at Fairfield University in Fairfield, Connecticut. She is currently working on a book focusing on Judaism, liberalism, feminism, and God. She contributed to *Who by Fire, Who by Water—Un'taneh Tokef* (Jewish Lights).

Like the biblical Jonah, whose story is read on the afternoon of Yom Kippur, we can run from God, but we cannot hide.

So we chant (or listen to) *Kol Nidre*, while standing alone before God, acknowledging our humanity. Our past is strewn with error, and however much we wish it would be otherwise, our future is unlikely to be better. *Kol Nidre* acknowledges how much we wish we could be free of religious obligation, commitment, and conviction. Yet before we admit that we will no doubt fail to do all we have promised, we get the preamble to *Kol Nidre*: the hope that those of us who are righteous will find both joy ("gladness") and illumination ("light"). I will return to this at the end, but first, let us look at the ritual's ending.

Immediately following *Kol Nidre* we encounter God's assurance that in the future Israel will be forgiven for sins committed "through error" (Numbers 15:26). So too with *Kol Nidre*, where the ritual denotes sins committed through error, rather than on purpose. Perhaps, then, if the *Kol Nidre* text expresses a desire to be free of vows and obligations, it is not because we are inherently sinful by desire, but because as humans, we have sinful inclinations that sometimes lead to sinful actions. We know that in the coming year, despite our best intentions, we probably will not achieve all of our goals and may well regret having set them.

So far so good, but this promise of forgiveness is not the only verse to follow *Kol Nidre*—the ritual concludes with two more, Numbers 14:19 and 14:20. A chart of the ritual as a whole will make this clear. What we have, following *Kol Nidre* itself, is the following:

1. Numbers 15:26 (a promise of forgiveness)
2. Numbers 14:19 (a prayer requesting forgiveness)
3. Numbers 14:20 (a response to the request, announcing that God has forgiven)

Now, in the Bible, #2 and #3 go together. Scouts have returned a negative prognosis of occupying Eretz Yisrael, and the Israelites have sinned by despairing of their mission and pleading instead to return to Egyptian servitude. So Moses prays for forgiveness (14:19) and receives it (14:20). Our ritual excerpts the two verses without saying the original prayer is by Moses, making it seem as if it is by us, on *Kol Nidre* night—a deft way of updating a specific biblical story to make its point current to every generation every Yom Kippur.

Numbers 15:26 (#1), however, seems to render the two verses after it (#2 and #3) irrelevant. Yet it has been added deliberately—in its original context, it has nothing to do with the narrative of the scouts; it is, as we saw, simply a promise of forgiveness for inadvertent failure to execute God's commandments in general. Either #1 or #2 and #3 would have made sense, but why all three verses? As the ritual stands, we have already been guaranteed forgiveness (in #1); why then follow it with a specific request for God's forgiveness, afterward? Why are these three verses combined this way?

In part, the purpose may be to underscore the centrality of prayer. Yes, we are guaranteed forgiveness (#1), but we must ask for it anyway (#2) to have it granted (#3).

Equally likely, however, is the possibility that we have a literary or liturgical trope, the deliberate use of three verses to match the threefold repetition of the *Kol Nidre*. Also, the ritual calls for the third verse to be repeated three times, and even though we nowadays take all the Torah scrolls from the ark during *Kol Nidre*, the minimal number is supposed to be two, so that the two people holding the scrolls and the prayer leader constitute the minimal number of a *bet din*—again, three.

In Judaism, the number three has long been a symbol of holiness. Yom Kippur, with its emphasis on purification and *t'shuvah* (returning to God), is a day of holiness and spiritual elevation. Hence, it is fitting that the *Kol Nidre* ritual preceding the evening service of Yom Kippur continually draws on the number three.

Another way of looking at the three biblical verses following the *Kol Nidre* text is to see the first (Numbers 15:26) as a direct response to *Kol Nidre*, with God's assuring us that we "shall be forgiven" in the future, with the second and third verses (Numbers 14:19–20) referring not to the future, but to the present and past. The same God of kindness who has "forgiven this people ever since [their enslavement in] Egypt" (Numbers 14:19) is asked (same verse) to pardon them, and God responds (14:20), not by saying, "I will pardon you in the future" (that is what we get in Numbers 15:26), but simply, "I have pardoned you." It is this last, short verse, repeated three times, that to me is the most powerful of the entire *Kol Nidre* ritual, for whatever the exact legal meaning of *Kol Nidre*, what matters is that we are accepted by God for who we are: weak and imperfect, yet filled with hope.

All of this returns us to the preamble, the promise of light and hope. The ritual implicitly returns to that theme, with its uplifting final note. In marked contrast to the somber and haunting, if not frightening, melody to which *Kol Nidre* is set, it concludes with the joyful chanting of *Shehecheyanu*. We are about to begin the set of Yom Kippur services, during which we will repeatedly confess our many sins. But we do so grateful to be alive and to have arrived once again "to this time of year" in which we can freely and humbly acknowledge our wrongdoings in anticipation of forgiveness. We stand accountable for all that we have said and done, hopeful that in voicing our prayers and asking for forgiveness, we, as individuals and as a community, will begin the important process of renewal.

⌘

All Vows? No!
Then, *Which* Vows?

Rabbi Margaret Moers Wenig, DD

"And God said, 'Let there be light,' and there was light."
—**Genesis 1:3**

We say that the world was created with words. Certainly financial and personal worlds can be created with words: verbal agreements are sealed with a handshake; written contracts are drafted by legal teams. Words matter. "I do," "Yes, I will," "I promise," "You can count on me," "I love you"—these are foundations on which we can stand, rest assured, and build a life. Or so they should be.

God's words turned chaos into a universe with at least some measure of order. Many things seem unpredictable in our world, but at least the sun does "rise" every day, and the moon does give light to the night sky. Imagine if we could not count on the daily rotation of the earth and the appearance of sun and moon.

Imagine also the chaos in our financial and personal lives if we could not rely on the promises made to us. It's destabilizing to be at the receiving end of promises people cannot or do not keep, to be in relationships with people who regularly promise more than they can deliver, who

Rabbi Margaret Moers Wenig, DD, teaches liturgy and homiletics at Hebrew Union College–Jewish Institute of Religion in New York and is rabbi emerita of Beth Am, The People's Temple. She contributed to *Who by Fire, Who by Water—Un'taneh Tokef* (Jewish Lights).

forget about or simply renege altogether on promises they made, who fail to remain true to their word.

Kol Nidre cannot possibly annul vows simply because we have failed to fulfill them. Were that the case, we could depend on nothing, depend on no one. (On the basis of this misreading of *Kol Nidre*, Jews have at times been accused of being undependable.)

A verbal promise is considered as good as a written contract. According to Jewish law, vows made to another person can be legally and officially annulled, but only (1) by an appropriate third party, normally a court, (2) in the presence of (and with the consent of) the person to whom the vow was made, and (3) if sufficient reason is provided to satisfy the court.[1] Simply having failed to fulfill a vow is not sufficient grounds to be granted release from it. It is not the function of *Kol Nidre* to release us from promises we have failed or will fail to fulfill!

Yet, as if the above requirements could be abrogated, translation after translation and commentary after commentary identify the vows annulled through the recitation of *Kol Nidre* simply as "unkept promises," "unkept pledges," "unfulfilled vows," "vows we will make today that we will not fulfill and vows we made last Yom Kippur and then forgot." While, of course *Kol Nidre* has to refer to *unfulfilled* vows—had the vows been fulfilled, it would be too late to annul them—nonetheless simply failing to fulfill a vow is insufficient grounds to annul it.

Other translations and commentaries refer to the vows of *Kol Nidre* as "impulsive vows," "vows made in error by the entire congregation," "vows unwittingly neglected," "vows improperly made," "thoughtless or impossible vows," vows whose implications we did not understand at the time we made them.[2] These interpretations attempt to limit the scope of the vows annulled by the recitation of *Kol Nidre*.

But even these limitations are insufficient. Aren't we inevitably unaware of all the implications of the decisions we make and vows we utter? None of us can see well enough into the future to anticipate all the implications of our actions and words. But shouldn't we still be held accountable for them? "I didn't know" or "I didn't mean it" can't be considered a sufficient excuse to release a person from a pledge. How was the person to whom the pledge was made, who may have proceeded to make plans or investments of time, heart, or money on the basis of that pledge, to have known that the pledge was made "in error," "impulsively," or "thoughtlessly"?

There have to be ways to obtain release from a contract, promise, or pledge that after the fact a person regrets having made or that was a good idea at the time but later turned out to be excessively burdensome, unhealthy, or downright dangerous. But that release can only be granted by the party to whom the promise or pledge was made. And the person who made the pledge may have to pay a penalty to obtain release from it. A person can even be released from a Jewish marriage contract but not through the simple recitation of *Kol Nidre*.

Standard versions of *Kol Nidre* limit the time period of the vows in question to the prior or the coming year. But it matters not whether the year in which those vows were or would be made is the year just past or the year to come. In neither case could we live in a world where promises could be annulled this simply.

Appreciating the chaos that would ensue were *all* vows so blithely annulled, other translations and commentaries have limited the vows in question to the following:

1. Vows made *to God* alone
2. Vows taken upon ourselves (*al nafshatana*) that affect no one else
3. Vows of abstinence, austerity, or self-deprivation that go above and beyond the requirements of Jewish law.

Some *machzorim* explicitly avoid limiting *Kol Nidre* to vows between ourselves and God (limitation 1). A Sephardi version, for example, cites *Keter Shem Tov* to say that vows made to God *and vows made to other people* are included in the prayer. "We seek the consent of the heavenly court [*biyshivah shel maʾalah*] to annul vows that pertain only to matters between man and God. And we seek the consent of the earthly court [*biyshivah shel matah*] to annul vows that pertain only to matters between man and his fellow.[3]

Most others explicitly demand that limitation—the Reform *machzor* of Great Britain, for instance, which carries two alternative versions of *Kol Nidre*. The first reads, "May we be absolved from all the vows and obligations we make *to God* in vain." The second concurs in even more definitive terms: "We ask to be forgiven and released from our own failings. All our promises to our fellow man stand. May God annul the empty promises we made *to Him alone* and shield us from their consequences."[4] The *machzor* used by the Spanish and Portuguese synagogue in New York also stipulates, "Every kind of oath, vow, penalty or renunciation *between ourselves and our God....*"[5] Similarly the North American Reform Movement's *Gates of Repentance* adds, "Let all our vows ... we incur *to You, O God* ... be null and void should we, after honest effort, find ourselves unable to fulfill them. Then may we be absolved of them."[6]

The translation in Birnbaum's *machzor* imposes the second limitation in its translation of *al nafshatana*, "All *personal* vows...."[7]

The current Reconstructionist *machzor*, *Kol Haneshamah*, implies all three of the above limitations, by saying, "All solemn vows, all promises of abstinence, and formulas of prohibition, and declarations of austerity, and oaths which bear the name of God, and pledges to ourselves assumed on penalty...."[8]

I wonder, however, if any vows we make impact no one but ourselves. Suppose we vow to change our eating, drinking, or exercise habits or the amount of money or time we spend on something in particular. Won't such supposedly "personal" vows affect those closest to us? I balk at the notion that we can take actions as individuals (*al nafshatana*) that affect *only* ourselves or *only* our relationship with God. I think it's dangerous to imagine that's the case. "No man [*sic*] is an island," as John Donne famously said. We are all connected. We are all part of a social organism. Our behavior affects those around us, and vows to change that behavior do as well. So I, for one, would not want to accept any of the above three categories of limitations as sufficient solutions to the problem of *Kol Nidre*.

But I do think there *are* vows that *Kol Nidre* ought to be able to annul: *vows made in anger or despair to hurt oneself or someone else.*[9] Haven't many of us found ourselves in conflicts that left us vowing to hurt another or ourselves?[10]

The notion that vows to harm someone may be the vows annulled by *Kol Nidre* may have ancient roots. In 1966, Cyrus H. Gordon pointed out "striking parallels between the Aramaic text of *Kol Nidre* and the Aramaic text inscribed on magical incantation bowls, which were popular in Babylonia around 500 CE. According to this view:

> [The original function of *Kol Nidre* was] the annulment of curses or oaths (originally not in the sense of promises or contractual obligations) that touch off evil forces in the community.... Its purpose is to give the community a fresh start by annulling the evil forces set in motion by destructive (even if unpremeditated) words.'"[11]

This interpretation was made explicit in both the Aramaic/Hebrew and English versions of *Kol Nidre* in the 1948 *machzor* of the Jewish Reconstructionist Foundation: "All vows ... so as to estrange ourselves from those who have offended us [*b'dil l'itrachaka min dialvu lan*], or to give pain to those who have angered us [*uv'dil l'zat'urei l'ilein d'argizu lan*]—they shall be absolved.... These our vows, and these only [*ilein l'chad*], shall not be vows."[12]

The recitation of *Kol Nidre* cuts right to the core of the relationship between intention and action. On the one hand, words must be uttered with the intent that they be fulfilled through action; on the other hand, our intent may turn out to have been flawed, in which case, for the sake of peace, we must sever intent from action.[13]

In that vein I offer a new interpretive translation of *Kol Nidre*. In the congregation I serve, the musical rendition of *Kol Nidre* pauses twice for spoken recitations of *Kol Nidre* in English translation. The first time, those on the bimah petition for the annulment of their vows, and the congregation serves as the court. The second time, the congregation petitions, and those on the bimah serve as the court. Finally, the choir, in effect, petitions for itself (as it sings *Kol Nidre* in the original Aramaic, but with the English translation understood), and the rabbi and congregation serve as the court. (*Kol Nidre* is preceded by *Or Zarua, Biy'shivah shel ma'alah* and followed by *V'nislach, S'lach na, Vayomer*, and *Shehecheyanu*, as provided in the liturgy of this book.)

Kol Nidre

Petitioners:
Every vow to withhold
every threat to prohibit
every commitment to cut off
every curse explicitly pronounced
every curse implicitly pronounced
every pledge to punish
and every oath to avenge[14]

that we have vowed and will vow[15]
that we have threatened and will threaten
that we have committed and will commit
that we have pronounced and will pronounce

that we have pledged and will pledge
that we have sworn and will swear
to take upon ourselves,

all those that we have sincerely regretted and may sincerely regret,[16]
from the past Yom Kippur to this Yom Kippur (may it bring us peace[17])
and from this Yom Kippur to next Yom Kippur[18] (may it bring us peace)

let those vows not be binding vows[19]
let those threats not be binding threats
let those commitments not be binding commitments
let those curses not be binding curses
let those pledges not be binding pledges
and let those oaths not be binding oaths.

Court:[20]
They are all hereby dismissed, forgiven, put to rest, canceled and annulled.
They are now without power and without standing.[21]

ﮥﮥﮥﮥﮥ

Many thanks to the following people who read and commented on an earlier draft of this piece: Dr. David Blumenthal, Ursula Blumenthal, Rabbi Marc Boone Fitzerman, Rabbi Gary Bretton-Granatoor, David Deschamps, Dr. Roger Gradess, Connie Heymann, Dr. Lawrence A. Hoffman, Ted Lowitz, Dr. Dalia Marx, Rabbi Michael Michlin, Dr. Judith Plaskow, Elizabeth Lorris Ritter, Steven Rosenberg, and Rabbi Judy Shanks.

How Is *Kol Nidre* Like a Dodgers Game?

Dr. Ron Wolfson

How, indeed, is *Kol Nidre* like a Dodgers game?
This is the question I asked my students in the Fingerhut School of Education at American Jewish University. We were beginning a practicum in experiential education, and I cannot think of a more compelling worship "experience" than the first moments of Yom Kippur evening.

The answer lies in the distinction made by my colleague, Rabbi Lawrence Hoffman, between the "game" and the "spectacle" that compose an experience of prayer. So, I took my students to Dodger Stadium to make the point.

We arrived ten minutes before the first pitch. Thousands of people were driving into the site, trying to find a parking spot, rushing into the building so as not to miss the beginning of the game. We showed our tick-

---

Dr. Ron Wolfson is Fingerhut Professor of Education at American Jewish University in Los Angeles and a cofounder of Synagogue 3000. He is author of *The Seven Questions You're Asked in Heaven: Reviewing and Renewing Your Life on Earth; God's To-Do List: 103 Ways to Be an Angel and Do God's Work on Earth;* the three volumes *Hanukkah, Passover,* and *Shabbat,* all family guides to spiritual celebrations; *The Spirituality of Welcoming: How to Transform Your Congregation into a Sacred Community; A Time to Mourn, a Time to Comfort: A Guide to Jewish Bereavement and Comfort;* and, with Rabbi Lawrence A. Hoffman, *What You Will See Inside a Synagogue* (all Jewish Lights). He contributed to *Who by Fire, Who by Water—Un'taneh Tokef* (Jewish Lights).

ets to the usher, located our seats, and took in the amazing sight. The players were on the field, warming up. The umpires met with the managers to receive the line-up cards. The soloist took her place behind the microphone, ready to sing the national anthem. The game was about to begin.

In the stands, there was activity galore. From wherever people sat, emissaries were dispatched to the concession stands to buy peanuts and Cracker Jack. Fans lined up to buy souvenirs. Serious students of the game were preparing scorecards to keep track of how each play unfolded. Hawkers trolled the narrow steps in each section, barking out their offerings: "Get y'r Dodger Dogs! Cotton candy! Coca-Cola!" Even after the game began, it was often more entertaining to watch the people than the players. One group of spectators batted around a beach ball, until an usher confiscated it. They did the "wave." They cursed the opposing team. And in the seventh-inning stretch, they sang "Take Me Out to the Ballgame."

The "game" is what happens on the field; the "spectacle" is everything happening surrounding the game. Both are integral to the experience.

On Yom Kippur eve, we begin this most transformative day with *Kol Nidre*—which is both game and spectacle. The "game" is the actual prayer, which I leave to the other commentators in this volume to illuminate. The experience of the "spectacle," everything else that surrounds this night, is what intrigues me most. I suspect the same is true for many congregants for whom the ancient legal formulation of *Kol Nidre* has little meaning; most do not even understand the Aramaic words, which, if translated in their prayer books, they do not even bother to read. But they are most definitely engrossed in the spectacle.

Here then are the top ten things about the spectacle of *Kol Nidre* that make it one of the most powerful experiences of communal prayer:

1. I grew up in a Conservative synagogue in Omaha, Nebraska, where I learned early on in my life that the most amazing thing about *Kol Nidre* was that everyone came to shul on time. On Shabbat and holidays, it was not unusual for people to trickle in throughout the morning. For *Kol Nidre*, there was a palpable rush through the late afternoon—getting dressed, scarfing down dinner, lighting the *yom tov* and memorial candles—all to be sure we would arrive in time to find seats with our large extended family.

2. At the old Beth El Synagogue in Omaha, people normally used the side door, as if we were synagogue "family" using the familiar entrance; no one, that is, entered through the massive front doors of the building—except for *Kol Nidre*. Just inside the entrance was a foyer, its walls lined with bronze memorial plaques. Next to each name was a small lightbulb. On the day of the *yahrzeit* anniversary of the person's death, the lightbulb was switched on. So, during most days, there was only a sprinkling of lights. But on *Kol Nidre* night, all the bulbs were illuminated, creating an awe-inspiring aura of mystical spirituality. The lights were so bright the synagogue seemed on fire. This was done to remind the living to remember the dead. Yet, it felt as if the souls of the dead had gathered to remind the living that they, too, faced the same inevitable fate. The way the stanchions of lights at Dodger Stadium lit up the field, the *yahrzeit* lamps lit up the synagogue, confronting us with our mortality.

3. No one was hungry. In fact, most people were downright stuffed, having carbo-loaded in anticipation of the fast. Nobody is hungry in Dodger Stadium.

4. There was a change in uniform. *Kol Nidre* is the only night of the year when the *tallit* is worn, a palpable symbol that this game was different. If daily, Shabbat, and *yom tov* services were the regular season, Yom Kippur was the World Series.

5. The change in uniform was apparent on the pulpit, as well. The choir wore white robes, replacing the usual blue. The cantor's tall, square *yarmulke* was white, not black. The rabbi wore white, too. Even the Torah mantles had been changed from the everyday multi-colored cloth to all white. In most ballparks, the home team wears white.

6. The "game," the worship service itself, begins with a bang—the *Kol Nidre* prayer. It's like a lead-off home run. Boom! There it is … this most holiest of days is off and running.

7. At Dodger Stadium, the singing of "Take Me Out to the Ballgame" is so popular, it is sung not once, but twice. *Kol Nidre* is repeated three times … three chances to get a hit.

8. Even if you do not understand the words, the haunting melody of *Kol Nidre*, especially those first four notes, transports you to another place. Even though we are essentially singing a legal contract, there is something about the music of *Kol Nidre* that moves the spirit.

9. There is often a sellout crowd, a packed stadium. The game is much more exciting when the place is full. Back in Omaha, an average crowd for Shabbat morning was 150. For *Kol Nidre*, 2,000. There is strength in numbers.

10. At the Dodgers game, the umpires reviewed the rules with the managers before play began, pointing to the fences that marked out-of-bounds. My rabbi, Ed Feinstein, tells his congregation that prayer, even a prayer as powerful as *Kol Nidre*, is no substitute for personal forgiveness. And, so, as the service begins, he invites people to turn to each other, to their spouses and their children, to ask for and to offer forgiveness.

Our teacher Elliot Dorff likens prayer in general to a baseball game. Sometimes you get a hit. Sometimes you strike out. But, sometimes, when everything is just right—your preparation, your stance, your eye on the ball, your timing—you swing for the fences and hit it out of the park. This volume of essays is your playbook, a tremendous guide for playing the game and enjoying the spectacle. May *Kol Nidre* be for you a spiritual home run, a game and a spectacle that are truly spectacular.

ᎼᏇᎷ

We Are the Image of God That God Leaves Behind for History to Know

Rabbi Daniel G. Zemel

Kol Nidre, the most powerful moment of the Jewish year, is also cloaked in the year's greatest mystery and ambiguity. It is impossible to comprehend. I once read that a search for meaning can erode meaning. We therefore approach *Kol Nidre*'s meaning with the greatest caution.

I can never really grasp the message from the words. Whatever we are being told must come from somewhere else—from the ritual, which speaks in its own language. To begin with, the primary text, *Kol Nidre* itself, is in Aramaic, virtually guaranteeing that no one understands the words. Is there a congregation anywhere that reads the prayer aloud in English? It would be hard to fathom. Then too, everyone is standing up, honoring that haunting melody that opens up the soul. And the Torah scrolls are dressed in white and removed from the ark.

This is the most highly choreographed of synagogue moments, deliberately designed to evoke the sacred. But read the words and they come at you like a sucker punch: all of your promises and oaths that you take this year—they don't matter. Simply say after you've blown it that you tried your hardest, and you're clean. It's all okay.

Rabbi Daniel G. Zemel is the senior rabbi of Temple Micah in Washington, D.C. He contributed to *Who by Fire, Who by Water—Un'taneh Tokef* (Jewish Lights).

We then can "go and study" the history of the prayer and learn how everyone tried to keep it out of the official liturgy; all of the way back to the *geonim* of the eighth and ninth centuries, our rabbis were embarrassed by it. Saadiah tried to find an excuse for it. Nineteenth-century European reformers tried to eliminate it. Their American successors who designed the *Union Prayer Book* could not bring themselves to include it. Eventually, they settled for the simple instruction (without the text) "The Kol Nidre is Chanted."

Even without the words, the truth about *Kol Nidre* is there in black and white on the page of almost every *machzor* you will ever see: "the *Kol Nidre* Chant." Its words just do not matter. That is far from the complete story. We tread softly here because, as I said, the search for meaning can erode meaning, and the meaning here is so elusive. But what meaning there is comes from somewhere beyond the words.

Didn't Marx teach (based on a teaching from Hegel) that sometimes things appear as their opposite—that what you see is not what you get? I never really understood that idea, except intuitively, but I think *Kol Nidre* is an example of this paradox, because the *idea* of *Kol Nidre* is the opposite of the *words* of *Kol Nidre*.

The annual *Kol Nidre* moment sends a ripple, a shiver, down the spine. In its wording, it may look like an irresponsible annulment of promises, but it is actually the complete reverse: a clear call for honesty and integrity, a demand to stand spiritually naked before our creator. Yom Kippur is nothing if not that, and *Kol Nidre* is nothing if not the means of making that message real. But here, now, is the real point. *Kol Nidre* requires us to stand naked not just before this elusive God, but before ourselves as well. This is the moment of no hiding, anywhere.

Kol Nidre in this sense is like other symbol-words: words that are simply larger than their literal meanings:

"In the beginning, God ..."
"We the People ..."
"Four score and seven years ago ..."

How many of us have really closely studied Genesis, the United States Constitution, or the Gettysburg Address? Yet we know what these words mean when we say them. They are all symbol-words: words with messages beyond themselves; messages that resonate with historic and life-changing consequences.

Genesis signals monotheism and a new conception of God and humanity. The Constitution signals the birth of American pluralistic democracy and a New World defined by human freedom. Lincoln's address stirs in us the realization that freedom must be attained in every generation.

In all of these words, the meaning is supplied by the context: associations, memories, and usage far more than by the dictionary meaning of the words themselves. History and experience impose their own meanings on these texts. Such is *Kol Nidre*.

With *Kol Nidre*, the meaning is implicit in the extreme. Who has ever heard a sermon preached on the meaning of the words of the prayer? How many worshipers focus their attention on understanding the prayerbook text? As we stand for *Kol Nidre*, our eyes leave the pages altogether; they are inevitably riveted instead on the ritual unfolding of the surrounding symbols: Torah scrolls, white robes, haunting melody, everyone standing, endless repetition. All of these conspire to send the signal of what really counts.

It all starts with Leviticus 23, where Rosh Hashanah and Yom Kippur, the first and tenth day of the seventh biblical month of Tishrei, occur together—but unconnected. The Torah simply does not associate the ritual practices of one with the other. They are presented as two separate observances: first, a day of blowing of horns, and then, a day of atonement and soul affliction. It is only with the Rabbis that we have the institution of the *Yamim Nora'im* ("Days of Awe") connecting the two.

If the meaning of *Kol Nidre* is dependent on context and association, we can partially tease out its power through its connection to Rosh Hashanah and its new-year theme of creation. On Rosh Hashanah we are asked to consider the God who gave us and the universe life. Ten days later, by Yom Kippur, we are forced to reckon with the burden, the real load this creator God imposed on us by being created in God's image—not just gifted with life, but conscious of that gift and of what it entails. As Rabbi Akiva taught, "Beloved is humanity, for human beings were created in the image of God; it is a sign of even greater love that it has been made known to them that they were created in the image, as it is says, 'For in the image of God, He made man' (Genesis 9:6)."

Kol Nidre drums home that awesome reality. Here on earth, where God is invisible, all that we have is ourselves, God's image. *Kol Nidre* has us reflect on that deep reality: we human beings are created in the image of God.

Those pesky words of *Kol Nidre* are backdrop for this larger message. We allow a suspension of all oaths as a way of taking stock. But it is the taking stock that matters. Perhaps we realize that complete candor comes only when what we say, think, and feel cannot be used against us in a court of law. Suspending all judgment for a moment, we can come clean. And it is only when we can safely come clean with ourselves that we realize the truth: that our lives are oaths.

Some oaths are formal, written out for future reference—like employment contracts and mortgage loans, for instance. Our lives are daily oaths, a steady practice of working out how we are doing in pursuing the consequences of being made in the image of God. Daily life—not contracts and loans: that's the real challenge for us.

Once a year, on Yom Kippur, we are told to reckon our accounts. *Kol Nidre* is the signal that we may do so safely. We may strip ourselves bare and confess how hard it all is, as if the words of *Kol Nidre* were really the case, as if, that is, the terrible burden we will admit to carrying doesn't count—even though we know it does. We are being asked to consider our place in the universe as the image of God that God has left behind for all of history to find and know.

Kol Nidre creates a safe space for this consideration of the everyday. Where do my allegiances lie? How do I spend my time? Who is important to me? How do I treat the people I love most? How do I treat the people I see least—the garage attendant who brings me my car, the restaurant server, the busboy? What kind of competitor am I? How do I look in the eyes of others? Am I a friend?

Kol Nidre suspends normality for this introspective analysis. It is a moment out of time, no longer day but not yet sundown and evening. It is a moment of suspended judgment: our oaths don't count. The Torah is taken from the ark but not read. We are wearing white as if we are angels. At that moment, the search for meaning erodes meaning. *Kol Nidre* is meaning.

I like to think that the whiteness of everything on *Kol Nidre* is itself a signal. White is a backdrop, an empty canvas on which we, the artists, will design our lives, a perfectly clean slate that inspires us to color in anew the days ahead.

The Oath, or My Family Story

Dr. Wendy Zierler

My grandfather William, after whom I am named, was an insurance salesman by week and a cantor by weekend. How he came to adopt this weekend religious vocation is, in effect, *the* story of my family. Upon coming to America, my/his family maintained little Jewish religious practice, his mother, Shifra, having enjoyed a certain notoriety in family lore for her habit of standing on street corners and hollering out Communist slogans to passersby. An immigrant from Bialystok, William and his siblings sought in America to be American in all ways, without the encumbrances of Judaism. He married my grandmother, Shirley (formerly Sarah); they had a son and then a daughter (my mother); they lived in the Bronx. They attended synagogue, only sparingly, on the High Holy Days, if at all.

At age two and a half, however, my mother, Marion, fell deathly ill with pneumonia. As these were the days before antibiotics, her situation was grave, and my grandparents were terrified they would lose her. The doctors hurried my mother into emergency surgery to remove a rib that had disintegrated from the infection. In the moments before the surgery,

---

Dr. Wendy Zierler is associate professor of modern Jewish literature and feminist studies at Hebrew Union College–Jewish Institute of Religion, New York. She is the author of *And Rachel Stole the Idols* and the feminist Haggadah commentary featured in *My People's Passover Haggadah: Traditional Texts, Modern Commentaries* (Jewish Lights), a finalist for the National Jewish Book Award. She contributed to *Who by Fire, Who by Water—Un'taneh Tokef* (Jewish Lights).

my grandfather, despite his long-standing ritual and theological disengagement, made a vow before God that if my mother survived this surgery and this illness, he would once again become a practicing Jew.

As it turns out, my mother survived, and my grandfather fulfilled his vow. In stark contrast to all of his brothers and sisters, who had rid themselves entirely of all signs and mores of Orthodoxy, he began going to synagogue regularly, keeping strictly kosher, studying with a neighborhood rabbi. And he developed his vocal talents into a side job as a cantor. My uncle, Martin Halpern, was sent to Salanter Yeshiva and went on to become a congregational rabbi. As he was a rabbi, his Hebrew name was Moshe, and my mother's was Miriam—like the heroes of the Exodus story—the family coined a rhyme-tag for my mother: *Miriam Esther, Moshe rabbenu's shvester.* A cute rhyme, it also carried deep resonance. Like Moses's sister, whose standing from afar to see what would be with her baby brother greatly influenced the progress of her brother's life story, my mother's toddler-age illness cast a long deterministic shadow over my uncle's life, and indeed all of our lives. If she had not become sick, my grandfather would never have "repented," and my uncle would never have been given the education that led him to become a rabbi. If he had not become a rabbi, he never would have moved to the small town in Western Ontario where my father lived to assume a pulpit, and my mother, who came to that town to visit her rabbinic brother, would never have met my father. And I would never have been born.

My whole life, it appears, is the outgrowth of an oath. A seemingly impulsive, theologically naïve promise, my grandfather's oath, in being honored, went against the grain of much that was transpiring in North American Jewish communities in the early twentieth century. And it changed the life course of an entire family. Given that, I confess that I have something of an odd relationship with *Kol Nidre*. My life is an extension of what happens when a person keeps a vow. *Kol Nidre*, a prayer that doubts the ability of any of us to really follow through, that annuls vows before the fact, seems to stand against the very idea of using language this way. How is it that we begin a day of fasting for and confessing our sins with the abrogation aforethought of verbal commitments?

I mentioned at the beginning of these remarks that as part of the fulfillment of his vow, my grandfather became a cantor. That means, for several years, he led various congregations in the *Kol Nidre* service. I have often wondered what this vow maker felt each year when he stood before the men and women he served and to whom he sang this prayer that enumerates the various vows we do not want to be held responsible for. Did it ever strike him as ironic that the only reason he was standing there in the first place was because of a vow for which he took responsibility? And did he really believe that God had responded to his vow and healed my mother? Add to this the additional irony that from a relatively young age, my grandfather had a heart condition that made the task of leading services on the High Holy Days, especially Yom Kippur, potentially dangerous to his health. Here was a man who renewed his commitment to Judaism and became a cantor in response to my mother's precarious health, but who now was potentially endangering his own! To this day, my mother recalls the fear they all had that that he would have a heart attack right there on the spot, during some climactic and musically demanding prayer—*Un'taneh Tokef*, say, or *Kol Nidre*.

To be sure, my family did not invent the many ironies, contradictions, and controversies that have swirled around this prayer. Since its inception, *Kol Nidre* has garnered more than its share of opponents: those who feared that this prayer would lead to excessive meaningless vowing; those who rejected its meaning because vows could be annulled only in the presence of a *bet din* of three; and those who feared the gentile impression that Jews, who apparently do not keep their word, cannot be trusted to honor business commitments. And despite all this, *Kol Nidre* has come to carry such intense emotional weight; for many, it is an inviolate liturgical and musical moment, standing somehow for the core of Yom Kippur, and even of Judaism, as indicated by the centrality of *Kol Nidre* in the Jewish identity drama of *The Jazz Singer*, for example. And yet the prayer is inherently about the tenuous nature of words, commitments, and deeds. It strikes at the very heart of our fears that we cannot live up to the pronouncements we make before God, that we cannot even follow through on our most resolute of resolutions. Better to disavow them before the fact than be held mortally liable for dismissing them afterward. And this is the prayer that has lent its name to the evening service of Yom Kippur? Is not Yom Kippur about taking words and deeds seriously and about our ability to commit ourselves to fundamental change?

Many times I have heard from my mother how difficult it was for her growing up as she did, in a newly religious home, within a larger Jewish community that had largely divorced itself from Jewish practice. In making his vow, my grandfather gave little consideration to what his sudden transformation would entail for his family. Did it never even occur to him that my mother would have no other observant Jewish children in the neighborhood with whom to play on Shabbat, that everything about his life and theirs would now be oddball in comparison to those around them? To this day, my mother says that as a young married woman, she remained observant not because of but in spite of her father's fanatic oath. Had it not been for my father and his deep, small-town Canadian longing for a more substantial Jewish life, she would have long ago abjured her father's commitments, at least as they pertained to her. She would have liked the *Kol Nidre* abrogation of vows to apply to what her father had put her through in making her so different from every other little girl in the neighborhood. And yet, she was the reason the oath was made in the first place!

As a child, what always discomfited me about this story was that my grandfather's "conversion" resulted in my uncle—Moshe rabbeinu, in the rhyme—being sent to a Jewish school, and not my mother; there just was not enough money for two private school tuitions. My uncle's transition to observance was, as a result, more seamless, less lonely. As a teenager, I remember coming to the incipient, feminist conclusion (and sharing it with my mother) that like the biblical Miriam, my mother was unfairly marginalized and cast aside, that her parents' choice of Jewish education for my uncle and not for her was the outgrowth of a biased system that prized Torah study above all other activities, but obliged fathers to teach Torah to their sons and not their daughters. My mother, as it turns out, did not look at it that way. Struggling with my father, at that time, to put my brother and me through Jewish day school, she seemed to have a more forgiving attitude and a better understanding of how difficult it was for her parents, in those difficult economic times, to make the choices they did. While she supported educating girls, she did not condemn her parents for not doing what they simply could not manage.

Our family's story is a quintessentially American/Canadian one, bound up with all the myriad possibilities that North American Judaism has afforded Jews: the ability to shed as well as to (re-)embrace one's Judaism, the choice to blend in or stand apart, and the gradations of affiliation and education that fall somewhere between these poles. Might the various, seemingly alien terms for vowing offered in the *Kol Nidre* declaration—prohibitions, oaths, consecrations, *konam*-vows, *konas*-vows—and the diverse terms used for their negation—permission, abandonment, cancellation, nullification and voiding, disempowerment and without standing—be seen in this metaphorical light, as an encapsulation of these many choices we have as American Jews to vow as well as disavow, to use or misuse words, intentions, rituals, and courses of study in the writing of our own contemporary Jewish stories?

៚

Notes

Morality, Meaning, and the Ritual Search for the Sacred, by Rabbi Lawrence A. Hoffman, PhD

1. Cf. Moshe Benovitz, *Kol Nidre: Studies in the Development of Jewish Votive Institutions*, Brown Judaic Studies 315 (Atlanta: Scholars Press, 1998), 170, and literature cited there.
2. See Moshe Benovitz, cited in note 1. Cf. also Jacob Milgrom, *Numbers*, The JPS Torah Commentary (Philadelphia: Jewish Publication Society, 1990).
3. Charles Taylor, "Disenchantment—Reenchantment," in *The Joy of Secularism*, ed. George Levine (Princeton: Princeton University Press, 2011), 65–66, 73.
4. Jane Bennett, *The Enchantment of Modern Life* (Princeton: Princeton University Press, 2001); George Levine, *Darwin Loves You: Natural Selection and the Re-enchantment of the World* (Princeton: Princeton University Press, 2006).
5. "What It All Means," *New York Times Review of Books*, January 23, 2011, reviews by Sarah Bakewell and Susan Neiman of James Miller, *Examined Lives: From Socrates to Nietzsche* (New York: Farrar Strauss and Giroux, 2011) and Hubert Dreyfus and Sean Dorrance Kelly, *All Things Shining* (New York: Free Press, 2011).
6. Terry Eagleton, *The Meaning of Life* (Oxford and New York: Oxford University Press, 2007); John Cottingham, *On the Meaning of Life* (London: Routledge, 2003); Julian Baggini, *What's It All About?* (Oxford and New York: Oxford University Press, 2004).

What's in a Bowl? Babylonian Magic Spells and the Origins of *Kol Nidre*, by Rabbi Dalia Marx, PhD

1. Cyrus H. Gordon, "Leviathan: Symbol of Evil," in *Biblical Motifs*, ed. Alexander Altmann (Cambridge, MA: Harvard University Press, 1966), 7.
2. Joseph Naveh and Shaul Shaked, *Magic Spells and Formulae: Aramaic Incantations of Late Antiquity* (Jerusalem: Magnes Press, 1993), 132.

Sermons and History: The "Marrano" Connection to *Kol Nidre*, by Rabbi Marc Saperstein, PhD

1. Cf. the debate on the report of the Committee on Liturgy over whether to include *Kol Nidre*, in the original text or in new Hebrew words, in the

forthcoming *Union Hymnal*, in *Yearbook of the Central Conference of American Rabbis* 40 (1930): 101–3.

2. First came a hymn: "Great Day of God! Thou art nigh ..." (*UPB II*, 1894), slightly revised as "Day of God, O come!" (*UPB II Revised*, 1922)—both based on the German hymn *O Tag des Herrn, Du Naehst* (which may have been sung to the melody of *Kol Nidre*). There followed Psalm 130, which begins, "Out of the depths, I call upon You O God," and concludes with the guarantee that God would "redeem Israel from all their iniquities." On the German background, see Annette Boeckler, pp. 39–66.

3. Joseph Stolz, "Out of the Depths, Into the Heights: A Sermon for," in *A Set of Holiday Sermons* (henceforth *SHS*) *5689—1928* (Cincinnati: Tract Commission, 1928), 24. An exception to this rule was Hyman G. Enelow, rabbi of New York's Temple Emanu-El and a prolific scholar. His 1926 Yom Kippur evening sermon begins by evoking positive memories of listeners who apparently grew up in an Orthodox environment (perhaps recalling his own childhood in Kovno): "How many of us remember the old ritual of *Kol Nidre* night—remember it with its awe-inspiring ceremony, the silent tread, the hushed voices, the muffled supplications, the white-robed precentor raising his lamentful chant in the midst of a sobbing assemblage of penitent men and women? Gone from our synagogue is the stir of that solemn rite, gone the emotions that led up to it, gone the life that made that chant, those cries, those deep devotions.... What does *Kol Nidre* night mean to us, to the men and women who, having forsaken the old forms, want to preserve the ancient spirit?" H. G. Enelow, "Broken Vows: A Sermon for Kol Nidre," in *SHS, 5687—1926* (Cincinnati: Tract Commission, 1926), 18. Enelow returned to a similar theme in a 1932 sermon, focusing more on the melody, "On Yom Kippur Eve: A Sermon for *Kol Nidre*," *SHS 5693—1932*, 19–21.

4. Sidney Tedesche, "*Kol Nidre*," in *SHS 5701—1940* (Cincinnati: Tract Commission, 1940), 22. On the allusion to the Blitz, compare Harold I. Saperstein on Rosh Hashanah evening 1940: "While we are praying here, bombs are falling on the city of London, heroic citadel of human liberty and dignity" (in *Witness from the Pulpit* [Langham MD: Lexington Press, 2000], 76). Louis I. Newman, in his 1940 sermon cited below (at p. 36), refers to a recent report of two Jewish children in a London air-raid shelter: one was reading the text of a Yom Kippur 1925 sermon by Abraham Cohen of Birmingham, and the other an address by Joseph H. Hertz delivered at the Conference of Anglo-Jewish Preachers 1935!

5. Louis I. Newman, "*Kol Nidrei*: The Secret of Its Power," in *Sermons and Addresses* (New York: Bloch Publishing Company, 1941), 2:29–36. Much of the background material in the sermon was apparently taken from the 1901–6 *Jewish Encyclopedia* article on *Kol Nidre*, which states explicitly that "the assertion that the *Kol Nidre* was introduced on account of the Spanish Marranos is incorrect."

6. The planned deportation of Jews from Central Europe and western Poland to the easternmost area of occupied territory, where they would be concentrated under appalling conditions, was first publicized in an article published by the *Times* of London on December 16, 1939, entitled "A Stony Road to Extermination," stating that the program "amounts to a mass massacre."

7. Cf. the more general statement made in the aforementioned 1930 debate (see above, n. 1) by David Philipson of Cincinnati: "To me the 'Kol Nidre' brings to mind the picture of the enemies of my people throughout the ages and the persecution of your fathers and mine" (*CCAR Yearbook* 40 [1930], 103).

8. Norbert L. Rosenthal, "*Kol Nidre*: The Song of the Heart; A Sermon for Yom Kippur Eve (*Kol Nidre*)," *SHS 5712 (1951–52)* (New York: UAHC Press, 1952), 16.

9. Louis I. Newman, "Beyond *Kol Nidrei*: A Loyalty Oath Before the Lord," in *The Search for Serenity: Sermons and Addresses*, vol. 8, 1952–1954 (New York: Bloch, 1954), 136–37; cf. his 1940 sermon, "*Kol Nidrei*: The Secret of Its Power," 31–35. He asserts also that the word *avaryanim* ("sinners") in the liturgy immediately following *Kol Nidre* was a code word for "Iberians." Cf. Cecil Roth, *A History of the Marranos* (Philadelphia: Jewish Publication Society, 1932), 379n4, where this scenario is introduced as "According to one theory" and concludes with an exclamation point expressing apparent disbelief that such a theory could be taken seriously.

10. Max Nussbaum, "Hail the Marrano," in *SHS 5716 (1955–1956)* (New York: CCAR, 1956), 16, 18; on Visigothic intolerance of Judaism, see Bernard S. Bachrach, *Early Medieval Jewish Policy in Western Europe* (Minneapolis: University of Minnesota Press, 1977), 3–26, with bibliography p. 146n1; on the theory of a seventh-century Visigothic origin for *Kol Nidre*, see below. Note the difference between this scenario—a gathering entirely of Marranos—and that of Newman in both sermons cited: Marranos secretly entering an actual synagogue on the eve of Yom Kippur. It might be noted that in the recent comprehensive survey of the religious practices of "secret Jews," which devotes fifteen pages to Yom Kippur, there is no mention of *Kol Nidre* as playing any significant role (David M. Gitlitz, *Secrecy and Deceit: The Religion of the Crypto-Jews* [Philadelphia: Jewish Publication Society, 1996], 357–71).

11. Nussbaum, "*Kol Nidrei*: The Secret of Its Power," 19.

12. Leo Jung, "Moral Accounting," in *Best Jewish Sermons of 5713*, ed. Saul Teplitz (New York: Jonathan David, 1953), 47–59. For a plausible candidate of the "nineteenth-century scholar," see below, n. 18.

13. "G-d Hath Not Turned Away from Thee," in *Rabbinical Council Manual of Holiday and Sabbath Sermons, 5716, 1955* (New York: RC Press, 1955), 102. Compare the rather different use of the *Kol Nidre*–Marrano connection by the British Orthodox rabbi Abraham Cohen, *Jewish Homiletics* (London: Cailingold, 1937), 35, referring to the first Yom Kippur sermon in his career, delivered in 1913.

14. Max Nussbaum, "Hail the Marrano," 22.

15. Eugene Borowitz, *The Masks Jews Wear: The Self-Deception of American Jewry* (New York: Simon and Schuster, 1973), 10.

16. Joseph S. Bloch, *Kol Nidre und seine Entstehungsgeschichte* (Vienna: Löwit, 1917, Berlin: Philo Verlag, 1922); Joseph S. Bloch, *Israel and the Nations* (Berlin and Vienna: Benjamin Harz Verlag, 1927), 278.

17. See Israel Davidson, "*Kol Nidre*," in *American Jewish Year Book* 29 (1923): 180–94, citing Bloch, yet concluding, "Appealing as this theory is for the sentimental side, it is not free from flaws" (p. 187).

18. Leon J. Mandelstamm, *Horae Talmudicae* (*Thalmudische Studien*) 2: "Reform in Judenthum" (Berlin: 1860), 6–16, esp. 10–12.

19. Cecil Roth, "The Religion of the Marranos," *Jewish Quarterly Review*, n.s., 12 (1931), reprinted in Cecil Roth, *Gleanings: Essays in Jewish History, Letters and Art* (New York: Bloch, 1967), 119 on "popular fantasy," 141–42 on the Day of Atonement; Cecil Roth, *A History of the Marranos* (New York: Meridian Books, 1959), 183–84 on the Day of Atonement, chap. 6 (pp. 146–67) on "Saints, Heroes and Martyrs." In his 1940 sermon on the *Kol Nidre*, Newman refers to "the story of the saints, heroes and martyrs of the Jewish past" as one that "comes to us at this season of the year as a challenge and a summons" (p. 32).

20. Roth, *History of the Marranos*, xiv. See also Roth's book *The Spanish Inquisition* (London: R. Hale, 1937), the preface to which explicitly makes a parallel with contemporary Nazi Germany. Roth's view of the conversos is that "the vast majority had accepted Christianity only to escape death, and remained at heart as Jewish as they had ever been.... Behind this outward sham [of Christian observance], the recent converts remained for the most part nearly as Jewish as they had ever been" (p. 26).

21. *Jewish Quarterly Review* 48 (1957–58): 183–203.

22. Yitzhak Baer, *A History of the Jews in Christian Spain*, 2 vols. (Philadelphia: Jewish Publication Society, 1961–66). See the concise summary of the historiographical controversy in B. Netanyahu, *The Marranos of Spain* (New York: AAJR, 1966), 1–4.

23. An online Google search for "Kol Nidre/Marranos/sermon" will provide many examples.

The Magic of the Moment: *Kol Nidre* in Progressive Judaism, by Dr. Annette M. Boeckler

1. Ashkenazi is the term for a Jewish tradition that originates in medieval Germany. During the Crusades, however, refugees brought it to different countries in Western, Central, and Eastern Europe; progressive Judaism originates mainly in this tradition. Even today there remain important differences in the prayers, customs, and tunes between Ashkenazim and, for example, Sephardim, which is the tradition whose origins are in medieval Spain and Portugal.

2. European progressive prayer books followed later: *Forms of Prayer for Jewish Worship*, (London: 1985), 272 (as one of two options); *Seder haTefillot: Das jüdische Gebetbuch* (Gütersloh: Gutersloher Verlagshaus, 1997), 288; *Mahzor*

Sefat Hanechamah Yom Kippour (Geneva: GIL, 2002), 4; *Machzor Ruach Chadashah* (London: Liberal Judaism, 2003), 436 (in appendix). The custom, however, to use the traditional *Kol Nidre*, although not printed in the book, started earlier and can be traced by photocopies or stickers stuck into the prayer books.

3. See, e.g., the pamphlet by the Christian minister J. Deckert, *Jüdische Richter, Judeneid, Kol-nidre! Zeitgemäße Gedanken* (Vienna: Verlag der "Reichspost," 1898), 12–24, in which he takes Reform Judaism as an example that Orthodox Judaism should follow—i.e., that *Kol Nidre* indeed should be abolished.

4. See the Latin and Hebrew report about the disputation between Rabbi Jechiel before Ludwig the Holy in 1240 in Paris: "Disputatio R. Jechielis cum Nicolao," in *Wagenseil, Tela Ignea Satanae* (Altdorf: Joh. Henricus Schonnerstaedt, 1681). See also S. Gruenbaum (ed.), *Wikkuach Rabbenu Jechiel mi Paris* (Thorn: 1873). See also A. Kisch, "Die Anklageartikel gegen den Talmud und ihre Verteidigung durch R. Jechiel vor Ludwig dem Heiligen in Paris," *MGWJ* 23 (1874): 10–18, 62–75.

5. The description follows Deckert, *Jüdische Richter*, 17–18.

6. *Protocolle der ersten Rabbiner-Versammlung abgehalten in Braunschweig vom 12ten bis zum 19then Juni 1844* (Braunschweig: Friedrich Vieweg u. Sohn, 1844), 33–42 (7th session on the afternoon of June 16).

7. From the second half of the twentieth century, the American *Union Prayer Book II* offers an introductory part for Yom Kippur containing four of these possibilities to start Yom Kippur with: the hymn "Day of God O, Come!," Psalm 130, an English translation of a new Hebrew version, and finally the note "The Kol Nidre Chant." This shows that in the course of time the different options were added to one long opening passage.

8. Also the founder of modern Orthodoxy, Samson Raphael Hirsch, abolished the recitation of *Kol Nidre* once; see Stuart Weinberg Gershon, *Kol Nidre: Its Origin, Development, and Significance* (Northvale, NJ: Jason Aronson, 1994), 100.

9. E. Kley and C. S. Günsburg, *Die Deutsche Synagoge* (Berlin: 1817). The English translation can be found in Jakob J. Petuchowski, *Prayerbook Reform in Europe: The Liturgy of European Liberal and Reform Judaism* (New York: World Union for Progressive Judaism, 1968), 341–42.

10. Psalm 69:33; Genesis 25:22 et al.

11. Leviticus 25:35 et al.

12. Deuteronomy 29:9, 29:14.

13. Psalm 134:1.

14. Malachi 3:23.

15. Leviticus 16:30.

16. Numbers 15:26.

17. Genesis 8:21.

18. Genesis 4:7.

19. Cf. Isaiah 40:30.

20. Ezekiel 33:11.

21. Leviticus 16:30.
22. Cf. Haggai 1:5, 1:7.
23. Hosea. 14:3.
24. Isaiah 1:6. Cf. also the priestly ritual in Leviticus 16.
25. Cf. Psalm 102:1, 142:3.
26. Leviticus 16:30.
27. Original German:

> Fromme Gemeinde! Fremdlinge und Einheimische! die ihr den Herrn suchet und hier versammelt seyd im Gotteshause, vor dem Ewigen Zebaot: Bereitet euch, heiligt euch, und seyd reines Sinnes an diesem großen, heilig furchtbaren Tage: denn an diesem Tage versöhnt man euch, um euch zu reinigen.

> Die Gemeinde: "Der ganzen Gemeinde Israels sowohl, als dem Fremden, der sich unter ihnen aufhält, sey vergeben: denn es geschah der ganzen Gemeinde aus Irrthum."

> Der Vorbeter: Schwach ist der Mensch, das Dichten seines Herzens nur Böses von Jugend auf und vor seiner Thüre lauert die Sünde. Schlüpfrig ist sein Weg, wie leicht gleiten seine Tritte:—O kehret zurück, kehret reuig wieder, auf daß ihr von allen Sünden vor dem Herrn gereinigt werdet.—

> Die Gemeinde: (wie oben.)

> Der Vorbeter: Nehmet euer Thun euch zu Herzen, untersuchet euren Wandel, bringet mit euch Worte der Reue und kehret wieder zu dem Ewigen, eurem Gott.—Reiniget den Sinn, läutert die Gedanken, bessert eure Herzen, dann schüttet aus euer inbrünstiges Gebet vor dem Höchsten, denn an diesem Tage versöhnt man euch u.s.w.

> Die Gemeinde: (wie oben.)

28. The order of the verses is changed; *V'nislach* was moved to the end, instead of heading the verses as in the traditional order. This way of opening Yom Kippur was taken over by David Einhorn in *Olat Tamid: Gebetbuch für Israelitische Reform-Gemeinden*, Zweite Auflage (Baltimore: C.W. Schneidereith, 1862), 201.
29. *Allgemeines Israelitisches Gesangbuch eingeführt in dem Neuen Israelitischen Tempel zu Hamburg* (Hamburg: Perthes und Besser, 1833), hymn no. 385, p. 472.
30. Translation by Dr. Annette M. Boeckler.
31. The melodies used for the hymns in the Hamburg Temple Hymnal can be found in *Gesaenge und Melodien zum Gebrauch fuer die Jacobson Schule in Seesen, Wolfenbuettel* (L. Holle, s.a. [after 1840]), 19. One of the very rare copies of this little fragile booklet can be found in the "Hyams Collection" within the rare books collection of Leo Baeck College Library, London.
32. In my research I could not find any Christian hymn using this melody, as it is the case with most of the other melodies used in the early Reform service. It seems, therefore, that this melody is a new composition.

33. The famous Chanukah song "Rock of Ages," for example, is also based on a text by L. Stein. A collection of his poems was published by H. and B. Landauer, *Briefe und Gedichte von Leopold Stein* (Augsburg: 1916).
34. David Philipson, *The Reform Movement in Judaism* (New York: Macmillan, 1931), 460n46; the original quote by Rev. D. W. Marks, whom L. Stein had told this, can be found in *Jewish Chronicle*, Jan 11, 1907, 18.
35. Leopold Stein, *Chizuk Habayit: Gebete und Gesänge zum Gebrauche bei der öffentlichen Andacht der Israeliten. Oder: Bausteine zur Auferbauung eines veredelten Synagogengottesdienstes. Erste Lieferung: Neujahr und Versöhnungstag* (Erlangen: 1840), 81–82. Quoted from the English translation by Jakob J. Petuchowski, *Prayerbook Reform in Europe*, 339.
36. Isaac M. Wise, *B'nei Y'shurun L'yom Hakippurim: The Divine Service of American Israelites for the Day of Atonement* (Cincinnati: Bloch, 1866), 30, 32.
37. Translation quoted from Isaac M. Wise, *Day of Atonement*, 30, 32.
38. *Israelitisches Gebetbuch. Im Auftrage des Verbandes der Synagogengemeinden Westfalens bearbeitet von Dr. Vogelstein. Zweiter Theil* (Westfalen: Selbstverlag des Verbandes der Synagogen-Gemeinden Westfalens, 1896), 274; *Israelitisches Gebetbuch für den öffentlichen Gottesdienst im ganzen Jahre. Zweiter Teil. Bearbeitet von Abraham Geiger* (Berlin: 1870), 140; *Avodat Yisrael: Israelitisches Gebetbuch für den Oeffentlichen Gottesdienst im ganzen Jahre, Geordnet und übersetzt von Benjamin Szold, 3. Aufl.* (Baltimore: 1871), 246; Wise, *Day of Atonement*, p. 31; and others.
39. The melody appeared already in the 1840s at the end of the booklet *Gesänge und Melodien zum Gebrauch für die Jacobson Schule in Seesen*, Melody No. 236. With only some minor variants, this melody and text are today widely accessible in Abraham Baer, *Ba'al Tefillah: Der practische Vorbeter; Zweite vermehrte und verbesserte Auflage*; reprint: Out of Print Classics Series of Synagogue Music 1 (New York: Sacred Music Press, s.a.), p. 295, no. 1302a.
40. L. Lewandowski, *Todah W'simrah: Vierstimmige Chöre und Soli für den israelitischen Gottesdienst mit und ohne Begleitung der Orgel* (Berlin); reprint: Out of Print Classics Series of Synagogue Music 12 (New York: Sacred Music Press, s.a.), no. 70.
41. According to a remark in *Liberal Jewish Prayer Book* (London: ULPS, 1945), 2:68.
42. Quoted from *The Union Prayer-Book for Jewish Worship*, part II (New York: Bloch, 1912), 89. A revised translation can be found in *The Union Prayer Book II*, newly rev. ed. (New York: Central Conference of American Rabbis, 1957), 127.
43. Ludwig Philippson, *Neues Israelitisches Gebetbuch für die Wochentage, Sabbathe und alle Feste zum Gebrauche während des Gottesdienstes und bei der häuslichen Andacht* (Berlin: Louis Herschel, 1864).
44. The "first" according to Petuchowski, *Prayerbook Reform in Europe*, 342. The original Geiger text can be found in A. Geiger, *Israelitisches Gebetbuch* (Breslau: Julius Hainauer, 1854), 358. In the second edition of his prayer book, however, Geiger rejected his own text and used L. Stein's hymn.

45. Geiger's translation does not follow the Hebrew syntax but renders the content in liturgical German prayer language. The original German read:

> Entferne, Allerbarmer, alle meine Vergehungen, alle Sünden dieser Versammlung und Deiner ganzen Gemeinde Israel. Entferne sie von Dir, reinige Du unser Herz, daß wir an Frömmigkeit wachsen von dem heutigen Tage der Versöhnung bis zum kommenden Sühnetage, den du uns vergönnst! Unser Herz ist gebrochen, unser Geist gedemüthigt; nicht unsere Werke können wir Dir vorzeigen, nur auf Deine Huld vertrauen wir. Gnadenvoller, Du wirst uns nicht verlassen, sind wir ja nur Staubgeborene, Du wirst uns nicht nach unserer Missethat vergelten.

46. An overview of different versions can be found in Petuchowski, *Prayerbook Reform in Europe*, 342–47.
47. The text appeared in the periodical *Israelitische Wochenschrift* (Breslau) 2 (1871), 301–2. The English translation is quoted from Petuchowski, *Prayerbook Reform in Europe*, 343–44.
48. That Lewandowski published a composition using the Munich text in his work *Todah ve-Zimrah* may have contributed to its fame.
49. Cf. *Esa einai el heharim* ("I lift my eyes to the mountains") (Psalm 121:1).
50. Cf. *Hayoshev al kisei ram v'nisa* ("who dwells on a high and lofty throne"), the High Holy Days' opening verse for the cantor.
51. Cf. Hosea 14:2, the beginning of the haftarah read on the Shabbat just before Yom Kippur.
52. Quoted from the *Sh'ma* (Deut. 6:5).
53. Quoted from *Kol Nidre*.
54. Quoted from the *Ya'aleh v'yavo*.
55. Cf. Psalm 51:12.
56. Cf. Jeremiah 25:5 and *Sarnu mimitzvotekha* from *Vidu'i* (quoted from Nehemiah 9:33).
57. Cf., Psalm 85:9.
58. See, e.g., the Dutch *machzor Seder Tov Lehodot, Gebeden voor Rosj Hasjana en Jom Kipoer ten gebruike in de Liberaal-Joodse Gemeenten in Nederland* (Amsterdam: Verbond van Liberaal Religieuze Joden in Nederland, 1964), 163. A very similar version was used in the Hamburg Temple and later entered into the British Reform *machzor Seder haTefillot* (London: Reform Synagogues of Great Britain, 1985), 3:272.
59. *Machzor Ruach Chadashah: Services for the Days of Awe* (London: Liberal Judaism, 2003), 174.
60. Ibid., 489n174.
61. Already the first edition of the Hamburg Temple Prayer Book offered in an appendix a list of psalms suitable to be read on Yom Kippur: Psalms 17, 25, 32, 51, 65, 85, 86, 102, 103, 104, 123, 130, 134.

62. *Gebetbuch für Israeltische Reform-Gemeinden* (New York: 1858), 2:202.

63. Baer, no. 1302b, p. 296 [for organ, solo, and choir]. According to Petuchowski (*Prayerbook Reform in Europe*, 347), the Swedish Progressive prayer books had Psalm 103 before 1931.

64. *Seder Tefillah Israelitisches Gebetbuch: Im Auftrage des Verbandes der Synagogengemeinden Westfalens bearbeitet von Dr. Vogelstein*, Zweiter Theil (1896), 273; *Seder Tefillot Kol Hashanah: Gebetbuch für die neue Synagoge in Berlin* (Berlin: 1914), 2:185; *Gebetbuch* (Berlin: Verlag der Jüdischen Reformgemeinde zu Berlin, s.a. [created between 1925–1932]), 40; *The Union Prayer-Book for Jewish Worship* (New York: Bloch, 1912), 2:89 [after "Day of God O Come"]; Jakob J. Kokotek, *Prayer Book for Jewish Worship throughout the Year*, rev. ed. (London: New Liberal Jewish Congregation, 1962), 2:226 [as an alternative text to a new Hebrew version]; *The Union Prayer Book for Jewish Worship*, newly rev. ed. (Cincinnati: Central Conference of American Rabbis, 1948), 2:129.

65. *Todah W'simrah*, no. 71, pp. 118–21 (for the congregations in Nuremberg and Stettin).

66. A performance of this piece in a concert by the American Conference of Cantors from Nov. 16, 2010, in Rome, Italy, can be seen on YouTube (accessed Jan. 2010): http://www.youtube.com/watch?v=WAJlmY8CAco&feature=player_detailpage.

67. *Gate of Repentance: Services for the High Holydays* (London: Union of Liberal and Progressive Synagogues, 1973), 131.

68. The first source to mention this custom was *Machzor Vitry*, eleventh century.

69. A. Z. Idelsohn, *Jewish Music in Its Historical Development* (New York: Schocken, 1967), 159.

70. Max Bruch in a letter to Eduard Birnbaum, Breslau, December 4, 1889. The German text can be found in A. Z. Idelsohn, *Jewish Music*, 513n22. My English translation was done with usage of http://www.chazzanut.com/bruch.html. See also Sabine Lichtenstein and Abraham Jacob Lichtenstein, "Eine juedische Quelle fuer Carl Loewe und Max Bruch," *Die Musikforschung* 49 (1996): 349–67.

71. Oral Information, but see, e.g., http://www.chazzanut.com/bruch.html.

72. *Gates of Repentance* (New York: Central Conference of American Rabbis, 1978). The history of the American debate within the CCAR can be found in Gershon, "*Kol Nidre* and Reform Judaism," in *Kol Nidre*.

73. *Forms of Prayer for Jewish Worship* (London: RSGB, 1985), 272. The Hebrew version is taken from from *Gebetbuch herausgegeben vom Israelitischen Tempelverband in Hamburg*, 6th ed. (1904).

74. *Seder haTefillot: Das jüdische Gebetbuch Band II Die Hohen Feiertage* (Gütersloh: Gutersloher Verlagshaus, 1997), 288.

75. *Mahzor Sefat Hanechamah Yom Kippour* (Geneva: GIL, 2003), 4.

76. *Machzor Ruach Chadashah* (London: Liberal Judaism, 2003), 436.

77. Anne J. Kershen and Jonathan Romain, *Tradition and Change: A History of Reform Judaism in Britain, 1840–1995* (London: Vallentine Mitchell, 1995), 3.

78. Quoted from the foundation document of the West London Synagogue of British Jews from April 15, 1840; see ibid.

79. An overview about non-Ashkenazi *Kol Nidre* tunes can be found in Gershon, *Kol Nidre*, 149ff.
80. I owe great thanks to David Jacobs from the Movement of Reform Judaism, who made his private collection of West London Synagogue prayer books available to me.
81. Translation quoted from *Forms of Prayer*, 1st ed. (London: J. Wertheimer, 1843), 4:1.
82. The text that is attributed to Hai Gaon (939–1038) is based on Mishnah Ta'anit 2:1.
83. Psalm 51:19.
84. Proverbs 28:13.
85. Psalm 19:15.
86. *Forms of Prayer according to the Custom of the Spanish and Portuguese Jews with an English translation by the Rev. D. A. de Sola*, vol. 3, *Day of Atonement Service* (London: J. Wertheimer, 5597 [= 1837]), 10; and *Forms of Prayer used by the West London Synagogue of British Jews with an English translation edited by the Rev. D. W. Marks*, vol. 4, *Prayers for the Day of Atonement* (London: J. Wertheimer, 5603 [= 1843]), 1.
87. Unpublished, typeset multiplied sheet used in North Western Reform Synagogue, found in a copy of the seventh edition of *Forms of Prayer* (1953).
88. The original German text "Ansprache zum Kol Nidre des Versöhnungstages 6. Oktober 1935" can be found in Michael A. Meyer, *Zusammenarbeit mit Bärbel Such, Briefe, Reden, Aufsätze: Leo Baeck Werke*, Band 6 (Gütersloh: Gütersloher Verlagshaus, 2006), 312–13.
89. Rabbi Dr. Werner van der Zyl (1902–84) came to London from Berlin in 1939 and served as rabbi at North Western Reform Synagogue (Alyth Gardens) from 1943 to 1958 and at West London Synagogue from 1958 to 1968. The other, bigger, and also influential Reform synagogue, Edgware and District Reform, was led by Rabbi Ignaz Maybaum (1897–1963); he, too, came to London in 1939 and served at Edgware from 1949 to 1963.
90. The last rabbi of the Hamburg Temple, Rabbi Dr. Bruno Italiener (1881–1956), served as minister in the West London Synagogue from 1943 to 1951.

Kol Nidre: A Halakhic History and Analysis, by Dr. Eliezer Diamond

1. There are scholars who believe that there is a reference to such a vow in Numbers 30:3; they translate *le'sor isar al nafsho* as "imposing a prohibition on oneself" and argue that it refers to a type of vow discrete from the afore-mentioned *sh'vu'ah*. However, this interpretation of the verse is highly debatable. See Moshe Benovitz, *Kol Nidre: Studies in the Development of Rabbinic Votive Institutions* (Atlanta: Scholars Press, 1998), 9n1.
2. Concerning the meaning, use, and abuse of prohibitive vows, see ibid., 9–40.
3. Numbers 30:6, 30:9, 30:13–14.

4. Judges 11:29–40. It is unclear whether or not Jephthah ultimately sacrifices his daughter. For a lengthy discussion of this question, see David Marcus, *Jephthah and His Vow* (Lubbock, TX: Texas Tech Press, 1986).

5. Josephus, *Antiquities* 5.2.12.

6. *Hypothetica* 7.3–5.

7. Mishnah Hagigah 1:8.

8. Benovitz, *Kol Nidre*, 149–64, esp. 162–64.

9. Lawrence A. Hoffman, *The Canonization of the Synagogue Service* (South Bend, IN: University of Notre Dame Press, 1979), 101, 216n40.

10. Cf. Hoffman, *Canonization*, 215n39; Benovitz, *Kol Nidre*, 172.

11. Benovitz, *Kol Nidre*.

12. *Responsa Sha'arehi Teshuva* 143:13. In fact, however, *Kol Nidre* is not found in the siddur of Saadiah Gaon.

13. See S. Y. Agnon, *Days of Awe* (New York: Schocken Books, 1995), 212–13. The author of the thirteenth-century halakhic work *Shibbolei Haleket* reports that Hai bar Sherira (eleventh century), the last of the great *geonim*, included *Kol Nidre* in his own siddur; see Hoffman, *Canonization*, 102.

14. For an explanation of the Talmudic basis for each of Rabbenu Tam's objections as well as counterarguments supporting the interpretation of *Kol Nidre* as *hatarat n'darim*, see the commentary of Rabbi Asher ben Yechiel (Rosh, Germany and Spain, thirteenth to fourteenth century) to Tractate Yoma, chap. 8, par. 28.

　　Another halakhic problem bedeviling halakhists was that legal proceedings like *hatarat n'darim* are proscribed on Shabbat and festivals; see Mishnah Shabbat 24:5 and Mishnah Betzah 5:2. This obstacle was overcome by adopting the custom, still followed by most communities, of chanting *Kol Nidre* before sunset, which marks the actual advent of Yom Kippur. See Benovitz, *Kol Nidre*, 172–73 and the sources cited in n. 45 on p. 173.

15. In fact, both formulations of *Kol Nidre* were circulating already in geonic times; see Hoffman, *Canonization*, 101.

16. For an exhaustive study of the various formulations of *Kol Nidre* and their history as well as the objections to its inclusion, see Naftali Wieder, "Past and Future in the Formulation of 'Kol Nidre'" [Hebrew], in *Mikhtam le-David*, ed. Y. D. Gilat and E. Stern (Ramat-Gan: Bar-Ilan University Press, 1978), 189–209. See also Daniel Sperber, *Minhagei Yisrael* (Jerusalem: Mosad Harav Kook, 1989), 1:35–36. From a manuscript published after Wieder wrote his article, it emerges that at least as late as the second half of the sixteenth century the Persian rite did not include *Kol Nidre*; see S. Tal, ed., *Nusach Hatefilah shel Yehudei Paras* (Jerusalem: Ben-Zvi Institute, 1981), Introduction, 2, 172.

17. Those interested in a thorough exposition of the history and meaning of each term should read Benovitz, *Kol Nidre*, 9–147.

18. Cf. Tosefta, Nedarim 5:1; Talmud, Nedarim 21a.

19. Benovitz, *Kol Nidre*, 172.

Choice, Commitment, Cancellation: Vows and Oaths in Jewish Law, by Rabbi Daniel Landes

1. Rav Kook, *Sh'monat Pirakim*, vol. 7, no. 87; translation Landes.
2. Moses Maimonides, *Mishneh Torah*, Laws of Vows (*Nedarim*) 3:6.
3. See Rosh (Rabbenu Asher ben Yehiel, 1250–1327, Worms, German, and Toledo, Spain) to Talmud, Nedarim 16b.
4. Maimonides, *Mishneh Torah*, Laws of Vows 3:6.
5. Ibid., Laws of Oaths 6:2.
6. Meir Hakohen (thirteenth century, Rothenburg, Germany), *Hagahet Maimoniyot*, Oaths 6:1.
7. Kook, *Sh'monat Pirakim*.

Kol Nidre from *Union Prayer Book* to *Gates of Repentance*, by Rabbi Lawrence A. Hoffman, PhD

1. The correspondence was saved by the late Rabbi A. Stanley Dreyfus, who drew them to my attention. I am grateful to him for this as I am for so much that he has taught me as my teacher throughout his lifetime.
2. Solomon B. Freehof, *Reform Jewish Practice* (New York: Hebrew Union College Press, 1944; reprinted, New York: Union of American Hebrew Congregations, 1963).
3. Rabbi Samuel Harry Goldenson (1878–1962) of Temple Emanu-El in New York; Rabbi Edward Nathan Calisch (1865–1946) of Congregation Beth Ahabah in Richmond. Cohon spells Goldenson incorrectly.
4. Founder of the Reconstructionist Movement, and author of his own Yom Kippur liturgy, which did not come out in official form until 1948, by which time (if Cohon is correct), Kaplan had apparently changed his mind, since the *High Holiday Prayer Book* published by the Reconstructionist Foundation in that year does have a version of *Kol Nidre* (pp. 2–3). It is very largely the traditional text, emended, however, by the addition of new Aramaic wording alongside English translation, to the effect that the vows being annulled were only those that had been made "so as to estrange ourselves from those who have offended us or to give pain to those who have angered us."
5. See *Gate of Repentance*, 132.
6. From the 1955 reprint of the newly revised *Union Prayer Book*, Temple Emanu-El of Livingston, NJ.

Memories of the Past, Guidelines for the Future, by Rabbi Andrew Goldstein, PhD

1. First edition published by the Liberal Jewish Synagogue in 1923. A revised edition appeared in 1937, reprinted in 1945 and published by the Union of Liberal and Progressive Synagogues, Jewish Religious Union.
2. See J. Petuchowski, *Prayerbook Reform in Europe*, 334–37, for a discussion on this subject as well as new versions of *Kol Nidre*. See also Eric L. Friedland,

"The Historical and Theological Development of Non-Orthodox Jewish Prayerbooks in the United States," doctoral thesis, Ann Arbor, MI, 1968.
3. Petuchowski, *Prayerbook Reform in Europe*, 334–37.
4. *A Time for Recommitment: Jewish Christian Dialogue 70 Years after War and Shoah* (Sankt Augustin/Berlin: Konrad-Adenauer-Stiftung, 2009). See www.iccj.org.
5. Ibid., 44–45.
6. To a large extent, the "Ten Points" were implemented in the years that followed, by the Roman Catholic and major Protestant Churches (though sadly not by all fundamentalist, Evangelical churches, nor, recently, by some individuals in the former bodies who are even now trying to return to the *status quo ante*).
7. *Encyclopaedia Judaica* 10:1167.
8. See Gershon, *Kol Nidrei*, 97ff.
9. Ibid., 98–114.
10. Ibid., 69.
11. See also ibid., 41–59.
12. Published by the Union of Liberal and Progressive Synagogues, London, 1973.
13. *Gates of Repentance* (New York: Central Conference of American Rabbis, 1978), 252.
14. Edited by Rabbi Dr. Andrew Goldstein and Rabbi Dr. Charles H. Middleburgh (London: Liberal Judaism, 2003).
15. "The Magic of the *Kol Nidre*," a sermon given at the Liberal Jewish Synagogue, Erev Yom Kippur, September 22, 1996.

What If Cleverness Is Foolishness and Righteousness an Illusion? by Rabbi Jonathan Magonet, PhD

1. *Forms of Prayer for Jewish Worship*, vol. 3, *Prayers for the High Holydays*, 8th ed., Assembly of Rabbis (London: Reform Synagogues of Great Britain, 1985), 273.
2. Ibid.
3. Ibid., 263.

Words of Wisdom or Legalese? by Rabbi Charles H. Middleburgh, PhD

1. *Liberal Jewish Prayer Book*, 2:67.
2. *Gate of Repentance*, 464–65.
3. Petuchowski, *Prayerbook Reform in Europe*, 343–46.
4. Ibid., 344.

At Least Credit Me with Being Compassionate, by Rabbi Tony Bayfield, CBE, DD

1. Andre Schwarz-Bart, *The Last of the Just* (New York: Overlook, 2000).
2. Adin Steinsaltz, *A Guide to Jewish Prayer* (New York: Schocken Books, 2000), 199.
3. Louis Jacobs, *A Guide to Yom Kippur* (London: Jewish Chronicle Publications, 1957), 31.

"Woe Is Me That I Have Sworn": The Power to Annul God's Vows, by Rachel Farbiarz and Ruth Messinger

1. As described in Rabbi Dov Peretz Elkins, ed., *Yom Kippur Readings: Inspiration Information Contemplation* (Woodstock, VT: Jewish Lights, 2005), 23; Rabbi Nosson Scherman, et al. (eds.), *Machzor Chaim Yechezkel: The Complete ArtScroll Machzor* (New York: Mesorah Publications: 1989), 52.
2. Rashi on Exodus 32:10, citing *Exodus Rabbah* 42:9.

Disruption, Disorientation, and Restarting: The *Kol Nidre* Road to Return, by Rabbi Shoshana Boyd Gelfand

1. The Talmudic interpretation of this phrase picks up on the ambiguity of its meaning. The Sadducees and Pharisees disagreed about whether it meant literally the day after Pesach, as reflected in our current practice of when we start counting the *omer*, or the Shabbat (i.e., the Saturday) after Pesach. Here I am following the accepted Pharisaic interpretation in suggesting that Shabbat can be used to refer to Pesach as well as Saturday.

"It's Rather Hard to Understand": Approaching God through Sound, Not Translation, by Rabbi Elie Kaunfer

1. A. Z. Idelsohn, "The Kol Nidre Tune," *Hebrew Union College Annual* 8–9 (1931–32): 493. See also A. M. Haberman, *Mipri Ha'et V'ha'et* (Jerusalem: Reuven Mass, 1981), 180: "It seems logical that the sweet melody kept/ guarded it."
2. Daniel Goldschmidt, ed. *Seder Rav Amram Gaon* (Jerusalem: Mossad Harav Kook, 1971), 162–63. See there for manuscript variations, including an Aramaic version for the first two lines, in the Oxford manuscript.
3. Moshe David Herr, "Matters of Palestinian Halakhah during the Sixth and Seventh Centuries CE" [Hebrew], *Tarbiz* 49 (1979–80): 68n29 end.
4. This was first noted in scholarly literature in the late 1870s and early 1880s. See J. Halevy, "Observation sur un vase judeo-babylonien du British Museum," *Comptes rendus de l'Academie des Inscriptions et Belles-Lettres*, 5 (1877): 291, cited in Charles Isbell, *Corpus of the Aramaic Incantation Bowls* (Missoula, MT: Scholars Press and the Society of Biblical Literature, 1975), 7n36. This similarity was also noticed by E. Babelon and M. Schwab in "Un Vase Judeo-Chaldeen," *Revue des Etudes Juives* 4 (1882): 170. See further, Herr, "Matters of Palestinian Halakhah," 68n29.
5. Gershom Scholem ("Havdallah De-Rabbi Akiva: A Source for Jewish Magical Tradition in the Geonic Period" [Hebrew], *Tarbiz* 50 [1980–81]: 262n61) notes how common such repetitions are in magical texts.
6. Claudia Rohrbacher-Sticker, "From Sense to Nonsense, From Incantation Prayer to Magical Spell," *Jewish Studies Quarterly* 3 (1996): 24–46.

7. Ibid., 25. She goes on to cite a case in which Rabbi Menahem ben Meir of Speyer allowed the use of Christian doctors who conjured Jesus's name "since it was not the *names* but the *sounds* of the conjuration which would make the treatment work." For further on this idea, see Lawrence A. Sullivan, "Towards a Hermeneutics of Performance," *History of Religions* 26, no. 1 (1986): 1–33, esp. 24–26; Naomi Janowitz, *Icons of Power: Ritual Practices in Late Antiquity* (University Park, PA: Pennsylvania State University Press, 2002), chap. 4; Patricia Cox Miller, "In Praise of Nonsense," in *Classical Mediterranean Spirituality*, ed. A. H. Armstrong (New York: Crossroad, 1986), 481–505.

All Bets Are Off, by Rabbi Lawrence Kushner

1. *Maggid D'varav Leya'akov, Likkutey Amarim*, 54 (Jerusalem, 1971). Cf. Rivka Shatz-Uffenheimer ed. (Jerusalem: Magnes Press, 1976), 30.
2. *Botzina Kaddisha*, ed. Rabbi Hayim Neta Donner.

The Room with No Back, Only Forward, by Rabbi Noa Kushner

1. In fact, *Kol Nidre* was sometimes carried out in the presence of an actual *bet din*, a court of law. See Rabbi Ronald Aigen, ed., *Renew Our Days* (Quebec: Congregation Dorshei Emet, 2001), 384.
2. This originally referred to the lifting of the ban of those who were in *cherem* (excommunication) and could not attend synagogue (ibid., 384).
3. See Everett Fox, trans., *The Five Books of Moses* (New York: Schocken Books, 1983), 735.

Imagining Nothing, by Liz Lerman

1. Adapted from Abraham Ibn Ezra, "I Have a Garment," translated by Robert Mezey; http://medievalhebrewpoetry.org/abrahamibnezraselection.html (accessed July 5, 2011).

A Vote of No Confidence, by Catherine Madsen

1. Ira Stone, "The Precarious Ties That Bind Us: Sotah 2a," *Cross Currents* 51 (Summer 2001): 279.
2. Jacob Taubes, *The Political Theology of Paul*, ed. Aleina Assman and Jan Assman, trans. Dana Hollander (Stanford, CA: Stanford University Press, 2004), 47.
3. "And it shall come to pass, that as Adonai rejoiced over you to do you good, and to multiply you, so Adonai will rejoice over you to destroy you, and to annihilate you" (Deuteronomy 28:63).
4. David Blumenthal, *Facing the Abusing God: A Theology of Protest* (Louisville, KY: Westminster/John Knox, 1993), 293.

Courting Inversion: *Kol Nidre* as Legal Drama, by Rabbi Aaron Panken, PhD

1. See the detailed discussion of the biblical and Rabbinic texts behind the releasing of vows in Moshe Benovitz, *Kol Nidre* (Atlanta: Brown Judaic Studies / Scholars Press, 1998).

The *Kol Nidre* Mirror to Our Soul, by Rabbi Sandy Eisenberg Sasso

1. For this understanding of Chagall's painting, I am thankful to Robert Coles, *The Secular Mind* (Princeton: Princeton University Press, 1999).
2. *Kol Haneshamah: Prayerbook for the Days of Awe* (Elkins Park, PA: Reconstructionist Press, 1999), 693.
3. Hayyim Herman Kieval, *The High Holy Days: A Commentary on the Prayerbook of Rosh Hashanah and Yom Kippur* (New York: Schechter Institute of Jewish Studies, 2004).

Release beyond Words: *Kol Nidre* Even on a Violin, by Rabbi Jonathan P. Slater, DMin

1. This is a paraphrase of a teaching from *Siach Sarfei Kodesh,* vol. 3 s.v. *parnasah* #14, ed. Yoetz Kim Kaddish of Pristik, my translation.
2. My translation.

Night Vision: A Gift of Sacred Uncertainty, by Rabbi David Stern

1. Paul Celan, "Speak, You Too," from *Selected Poems and Prose of Paul Celan,* quoted in Alan Lew, *This Is Real and You Are Completely Unprepared* (Boston: Little, Brown, 2003), 196.
2. Reuven Hammer, *Entering the High Holy Days* (Philadelphia: Jewish Publication Society, 1998), 110.
3. Lawrence A. Hoffman, *Gates of Understanding,* vol. 2, *Appreciating the Days of Awe* (New York: Central Conference of American Rabbis, 1984), 106.
4. I am grateful to Rabbi Jonathan Slater for the essence of this teaching.

All Vows? No! Then, *Which* Vows? by Rabbi Margaret Moers Wenig

1. Hayyim Herman Kievel, *The High Holy Days: A Commentary on the Prayerbook of Rosh Hashanah and Yom Kippur* (Jerusalem: Institute of Applied Halachah, Schechter Institute of Jewish Studies, Jerusalem, 2004), 267.
2. *Machzor M'soret Harav L' Yom Kippur with Commentary Adapted from the Teachings of Rabbi Joseph B. Soloveitchik,* Kasirer Edition (New York: K'hal Publishing, 2006), 70.
3. Eliezer Toledano, "The Order of Kal Nidre for Syrian Congregations," *in Machzor Kol Yehudah: The Orot Sephardic Yom Kippur Machzor* (Lakewood, NJ: Orot, 2002), 78n187.

4. *Forms of Prayer for Jewish Worship*, vol. 3, *Prayers for the High Holidays*, ed. Assembly of Rabbis of the Reform Synagogues of Great Britain (London: Reform Synagogues of Great Britain, 1985); italics added.

5. *Prayers for the Day of Atonement according to the Custom of the Spanish and Portugese Jews*, 9th ed., ed. and trans. David de Sola Pool (New York: Union of Sephardic Congregations, 1988), 26; italics added.

6. *Gates of Repentance*, 252; italics added.

7. *Machzor Hashaleim L'Rosh Hashanah v'Yom Kippur, High Holiday Prayer Book*, translated and annotated with an Introduction by Philip Birnbaum (New York: Hebrew Publishing Company, 1951), 490; italics added.

8. *Kol Haneshamah*, 693.

9. Some believe that the recitation of *Kol Nidre* is a mystical rite to induce God, by our own example, to renounce God's vow to exile Israel and the *Shekhinah*. And in response to our renunciation of the curses we have uttered, God declares: *Salachti kidvarekha*. Some *machzorim* even include a passage from *Tikkunei Zohar* prior to *al da'at hamakom* that speaks of absolving God from God's oath; e.g., *Machzor Shalom Yerushalaim, Yom Kippur, Seder T'filot K'minhag B'nai Aram Tzova (Aleppo)* (Monsey, NY: Sephardic Heritage Foundation, 2005), 63, and *Machzor M'soret Harav*, 62–63.

10. I thank David Blumenthal for insisting that I make explicit this nearly universal human experience.

11. Hayyim Herman Kieval, "The Kol Nidrei Service," in *The High Holidays: A Commentary on the Prayerbook of Rosh Hashanah and Yom Kippur*, ed. David Golinkin and Monique Susskind Goldberg (Jerusalem: Institute of Applied Halacha: The Schechter Institute of Jewish Studies, 2004). Cf. C. H. Gordon, "Leviathan: Symbol of Evil," in *Studies and Texts*, vol. 3, *Biblical Motifs, Origins and Transformations*, ed. Alexander Altmann (Cambridge, MA: Harvard University Press, 1966), 6–7, 23. Saul Lieberman, *Greek in Jewish Palestine* (New York: Jewish Theological Seminary of America, 1942), 119ff., provides the parallel use of terminology in vows and in magical incantations.

12. *High Holiday Prayer Book*, vol. 2, *Prayers for Yom Kippur* (New York: Jewish Reconstructionist Foundation, 1948), 2–3.

13. I thank Steven Rosenberg for urging that I make this essential insight of *Kol Nidre* explicit.

14. Sephardim and Ashkenazim use somewhat different verbs here and also list them in different orders. I followed the Ashkenazi list: *nidrei, esarei, charamei, konamei, kinuyei, kinusei, ush'vu'ot*.

15. Some versions of *Kol Nidre* refer only to the past, others to the future. Some refer to both in the same sentence. And in some traditions, separate versions referring to the past and to the future are both recited. I include both here, with this understanding of their meanings: A request to annul a past vow one has regretted is a sign of remorse. A request to conditionally annul a future vow one may regret is a sign of "determination" to refrain from repeating that very sin. (Based on Rav Soloveitchik's understanding of Rabbenu Tam's

formulation of *Kol Nidre*, annulling vows made during the coming year. See *Machzor M'soret Harav*, 68.)

16. This translation of *icharatna v'hon* ("we regret them") is from *Machzor M'soret Harav*, 66.

17. Sephardim say *l'shalom*, Ashkenazim say, *l'tovah*.

18. Toledano, *The Orot Sephardic Yom Kippur Machzor*, 84, includes both formulations (from last Yom Kippur to this one and from this one to the next) in a single recitation of *Kol Nidre*, as well as the reference to all vows "that we *have vowed* or that we *will vow*" (italics added) and the full repetition of *all* the verbs, first in the stanza that begins *dindarna* and again in the stanza that begins *nidrana la nidrei*.

19. Some translations interpolate "shall not be *valid* vows" or "shall not be *considered* vows." "Shall not be *binding* vows" (italics added) comes from *Kol Haneshamah*, 693.

20. Imagining that the court is actually answering the petitioners' request for annulment of vows is based on the ritual of *hatarat n'darim* performed, traditionally, by some, after the morning service on the day prior to Rosh Hashanah. See *Machzor M'soret Harav*, 3–7.

21. In Sephardi *machzorim*, *la sh'ririn, v'la kayamin* appears at the end. "Without power and without standing" comes from the translation in *Machzor M'sorot Harav*.

Glossary

The glossary presents names and Hebrew words used regularly throughout this volume and provides the way they are pronounced. Sometimes two pronunciations are common, in which case the first is the way the word is sounded in Hebrew, and the second is the way it is sometimes heard in common speech, under the influence of English or, sometimes, of Yiddish, the folk language of Jews in northern and eastern Europe (a combination, mostly, of Hebrew and German). Our goal is to provide the way that many Jews actually use these words, not just the technically correct version.

- The pronunciations are divided into syllables by dashes.
- The accented syllable is written in capital letters.
- "Kh" represents a guttural sound, similar to the German (as in "sprach").
- The most common vowel is "a" as in "father," which appears here as "ah."
- The short "e" (as in "get") is written as either "e" (when it is in the middle of a syllable) or "eh" (when it ends a syllable).
- Similarly, the short "i" (as in "tin") is written as either "i" (when it is in the middle of a syllable) or "ih" (when it ends a syllable).
- A long "o" (as in Moses") is written as "oe" (as in the word "toe") or "oh" (as in the word "Oh!").

Adonai (pronounced ah-doh-NA'I): The pronunciation for the tetragrammaton. See **Tetragrammaton**.

Alenu (pronounced ah-LAY-noo): The first word and, therefore, the title of a well-known prayer, compiled in the second or third century as part of the New Year (Rosh Hashanah) service, but from about 1300 CE on, used also as a concluding prayer for every daily service. *Alenu* means "it is incumbent upon us ..." and introduces the prayer's theme: our duty to praise God.

Am ha'aretz (pronounced ahm-hah-AH-rets; pl. *amei ha'aretz*, pronounced ah-MAY hah-AH-rets): Literally, "person of the land"; used Rabbinically to denote people other than the Rabbinic scholarly class, those presumed to be ignorant of Rabbinic food regulations such as tithing. By extension today, a pejorative term implying "ignoramus."

Amidah (pronounced either ah-mee-DAH or, commonly, ah-MEE-dah): One of three titles for the second of two central units in the worship service, the first being the *Sh'ma* and Its Blessings. It is composed of a series of blessings, many of which are petitionary, except on Sabbaths and holidays, when the petitions are removed out of deference to the holiness of the day. Also called *T'fillah* (pronounced t'-fee-LAH or, commonly, t'-FEE-lah) and *Shmoneh Esreh* (pronounced sh'-moh-NEH es-RAY or, commonly, sh'-MOH-neh ES-ray). *Amidah* means "standing," and refers to the fact that the prayer is said standing up.

Aseret hadibrot (pronounced ah-SEH-ret hah-deeb-ROHT): Literally, "the ten words," that is, "The Ten Commandments."

Aseret had'varim (pronounced ah-SEH-ret hah-d'-vah-REEM): A variant of *aseret hadibrot* ("Ten Commandments"). See *aseret hadibrot.*

Ashkenazi (pronounced ahsh-k'-nah-ZEE or, commonly, ahsh-k'-NAH-zee): From the Hebrew word *Ashkenaz,* denoting the geographic area of northern and eastern Europe. Ashkenazi is the adjective, describing not just the inhabitants but also the liturgical rituals and customs practiced there, as opposed to Sephardi (pronounced s'-fahr-DEE or, commonly, s'-FAHR-dee), meaning those derived from *Sefarad,* modern-day Spain and Portugal (see **Sephardi**).

Avaryanim (pronounced ah-vahr-yah-NEEM; sing. *avaryan,* pronounced ah-vahr-YAHN): Literally, "sinners."

Avodah (pronounced ah-voh-DAH): Literally, "work"; hence, (1) the name given to the sacrificial cult of old, which was thought to be a "public work," in that it represented the people to God (parallel to the Greek term *leiturgia,* from which we get "liturgy"); (2) used also to denote a benediction asking God to accept the sacrificial offering and, in its place, our communal prayers, taken to be "offerings of our lips." In context here, (3) it is the name for an entire section of the Yom Kippur additional service (*Musaf,* pronounced moo-SAHF or, commonly, MOO-sahf), which recalls the sacrificial cult of old and, in Orthodox services, requests its reinstitution as part of the messianic age.

BaCH (pronounced BAHKH): An acronym of the Hebrew initials for *Bayit Chadash,* the name of a legal commentary to the thirteenth-century law code known as the *Tur;* composed by Rabbi Joel Sirkes of Poland (1561–1640). *BaCH* refers to Sirkes and to his commentary.

Bet din (pronounced bayt DEEN): A law court, tribunal, or panel of judges.

Bimah (pronounced bee-MAH or, commonly, BEE-mah): Literally, "stage," "platform," or "pulpit"; in context here, the area in a worship space from which the worship service is led and the Torah publicly read.

Birkat b'tulin (pronounced beer-KAHT b'-too-LEEN): Literally, "blessing of virgins"; a custom, never formally accepted as halakhah but commonplace anyway in the Middle Ages, according to which a blessing was said following a couple's wedding night, acknowledging the bride's virginity.

Chametz (pronounced khah-MAYTS): Literally, "leaven." Hence, products forbidden on Passover because they are made with wheat, barley, spelt, oats, or rye that may have fermented or leavened through having come in contact with water for more than eighteen minutes.

Charamei: See *cherem.*

Charatah (pronounced khah-rah-TAH or, commonly, khah-RAH-tah): Literally, "regret," that is, the regret one feels when recognizing oaths and vows that one has taken and wishes to annul.

Chatzi Kaddish (pronounced khah-TSEE kah-DEESH or, commonly, KHAH-tsee KAH-dish): Literally, "half *kaddish*"; see *Kaddish.*

Cherem (pronounced KHEH-rem; Aramaic pl. *charamei,* pronounced khah-rah-MAY): (1) A particularly severe type of vow, originally by an entire community, but eventually, applying to individuals as well. (2) The state of excommunication, as in the expression, "placed in *cherem.*"

Converso (pronounced kon-VEHR-soh): A Jew forced to convert to Christianity during the period of the Spanish Inquisition.

Dayan (pronounced dah-YAHN; pl. *dayanim,* pronounced dah-yah-NEEM): Judge.

Esarei: See *issar.*

Gaon (pronounced gah-OHN; pl. *geonim,* pronounced g'-oh-NEEM): Title for the leading rabbis in Babylon (nowadays Iraq) from about 750 to 1038 CE. From a biblical word meaning "glory," equivalent (in the title) to saying, "Your Excellence."

Halakhah (pronounced hah-lah-KHAH or, commonly, hah-LAH-khah): The Hebrew word for Jewish law. Used adjectivally in the anglicized form, "halakhic" (pronounced hah-LAH-khic), meaning "legal." From the Hebrew root *h.l.kh,* meaning "to walk," or "to go," denoting the way one should walk or go through life.

Hatarat n'darim (pronounced hah-tah-RAHT n'-dah-REEM or, commonly, hah-tah-RAHT n'-DAH-reem): Literally, "the permitting of vows"; the name given to the Rabbinic method by which vows of an individual could, under certain circumstances, be legally voided.

Hin'ni (pronounced hee-n'-NEE or, commonly, HEE-n'-nee): Literally, "Here I am"; the opening word of (and, hence, the title for) the opening prayer at *Musaf* on the High Holy Days; moved to the opening of the Rosh Hashanah evening service by North American Reform Jews.

Issar (pronounced ee-SAHR or, commonly, EE-sahr; Aramaic pl. in *Kol Nidre* is *esarei*, pronounced eh-sah-RAY): Literally, "binding," hence, a type of binding oath, with different denotations over time.

Kaddish (pronounced kah-DEESH or, commonly, KAH-dish): From the Hebrew root *k.d.sh*, meaning "holy," and, therefore, the name given to a first-century prayer affirming God's holiness. It eventually found its way into the service in several forms, including one known as the Mourner's *Kaddish* (*Kaddish Yatom*, pronounced kah-DEESH yah-TOHM). It functions also as a form of oral punctuation, a "full *Kaddish*" (*Kaddish Shalem*, pronounced kah-DEESH shah-LAYM) representing a complete break between sections (a "period") and the "Half *Kaddish*" (*Chatzi Kaddish*, pronounced khah-TSEE kah-DEESH or, commonly, KHAH-tsee KAH-dish), a minor break (a "semicolon").

K'dushah (pronounced k'-doo-SHAH or, commonly, k'-DOO-shah): From the Hebrew word meaning "holy," and, therefore, a prayer from the first or second century occurring in several places and versions, all of them built upon Isaiah 6:3—*Kadosh, kadosh, kadosh …* (pronounced kah-DOHSH kah-DOHSH kah-DOHSH), "Holy, holy, holy is the Lord of hosts. The whole earth is full of his glory."

Kibbitz (pronounced KIH-bits): Yiddish for conversational banter, joking about.

Kinu'i (pronounced kee-NOO-ee; pl. *kinuyim*, pronounced kee-noo-YEEM; Aramaic pl., *kinuyei*, pronounced kee-noo-YAY): Literally, "an epithet," a term used here as a catchall word to stand for a variety of alternative epithets once commonly used to constitute a vow.

Kinusei: See *konas*.

Konam (pronounced koh-NAHM or, commonly, KOH-nahm; Aramaic pl. *konamei*, pronounced koh-nah-MAY): A euphemistic way of referring to *korban*, "sacrifice" (see *korban*).

Konas (pronounced koh-NAHS or, commonly KOH-nahs; Aramaic pl. *konasei*, pronounced koh-nah-SAY, or, by analogy with *kinuyei* [see *kinu'i*], *kinusei*, pronounced kee-noo-SAY). A euphemistic way of referring to *korban*, "sacrifice" (see *korban*).

Korban (pronounced kohr-BAHN or, commonly, KOHR-bahn; pl. *korbanot,* pronounced kohr-bah-NOHT): A sacrifice, offered up in the Temple cult of old.

Machzor (pronounced mahkh-ZOHR or, commonly, MAHKH-zohr; pl. *machzorim,* pronounced mahkh-zoh-REEM): Literally, "cycle," as in the annual cycle of time; hence, the name given to the prayer book for holy days that occur once annually and that mark the passing of the year. Separate *machzorim* exist for Rosh Hashanah and Yom Kippur.

MaHaRaM (pronounced mah-hah-RAHM): An acronym formed from the consonantal initials of Moreinu Harav Rabbi Meir, literally, "Our teacher, the Rabbi, Rabbi Meir" (Meir of Rothenberg, 1215–93); in context here, the author of the introduction to *Kol Nidre* permitting prayer alongside sinners.

MaHarIL (pronounced mah-hah-RIHL or, commonly, MAH-hah-rihl): An acronym of the Hebrew initials for *Moreinu Harav Rabbi Ya'acov Levi* ("Our teacher, Rabbi Jacob the Levite") of Mainz and Worms (1365–1427). The Maharil was an enormously influential founder of Ashkenazi tradition.

Marrano (pronounced mah-RAH-noh): A Jew forced to convert to Christianity during the period of the Spanish Inquisition. Nowadays, the term is generally avoided because of its pejorative etymology from the medieval Spanish for "pig." See preferred term, **converso**.

Matzah (pronounced mah-TZAH but, commonly, MAH-tzuh): Unleavened bread consumed during Passover as a recollection of the fact that the Israelites hastened out of Egypt without time to let their bread for the journey rise.

M'daber (pronounced m'-dah-BAYR): Literally, "speaking," hence, by extension, the medieval philosophical term for "human beings," the species that "speaks."

Me'ah b'rakhot (pronounced may-AH b'-rah-KHOHT but, commonly, MAY-ah b'-rah-KHOT): Literally, "One hundred blessings," a reference to the Rabbinic adage that a person should say one hundred blessings daily.

Mezid (pronounced may-ZEED): Literally, "willfully," hence, the technical term for a sin that is willfully committed. See opposite, *shogeg*.

M'ilah (pronounced m'-ee-LAH): The sin by which a layperson uses anything pledged to God (in practice, to the Temple) and, therefore, reserved for priestly use alone.

Minchah (pronounced meen-KHAH or, commonly, MIN-khah): Literally, "afternoon." Originally, the name of a type of sacrifice; but the name now of the afternoon service usually scheduled just before nightfall.

Misinai (pronounced mee-see-NAH-ee or, commonly, mee-SEE-nah-ee): Literally, "From Sinai," hence, the name given to the oldest known stratum of musical melodies from Ashkenaz, presumably (although not actually) dating back to Sinai; in actuality, *misinai* melodies can be traced back to the sixteenth century or so.

Mitzvah (pronounced meetz-VAH or, commonly, MITZ-vah; pl. *mitzvot*, pronounced meetz-VOHT): A Hebrew word used commonly to mean "good deed," but in the more technical sense, a commandment from God; from its Hebrew root *tz.v.h*, meaning "command."

Mizrachi (pronounced meez-rah-KHEE or, commonly, miz-RAH-khee): Literally, "eastern"; the term for "eastern" liturgical communities and customs, meaning those in and around the Land of Israel, as opposed to those of European Jews, who saw Jerusalem (and, by extension, the whole Land of Israel) as "the east."

Mochorat Shabbat (pronounced moh-choh-RAHT shah-BAHT): Literally, "day after Shabbat," but, by extension, "day after the time-off time." A biblical term (Lev. 23:15) denoting the time from which one is to count the days leading up the spring festival of Shavuot; interpreted by the Rabbis to mean the day after the onset of "Passover."

Musaf (pronounced moo-SAHF or, commonly, MOO-sahf): The Hebrew word meaning "extra" or "added," and, therefore, the title of the additional sacrifice that was offered in the Temple on Shabbat and holy days; now the name given to the additional service of worship appended to the morning service on those days.

Neder (pronounced NEH-der, pl. *n'darim*, pronounced n'-dah-REEM; Aramaic pl., *nidrei* [variant, *nidre*] pronounced need-RAY or, commonly, NID-ray): A vow, either assertory (testifying to a fact) or promissory (promising an act, positive or negative, in the future).

Nidre: See *neder*.

Nidrei: See *neder*.

N'ilah (pronounced n'-ee-LAH or, commonly, n'-EE-lah): Literally, "locking," hence, (1) the time at night when the gates to the sacrificial Temple of late antiquity were closed; and (2) additional worship services that developed then just for fast days, one of which, the final service for Yom Kippur, is still the norm today.

Petach (pronounced PEH-tahkh): Literally, "opening"; in context here, the "excuse," "reason," or "opening" that provides the opportunity to declare a vow legally annullable.

Pilgrimage Festivals: Passover, Shavu'ot and Sukkot, the three festivals associated originally with the spring and autumn harvests, and for which pilgrimage to Jerusalem is biblically mandated.

Piyyut (pronounced pee-YOOT; pl. *piyyutim*, pronounced pee-yoo-TEEM): A poem. In a liturgical context specifically, poetry added to the main prayers of the liturgy, and embedded in those prayers according to a complex set of rules that combine the nature of the poem in question with the content and structure of the prayer for which it is composed.

Rosh Chodesh (pronounced rohsh KHOH-desh): Literally, "head of the moon or month," hence, the twenty-four-hour holy-day period introduced by the new moon, the first of the month.

Rosh Hashanah (pronounced rohsh hah-shah-NAH or, commonly ROHSH hah-SHAH-nah): Literally, "head of the year," hence, the new year.

R'shut (pronounced r'-SHOOT): Literally, "permission," hence, (1) the name of a prayer offered by the cantor (or prayer leader) requesting permission to represent the congregation before God; (2) used also to denote a type of medieval poem (*piyyut*, pronounced pee-YOOT) that requests permission for the prayer leader to say a series of other poems that follow on behalf of the congregation.

Shabbat Shabbaton (pronounced shah-BAHT shah-bah-TOHN): Literally, "Sabbath of Sabbaths," a biblical name given to Yom Kippur.

Shehecheyanu (pronounced sheh-heh-kheh-YAH-noo): Literally, "who has kept us alive," hence, the popular name for a blessing praising God for "having kept us alive, sustained us, and brought us to this time of year." Also called *birkat hazman* (pronounced beer-KAHT hahz-MAHN), "the blessing of the time." It is recited at various "first-time" occasions, including wearing new clothes, eating the fruit of a new season, and the onset of holidays, including, here, the eve of *Kol Nidre*.

Sefer Torah (pronounced SAY-fer toh-RAH or, commonly, SAY-fer TOH-rah; pl. *sifrei Torah* (pronounced seef-RAY toh-RAH or, commonly, SIF-ray-TOH-rah): A Torah scroll.

Sephardi (pronounced s'-fahr-DEE or commonly, s'-FAHR-dee): From the Hebrew word *Sefarad* (pronounced s'-fah-RAHD), denoting the geographic area of modern-day Spain and Portugal. Sephardi is the adjective, describing not just the inhabitants but also the liturgical rituals and customs practiced there, as opposed to Ashkenazi, meaning those derived from *Ashkenaz*, northern and western Europe (see **Ashkenazi**).

Shekhinah (pronounced sh'-khee'NAH or, commonly, sh'-KHEE-nah): From the Hebrew root *sh.kh.n*, "to dwell." In Talmudic literature, therefore, the "indwelling" aspect of God, most immediately empathetic to human experience. As the feminine side of God, it appears in Kabbalah as the tenth, and final, emanation.

Sh'fokh chamotkha (pronounced sh'-FOKH khah-moht-KHAH): Literally, "Pour out your wrath...." A citation from Psalm 79:6, and the introductory line of a medieval prayer from the Passover seder, requesting revenge on those who had just decimated Jewish communities in the Rhineland as part of the First Crusade.

Shogeg (pronounced SHOH-gayg): "Mistakenly," denoting a sin that has been mistakenly committed. This is the opposite of *mezid*. (See *mezid*).

Shul (pronounced SHOOL): Yiddish for "synagogue."

Shulchan Arukh (pronounced shool-KHAN ah-ROOKH or, commonly, SHOOL-khahn AH-rookh): Literally, "the set table"; a compendium of law written by Joseph Caro (1488–1575), a prominent Sephardi rabbi and mystical teacher in medieval Safed, and published in 1565. The name refers to the ease with which the laws are presented—like a table set with food that is ready for consumption. Rabbi Moses Isserles of Cracow, Poland (1520–1572)—called, also, the *mapa* (pronounced mah-PAH, and meaning "tablecloth")—provided "corrective" glosses that fill in points where Ashkenazi custom differed from Caro's Sephardi practice.

Sh'vu'ah (pronounced sh'-voo-AH; pl. *sh'vu'ot,* pronounced sh'-voo-OHT): A promissory oath, positive or negative, assumed to involve (at least implicitly) the name of God.

Sh'vu'at bitu'i (pronounced sh'-voo-AHT bee-TOO-ee): Literally, "an oath of expression," denoting either an act in the past or in the future that one has or has not done, or will or will not do.

Sh'vu'at edut (pronounced sh'-voo-AHT ay-DOOT): Literally, "an oath of testimony," whereby those who might be in receipt of information regarding a monetary suit deny on oath that they have testimony to offer.

Sh'vu'at hadayanim (pronounced sh'-voo-AHT hah-dah-yah-NEEM): Literally, "an oath imposed by judges [in court]"; generally, the means by which a person charged with a monetary crime takes an oath of being in debt, so as to be free of incurring further monetary responsibility that would accrue through the penalty imposed on account of the crime.

Sh'vu'at pikadon (pronounced sh'-voo-AHT pee-kah-DOHN): Literally, "an oath of deposit"; an oath to the effect that something that one holds (as it were) "on deposit" from another person is not owed to that person.

Sh'vu'at shav (pronounced sh'-voo-AHT SHAV): Literally, "an oath in vain," that is, an oath that takes God's name in vain.

Sh'vu'at sheker (pronounced sh'-voo-AHT SHEH-ker): Literally, "a lying oath," a violation of Leviticus 19:1: "Do not swear by my name lyingly, so as to profane the name of your God."

Sh'vukah (pronounced sh'-vook-KAH): A euphemism for *sh'vu'ah*, "oath." See *sh'vu'ah*.

Sh'vu'ot: See *Sh'vu'ah*.

Sh'vutah (pronounced sh'-voo-TAH): A euphemism for *sh'vu'ah*, "oath." See *sh'vu'ah*.

Sifrei Torah: See *Sefer Torah*.

S'lichah (pronounced s'-lee-KHAH or, commonly s'-LEE-khah): Literally, "pardon"; hence, the name given to (1) the blessing for pardon within the daily *Amidah* (see *Amidah*); and (2) a liturgical poem (*piyyut*, pronounced pee-YOOT) inserted into the liturgy on the theme of pardon.

Sukkah (pronounced soo-KAH or, commonly, SOO-kah): Literally, "booth." A temporarily constructed booth in which Jews are commanded "to sit" during the autumn harvest festival of Sukkot (pronounced sook-KOHT, "Booths"), originally as grateful acknowledgment for autumn produce, but reinterpreted also to denote the fragility of desert wandering following the Exodus.

Tallit (pronounced tah-LEET or, commonly, TAH-lis): The prayer shawl worn for morning worship, featuring tassels called *tzitzit* (pronounced tsee-TSEET or, commonly, TSIH-tsis) on the corners. See *tzitzit*. In context here, worn also for just one evening service in the year, the one introduced by *Kol Nidre*.

Tetragrammaton: The technical term for the four-letter name of God that appears in the Bible. Treating it as sacred, Jews stopped pronouncing it centuries ago, so that the actual pronunciation has been lost; instead of reading it according to its letters, it is replaced in speech by the alternative name of God, *Adonai* (pronounced ah-doh-NA'I).

T'fillah (pronounced t'-fee-LAH or, commonly, t'-FEE-lah): A Hebrew word meaning, "prayer," but used technically to denote a specific prayer, namely, the second of the two main units in the worship service; known also as the *Amidah* or the *Sh'moneh Esreh* (see *Amidah*). Also the title of the sixteenth blessing of the *Amidah*, a petition for God to accept our prayer.

T'fillin (pronounced t'-fee-LEEN or, commonly, t'-FIH-lin): Two cube-shaped black boxes containing biblical quotations (Exod. 13:1–10, 13:11–16; Deut. 6:4–9, 11:13–21), and affixed by means of attached leather straps to the forehead and left arm (right arm for left-handed people) during morning prayer.

T'shuvah (pronounced t'-shoo-VAH or, commonly, t'-SHOO-vah): Literally "repentance"; also the title of the fifth blessing in the daily *Amidah*, a petition by worshipers that they successfully turn to God in heartfelt repentance.

Tz'dakah (pronounced ts'-dah-KAH or, commonly, ts'-DAH-kah): Charity.

Tzitzit (pronounced tsee-TSEET or, commonly, TSIH-tsis): A Hebrew word meaning "tassels," or "fringes," and used to refer to the tassels affixed to the four corners of the *tallit* (the prayer shawl, see *tallit*) as Numbers 15:38 instructs.

Un'taneh Tokef (pronounced oo-n'-TAH-neh TOH-kehf): A *piyyut* (liturgical poem) for the High Holy Days emphasizing the awesome nature of these days when we stand before God for judgment; but originally, the climactic part of a longer poem for the *Amidah* called *k'dushta* (pronounced k'-doosh-TAH or, commonly, k'-DOOSH-tah). Although widely connected with a legend of Jewish martyrdom in medieval Germany, the poem more likely derives from a Byzantine poet, circa sixth century. It is known for its conclusion: "Penitence, prayer, and charity help the misfortune of the decree pass." See full treatment in Lawrence A. Hoffman, ed., *Who By Fire, Who by Water—Un'taneh Tokef* (Woodstock VT: Jewish Lights Publishing, 2010).

Ya'aleh tachanuneinu (pronounced *yah-ah-LEH takh-ah-noo-NAY-noo*): Literally, "O let our prayer ascend," the opening words, and, hence, the title, of a Yom Kippur eve poem (*piyyut*, pronounced pee-YOOT), requesting that our prayers rise to God throughout the period of Yom Kippur that the poem inaugurates.

Yarmulke (pronounced YAHR-ml-kuh): Yiddish word for the standard skull cap (Hebrew, *kippah*, pronounced kee-PAH or, commonly, KIH-pah) worn during prayer.

Yeshivah shel ma'alah (pronounced y'shee-VAH shel mah-ah-LAH or, commonly y'-SHEE-vah shel MAH-ah-lah): Literally, "the academy [or, in context here, 'court'] on high," the heavenly court.

Yeshivah shel matah (pronounced y'-shee-VAH shel mah-TAH or, commonly, y'-SHEE-vah shel MAH-tah): Literally, "the academy [or, in context here, 'court'] below," the earthly court of law as opposed to the divine court in heaven.

Yom Hakippurim (pronounced YOHM hah-kee-poo-REEM): The formal Rabbinic term for "Day of Atonement," nowadays, shortened in common speech to Yom Kippur.

Yom Kippur (pronounced yohm kee-POOR or, commonly, yohm KIH-p'r): Day of Atonement.

Printed in the USA
CPSIA information can be obtained
at www.ICGtesting.com
JSHW012022140824
68134JS00033B/2820